Cross-Country Skiing

**A Guide to
America's Best Trails**

Also by Lucy M. Fehr

SKIING USA: A Guide to the Nation's Ski Areas

Americans-Discover-America Series

Cross-Country Skiing

A Guide to America's Best Trails

by Lucy M. Fehr

William Morrow and Company, Inc., New York

Library of Congress Catalog Card Number 79-90099
ISBN 0-688-08505-9

Printed in the United States of America

First Edition
1   2   3   4   5   6   7   8   9   10

To my mother and father

PREFACE

Every winter, more and more people are discovering the fun of gliding over a quiet, snowy landscape on cross-crountry skis. Sometimes called ski touring or Nordic skiing, the sport is easy to learn and only as physically demanding as you choose. The equipment is comfortable and lightweight, and just sensible, warm layered clothing is necessary.

Since cross-country skiing can be done almost anywhere there is snow, the possibilities of where to go are unlimited. This guide will tell you where to find some of the best commercial and non-commercial trail systems in the country, and what to expect when you get there. In recent years, many commercial touring centers have opened, offering ski rentals, instruction, manicured trails, food, lodging, and all the amenities for a winter vacation. An increasing number of downhill ski areas are clearing trails and renting cross-country skis, great for those who want the best of both worlds. For skiers who want to get away from the resort areas, city, state, and federal parks and forests are laced with miles of marked trails and unplowed roads suitable for skiing. Because of the growing interest in ski touring, park and forest personnel are beginning to cater to winter visitors by offering ski trail maps, plowed parking lots, restroom facilities, and in some areas, ski rentals, instruction, and naturalist-guided tours. For experienced skiers, professional guide services conduct overnight tours, snow camping tours, week-long backpack trips into remote wilderness areas, winter survival seminars, and tours tailored to suit the interests and ability of any group.

Trail ratings: Trail difficulty varies according to snow conditions. For example, ice or heavy wet snow is a challenge to novice or advanced skiers on any trail. The following evaluations apply to the difficulty of trails and the skill levels of skiers. They are meant for your general guidance.

Novice-rated trails are short, mostly flat, and may have some gently rolling terrain. The novice skier, with one or two lessons, knows the basic stride and the snowplow turn and stop. The novice trail requires a minimum of stamina and little or no knowledge of winter survival. The rank beginner can expect to handle and enjoy a novice trail after one lesson.

Intermediate-rated trails are longer, more rolling, and might have some short steep spots. Intermediate skiers have confidence in climbing, turning, and stopping skills, a good dose of endurance, and a knowledge of map reading and winter survival.

Advanced- and *expert*-rated trails are for experienced skiers only. The trails are usually long, often lead into remote areas, and can have long steep narrow climbs or downhill runs. A thorough knowledge of winter survival and map reading, as well as mental and physical stamina, are necessary.

A *maintained* trail is periodically cleared of brush, fallen trees, and other obstacles. A *groomed* trail has had the snow broken and packed by machine and in some cases a track set which provides skiers with an easy-to-ski trail. Areas with groomed trails almost always charge a trail usage fee, usually between $1.00 and $3.00, to help offset trail maintenance and grooming expenses.

Equipment: There are two types of cross-country skis, wax and no-wax. Wax skis require proper waxing for maximum climbing grip and a smooth fast glide. Learning how to wax is important, and nearly every ski lesson will include waxing instruction. There are different waxes for different temperature ranges, and the ranges are marked on the containers. One thing to remember is that a cold-temperature wax cannot be applied on top of a warm-temperature wax, but the reverse can be done. Since the wax-temperature ranges overlap, start with a colder wax when possible. Several waxes should be carried to deal with changing temperatures and snow conditions. Waxing is not complicated once you have learned how, and it is essential to an enjoyable ski tour.

No-wax skis have special bottoms that prevent backsliding on uphill climbs. Fish-scale bottoms (they look like big fish scales) and mohair strips are the common varieties. About the only disadvantage is a small sacrifice of speed; for a beginner, that may be a plus!

The whole package of skis, boots, bindings, and poles may be purchased for about $100. If you are a first-timer, rent equipment to be sure cross-country skiing is for you. Rental equipment is available for a reasonable daily fee in many sport shops and resort areas. Often an introductory lesson is included in the rental fee.

Some notes of caution: Listen to local weather reports so you don't get caught in a storm. If you are out touring and the weather turns bad, start back immediately. Falling snow can quickly cover your tracks and disorient you. Cold windy weather, because of the wind chill factor, can cause frostbite and hypothermia (loss of body heat, which if unattended is fatal very quickly.

Never ski alone in remote areas. At least three people should be in a ski party. In the event of injury, you may need help.

Tell your tour plans to a responsible person, or check in and out with a ranger or someone whenever possible.

For an all-day tour, carry a map and compass, an extra ski tip, a binding repair kit, and some high-energy food.

Estimate the hours your tour will take and allow enough time to get back with at least one hour to spare before sundown.

Respect thin ice and avalanche warnings.

Stay out of big-game areas during hunting seasons and always be alert for illegal hunters.

Never attempt a tour beyond your capabilities.

Information listed in this guide was as accurate as possible at press time. However, some errors may have crept in and some changes will have occurred since publication; for these, the author apologizes.

List of Abbreviations

km	kilometer
m	mile
CSIA	Central Ski Instructors Association
DNR	Department of Natural Resources
EPSTI	Eastern Professional Ski Touring Instructors
FIS	Federation Internationale de Ski
ISIA	Intermountain Ski Instructors Association
NASTAR	National Standard Race
NSTOA	National Ski Touring Operators Association
PNSIA	Pacific Northwest Ski Instructors of America
PSIA	Professional Ski Instructors of America
PSRA	Professional Ski Racers of America
RMSIA	Rocky Mountain Ski Instructors Association
USSA	United States Ski Association

CONTENTS

Cross-Country Skiing

**A Guide to
America's Best Trails**

ALASKA

Most of Alaska is covered with snow from November to April and cross-country skiing is done everywhere. A good number of the maintained and recommended trails for touring are in the Anchorage, Fairbanks, and Juneau areas. Skiers venturing beyond these areas should be experienced and would be well advised to ski with a guide.

For additional information, contact the individual area, guide, or Alaska Division of Tourism, Pouch E, Juneau, AK 99811.

ANCHORAGE: Kincaid Park (1 m W of Sand Lake Rd., off Raspberry Rd.; watch for "ski trails" signs), 22.5 km of marked trails on 390 acres; 1 novice loop around the lake, 6 intermediate and 2 expert interconnecting loops (expert trails are for advanced skiers only); site of 1978 National Cross-Country Ski Championships; 2 trailheads with parking areas; snow machines not allowed. **Centennial Park** (off Glenn Hwy. N of intersection of Muldoon Rd. and Glenn Hwy.), 5 km of marked trails and 1-km lighted trail for night skiing; novice to intermediate terrain on 78 acres; small downhill area with rope tow (small fee) operates Wed.-Fri., 4-6 pm and Sat., Sun., 1–10 pm; ice skating and free sliding hill; warm-up shelter, restrooms; snow machines not allowed. **Muldoon Park** (bordered by Patterson St., Northern Lights Blvd., and Muldoon Rd.), 4 km of marked trails for novice skiers on 80 acres; no snow machines allowed. **Bicentennial Park**, formerly Campbell Creek Resource Land (access from Abbott Rd. on W and Tudor Rd. on N), 30 km of marked cross-country trails for intermediates and experts; trails connect to Hillside Park and Chugach State Park; designated dog mushing and snow machine trails. **Russian Jack Springs Park** (off DeBarr Ave. W of Boniface Pkwy.), 320 acres with over 5 km of marked trails (some lighted) connecting to Chester Creek Trail; gentle rolling terrain for novice and intermediate skiers; downhill slope with rope tow (small fee), operated Mon.–Fri. 3–9 pm, and Sat. Sun. 1–9 pm; warm-up chalet with restrooms, food concession; no snow machines allowed in cross-country trail area S of DeBarr Ave. **Chester Creek Trail** (from Westchester Lagoon on the W to Goose Lake on the E; extension connects to Russian Jack Springs Park), long narrow park with trail follows Chester Creek across the

City of Anchorage; several road crossings require skis off. **Hillside Park** (access from Abbott Rd. or Service-Hanshew High School parking lot), 7 km of marked interconnecting, intermediate trails on 420 acres; trails connect to Bicentennial Park; downhill area with rope tow (small fee), operates Wed., 6–8 pm, and Sat., Sun., holidays, 10 am–3 pm; snow machines not allowed. **Campbell Park** (S of Tudor Rd. off Lake Otis Pkwy.), 18 acres open to cross-country skiers, maintained trails not available; snow machines not allowed. Maps and information on above trails: Municipality of Anchorage, Division of Parks & Recreation, Pouch 6-650, Anchorage, AK 99502. 907-274-2525.

Chugach State Park (abuts E edge of city), ½ million acre park with open alpine valleys, glaciers and rugged mountain peaks; many km of recently upgraded trails on varied terrain for all levels of skiers. Information: District Superintendent, Chugach State Park, 2601 Commercial Dr., Anchorage, AK 99501. 907-274-4679.

Chugach National Forest (E of Anchorage), 4.7 million acres of mountainous coastline with fiords, glaciers, lakes and rivers; because of extreme avalanche danger, always check current weather conditions: **Resurrection Pass** (to find north trailhead from Hope, turn at Resurrection Pass Trail sign on the Hope Hwy., follow Resurrection Creek Rd. for about 4 m to beginning of trail (road not maintained in winter); south trailhead is marked with large Resurrection Pass Trail sign at milepost 52.3 on the Sterling Hwy. near Cooper Landing), 38-m trail, originally established by gold miners, follows Resurrection Creek from Hope end, up to Resurrection Pass, then follows Juneau Creek down to Sterling Hwy.; 7 Forest Service cabins are located along trail (cabin use permits issued at forest offices); avalanche danger areas exist along trail, connecting Devil's Creek Trail should be avoided; snowmobiles permitted during certain winter months. **Russian Lakes Trail** (access from Russian Lake Campground at milepost 52 on Sterling Hwy.), 20-m trail; only first 2.6 m to Lower Russian Lake recommended for winter use, avalanche danger beyond; brown bear country; snowmobiles permitted. **Turnagain Pass** (off SR 1 at Granite Creek Campground), well-used area with gentle slopes, lots of snow, good off-road parking; separate area to west zoned for snowmobiles. **Nordic Ski Trail** (see Girdwood). Maps and information on above trails: Forest Supervisor, Chugach National Forest, Pouch 6606, 2221 E. Northern Lights Blvd., Suite 230, Anchorage, AK 99502. 907-272-4485. Avalanche situation: 907-274-4113.

Nordic Ski Club of Anchorage organizes an annual Ski Train trip into the Chugach National Forest. Usually scheduled for early March, the trip allows over 500 skiers to explore otherwise inaccessible territory near Grandview Glacier. It is one of the biggest events of the year for local cross-country skiers. Information: Nordic Ski Club of Anchorage, Anchorage, AK 99501.

Guide services operating from the Anchorage area include: **Alaska Wilderness Unlimited,** ski touring, winter camping, and mountaineering in the Arrigetch Peaks and the Arctic National Wildlife Range. Information: William Quirk III, Box 4-2477, Anchorage, AK 99509. 907-277-0197. **Bear Bros. Whole Wilderness Experience,** cross-country ski and winter dog mushing trips, 1- to 3-week expeditions into South Central Alaska. Information: Eric Singer, c/o BBWW, Box 4-2969, Anchorage, AK 99509. 907-344-5760. **Far North Ski Guides, Inc.,** see Girdwood. **Montain Trip, Inc.,** see Fairbanks.

FAIRBANKS: Mount McKinley National Park (120 m S on SR 3). There are few trails in the park and many natural routes; park is open all winter for ski touring, snowshoe hikes, and dogsled trips; park bus stops on request along the 85-m route, but park road may be closed after mid-September by snow at high passes; check-in and check-out at Park Headquarters during winter months; backcountry use permit (no cost) required for all overnight tours; maps, area descriptions, and general guidance are available at Riley Creek Visitor Orientation Center, near park entrance. Information: Superintendent, Mount McKinley National Park, P. O. Box 9, McKinley Park, AK 99755.

Guiding services available for Mount McKinley and Fairbanks area: **Mountain Trip, Inc.** offers Ski Mountaineering, High Altitude Tours, Ipitarod Dog Sled Ski Tour (famous dogsled trail from Anchorage to Nome). Information: Gary Bocarde & Jim Hale, P.O. Box 10078, South Station, Anchorage, AK 99502. 907-349-1161. **Mountains North** offers ski tours in Central Alaska. Information: Ed Wenrick, 351 University Ave., Fairbanks, AK 99701. **Sourdough Outfitters** offer ski touring and dogsledding wilderness trips in the Central Brooks Range. Information: David Ketscher, General Delivery, Bettles, AK 99726. 907-692-5252.

GIRDWOOD: Alyeska Resort (40 m SE of Anchorage via SR 1, Anchorage/Seward Hwy.), many km of scenic, unmaintained trails suitable for beginners through experts; varied terrain from forested slopes to frozen creek beds to open meadows. **Nordic Ski Trail** (in Chugach National Forest), from lodge area to Winner Creek, has 2 loops of 2.5 km and 5 km, plus 10-km competition loop; rentals available; heli-skiing and glacier skiing arranged. Alyeska, a year-round resort, has extensive downhill ski facilities, day lodge, cafeteria, restaurants, cocktail lounges, disco; lodge and condominium accommodations, convention facilities, sport and gift shops. Group and package plans. Transportation Services, Inc. operates daily bus service from Anchorage (907-279-5592). Information: Alyeska Resort, P.O. Box 249, Girdwood, AK 99587. 907-783-6000.

   Far North Ski Guides, Inc. offer heli-skiing, glacier skiing, fly-in ski tours, nordic and alpine tours, and hut skiing in the Talkeetna, Chugach, and Kenai Mtns. and Alaska Range. Reservations and information: 401 E. Northern Lights Blvd., Suite 203, Anchorage, AK 99504. 907-279-2314.

   Prism Nordic & Alpine Ski Touring offers guide service on a wide selection of routes in the Girdwood, Turnagain Pass, and Summit Lake areas of the Chugach-Kenai Mtns. and in the Hatcher Pass area of the Talkeetna Mtns.; rentals, instructor/guides available; group rates. Information: Prism/Bill Glude, Box 136, Girdwood, AK 99587. 907-783-4991.

JUNEAU: Spaulding Trail (trail begins a short distance NW of Auke Bay P.O., on the right before Wadleigh Creek), 3-m trail through muskeg meadows and wooded areas terminating in the rolling hills of Spaulding Meadows with unlimited skiing and views of Chilkat Mtns., Lynn Canal and Auke Bay; 3-m access trail closed to snowmobiles; no parking at trailhead. **Windfall Lake Trail** (off Glacier Hwy. at mile 27, just before Herbert River, then right onto gravel road for .2 m), 3.5-m trail along Herbert River, through spruce and hemlock forest to the lake; level terrain for a good portion of the distance; when river is safely frozen, many people ski from the parking lot to Herbert Glacier, about 5 m. **Herbert Glacier Trail** (trailhead and parking lot at mile 28 on Glacier Hwy.), 4.6-m relatively flat trail up the valley, crosses several small hills and ends just before a terminal moraine; a climb over the rocks to the left of the glacier provides a spectacular view of a waterfall; brown and black bear may be in the area and mountain goats may be seen on the surrounding mountain. **Dan Moller Ski Trail** (on Douglas Island; keep left after crossing Juneau-Douglas Bridge, then first right onto Cordova St., then left onto Nowell Ave. to the end; trail begins just beyond the last house on the right), 3.3-m trail beginning on an old road, then emerges into open muskeg and ends at the Don Moller Cabin; avalanche-prone area, caution should be observed; former snowslide paths should be crossed with haste and trail avoided during periods of high avalanche danger. **Mendenhall Glacier Recreation Area** (13 m N). Level terrain makes this a popular area for beginning skiers; visitor center open on a limited schedule in the winter. Many Juneau area trails are dangerous during winter and spring months due to avalanche activity; Perseverance and Sheep Creek Trails are especially dangerous. The Forest Service recommends the above trails for winter use. Information: Tongass National Forest, Juneau Work Center, P.O. Box 1049, Juneau, AK 99802. 907-586-7151. **Treadwill Ditch Trail** (access off Dan Moller Trail, 1 m from the beginning; see above), 3-m trail along the historic Treadwill Ditch; flat wide trail crosses Lawson Creek and leads to Gastineau Meadows, a popular area for cross-country skiers; trail will eventually extend to Cropley Lake, 12 m. **Cropley Lake Ski Trail** (turn right after crossing Juneau-Douglas Bridge, drive 5 m, then left onto Fish Creek Rd.; trailhead at end of road, a short distance past Eaglecrest Ski Lodge on the right), very steep 1.5-m trail to Cropley Lake; should not be attempted by beginners; terrain levels off once at Cropley Lake with views of Fish Creek Valley and the mainland; skiers are asked to register at ski lodge prior to skiing this trail. Information for above 2 trails: City & Borough of Juneau, 190 S. Franklin, Juneau, AK 99801. 907-586-3300.

Eaglecrest Ski Area (turn right after crossing Juneau-Douglas Bridge, follow North Douglas Hwy. 5 m, then left onto Fish Creek Rd.), 640 acres with cut trails at lower elevations and glade skiing in upper elevations; beginner to expert terrain; skiers should register at lodge for information on avalanche danger areas; instruction available; large downhill ski area with day lodge, fireplace, cafeteria, convenience store. Eaglecrest boasts 1 inch of fresh snow daily throughout the ski season. Accommodations, restaurants, and excellent ski shops for rentals, repairs, and clothing in Juneau. Information: City & Borough of Juneau, 190 S. Franklin, Juneau, AK. 99801. 907-586-3300, Ext. 26, 27. Recorded snow report: 907-586-6464.

WILLOW: Nancy Lake Recreation Area (Milepost 67 on Parks

Hwy., 1¼-hour drive N of Anchorage), 23,000 acres of rolling hills of birch forest broken by hundreds of lakes, ponds, and black spruce bogs; located in the Lower Susitna River Valley, the gentle terrain and calm winds make ideal conditions for winter activities; 3 interconnecting loops with 2 crossover trails for short tours; novice to expert maintained trails total nearly 10 m in area closed to snowmobiles and dog teams; trailhead and parking lot 2.3 m into recreation area on maintained gravel road (Alaska State Parks Entrance Permit, $10 per yr, no daily fee); skiing permitted in rest of park along with snowmobiling, snowshoeing, and dog mushing; winter camping permitted, but campsites not maintained; restaurants and accommodations in Willow. Trail map and information: Chief Ranger, Nancy Lake State Recreation Area, P.O. Box 116, Willow, AK 99688. 907-495-6273.

Located in the Talkeetna Mtns. E of Nancy Lake Recreation Area is **Hatcher Pass** (from Willow via Hatcher Pass Rd., milepost 71 on Parks Hwy.; from Palmer and Wasilla via Fishhook-Willow Rd.; from either end, continue until you see "State Road Maintenance Ends") 20 m of road across the pass is closed in the winter; pass elevation ranges from 1700 ft where maintenance ends to 3886 ft at the summit; a crossover trip would require a waiting vehicle at the other end of pass, and many opportunities for out-and-back trips are afforded by the open country, all above timberline; the trip should not be attempted alone or without an experienced skier. Hatcher Pass is a proposed State Recreation Area. Information: State of Alaska, Division of Parks, P.O. Box 182, Palmer, AK 99645.

ARIZONA

For additional information, contact the individual area or Arizona Office of Tourism, 1700 West Washington, Phoenix, AZ 85007.

FLAGSTAFF: Arizona Snow Bowl (14 m N in Coconino National Forest; 7 m N of US 180 to Snow Bowl turnoff, then 7 m to lodge), variety of terrain suited for beginners to advanced; 6- and 10-km maintained trails plus surrounding wooded areas; Rocky Mountain Ski Instructors Association-certified instructors offer group lessons and tours; rentals; no trail usage fee, trail maps available; major downhill ski area with day lodge, cafeteria, cocktail lounge, shop. Accommodations, restaurants in Flagstaff. Information: Norm Johnson, Arizona Snow Bowl, P.O. Box 158, Flagstaff, AZ 86002. 602-774-0562. Snow report: 602-779-4576. **Mormon Lake Ski Touring Center** (30 m SE via Lake Mary Rd.), unlimited skiing plus over 50 m of marked trails on old logging roads, across alpine meadows and over gentle pine-forested slopes in a 7200-ft lake basin of the Coconino National Forest; breathtaking mountain scenery; Forest Service trail map available; separate trails for snowmobiles; rentals, instruction, multi-day ski camping tours and guide service; special group package rates. Mormon Lake Lodge at trailhead with stone fireplace, restaurant, live band Fri. and Sat. nights in western-style saloon. Motel and cabin accommodations. Information: Mark and Deanna Brown, Mormon Lake Ski Touring Center, Mormon Lake, AZ 86038. 602-354-2240.

SPRINGERVILLE: Greer Ski Touring (15 m SW; 2.5 m N of Greer on SR 373), clearly marked trails pass through beautiful scenery in the Valley of the Little Colorado River: 5 interconnecting loops of 1.5 m for beginners, 3.5 for intermediates, 5.75 m for intermediate to advanced, 6.5 m and 7 m for advanced; varied terrain ranges from 8300 ft at parking lot to 9000 ft in the meadows on loop 5 trail; free maps, no trail fee; trails periodically compacted and tracked; sign-in and sign-out log at trailhead checked daily at 5 pm; accident assistance, instruction, rentals, and sales available from Charles S. Tripp (Ski Area Manager), Circle B Market in Greer, 602-735-7540. Lodges, cabins, restaurants, cocktail lounge; shops, grocery store, gas stations in Greer. Information: Charles S. Tripp, Box 121, Greer, AZ 85927; or, Greer Chamber of Commerce, Box 254, Greer, AZ 85927. 602-735-7201. **Alpine Country Club** (25 m S in Alpine), 2-m cross-country trail in addition to skiing on the golf course. Information: Alpine Country Club, Alpine, AZ 85920. 602-339-4574.

TUCSON: Mt. Lemmon Ski Valley (35 m N of Tucson via Catalina Hwy. in the Coronado National Forest), downhill ski facilities with area for cross-country skiers; best skiing is right after snowstorms; good conditions are short-lived because of snowmobiles; rental equipment available; restaurant, bar, public shelter. Bus service from Tucson on weekends by reservation from Mt. Lemmon Ski

Valley. Accommodations in Tucson or nearby Summerhaven. Information: Box 612, Mt. Lemmon, AZ 85619. 602-791-9721.

CALIFORNIA

For additional information, contact the individual area or San Francisco Convention & Visitors Bureau, 1390 Market St., San Francisco, CA 94102; Southern California Visitors Council, 705 W. 7th St., Los Angeles, CA 90017; National Park Service, 450 Golden Gate Ave., San Francisco, CA 94102.

BEAR VALLEY: Bear Valley Nordic Ski School (on SR 4 in Bear Valley; 100 m E of Stockton), 20 m of marked and groomed trails plus unlimited skiing possibilities in Stanislaus National Forest; gentle to challenging terrain for all levels of skiers; trail map available; certified instructors offer group and private lessons; guided day tours (bring your own lunch; reservations 2 days in advance), overnight tours to Duck Lake Hut, Bear Trap Basin Hut, or Jelmini Hut with breakfast and dinner provided (reservations 1 week in advance); annual cross-country races; rentals; package plans; downhill ski facilities on Mt. Reba with day lodge, cafeteria, bar; day-care center for children 2–8 yrs. old. Accommodations at Bear Valley Lodge and area condominiums; restaurants, cocktail lounges, après-ski; shops and services. Touring information: Bear Valley Nordic Ski School, Box 5, Bear Valley, CA 95223. 209-753-2844. Accommodations: Bear Valley Reservations, Box 8, Bear Valley, CA 95223. 209-753-2311.

FRESNO: Tamarack Mtn. Area (50 m NE via SR 168 at Tamarack Ridge), 10.6 km of marked and maintained trails for intermediates in the Sierra National Forest; beautiful vista of Huntington Lake and Sierra Crest; no snowmobiles; plowed parking area. Information: District Ranger, Pineridge Ranger District, U.S. Forest Service, P.O. Box 300, Shaver Lake, CA 93664. 209-841-3311. **China Peak Ski Area** (62 m NE via SR 168 at Lakeshore), trails for cross-country skiers; primarily a downhill ski area with day lodge, cafeteria, restaurant and cocktail lounge; lodging at area and in Canadian

Village and Shaver Lake. Information: China Peak Ski Area, P.O. Box 236, Lakeshore, CA 93634. 209-893-3316. See also Sequoia and Kings Canyon National Parks.

KIRKWOOD: Kirkwood Ski Touring Center (35 m S of South Lake Tahoe on SR 88; 110 m E of Stockton on SR 88), located in an old horse barn on the hill behind historical Kirkwood Inn, home of Zacary Kirkwood, dating to 1864; touring center has wood-burning stove, Nordic library, and many necessary Nordic accessories in the shop; 35 m of marked trails plus unlimited touring possibilities in Eldorado National Forest; trail map (25¢) with brief description of terrain, mileage, and recommended skill level of skier; tours vary from easy 2-m beginner loops through gentle aspen glades to Martin Meadow to more advanced all-day tours above timberline at Carson Pass; Nordic Ski Patrol on duty every weekend; trail donation ($1); group and private instruction for all levels, plus downhill lessons for skate, telemark, and parallel turns on both packed and powder snow; all-day guided tours; lesson lunch tour; all-day snow camping instruction; moonlight tours; overnight tours by arrangement; Far West Ski Assoc. and citizens' races; 12-m endurance and ability race from Echo Summit to Kirkwood; rentals for adults and children. Accommodations at Kirkwood condominiums (Kirkwood Condominiums Reservations, P.O. Box 2, Kirkwood, CA 95646. 209-258-6000); hearty meals and spirits in rustic Kirkwood Inn; extensive downhill ski facilities with day lodge, cafeteria, restaurant, bar, and apres-ski; grocery store next to Inn. Touring information: Kirkwood Ski Touring Center, P.O. Box 77, Kirkwood, CA 95646. 209-258-8864. Additional lodging, housekeeping cabins, restaurant, grocery store, and gas at Caples Lake Resort (½ m W on SR 88); package plans with Kirkwood Touring Center. Information: Caples Lake Resort, Box 8, Kirkwood, CA 95646. 209-258-8888.

LASSEN VOLCANIC NATIONAL PARK (79 m E of Redding via I-5 and SR 36; 49 m E of Red Bluff): **Lassen Ski Touring** (at SW entrance to park), over 50 m of marked trails on gentle rolling hills with steaming fumaroles, mud pots, volcanic remnants, mountain lakes, and towering alpine peaks; map available showing both marked and unmarked trails; instruction and rentals (group rental rates); full-day guided tours to Ridge Lakes, Bumpass Hell Thermal Area, and Forest Lake; winter survival classes; 3-day guided tour over Lassen Park Rd. for the hearty willing to snow camp, meals included; cafeteria and restrooms at chalet adjacent to touring center. Information: Lassen Ski Touring, Mill Creek, CA 96061. 916-595-3376. Accommodations at nearby **Childs Meadows Resort** (in Mill Creek); motel and housekeeping cabins, restaurant and bar; cross-country ski rentals and lessons. Information: Childs Meadows Resort, Mill Creek, CA 96061. 916-595-3391. Additional lodging, restaurants, and services in Mill Creek.

MAMMOTH LAKES: Mammoth Ski Touring Center (at Twin Lakes, next to Tamarack Lodge on Lake Mary Rd.), marked and groomed trails on 35 acres; unlimited wilderness tours into the High Sierra Basin of the **Inyo National Forest;** Far West Ski Assoc. certified instructors offer individual and group classes; guided day tours include lunch and some instruction; moonlight and overnight snow camping tours; races; rental and retail shop; annual heavy snowfall insures a long season, usually from Nov. to June. Accommodations and restaurant at Tamarack Lodge; additional lodging, restaurants, and services in Mammoth Lakes (2 m); nearby Mammoth Mtn. Ski Area, with extensive downhill ski facilities, has 2 day lodges with cafeterias. Information: Mammoth Ski Touring Center, P.O. Box 102, Mammoth Lakes, CA 93546. 714-934-6955. **Sierra Meadows Ski Touring Center** (on Sherwin Creek & Old Mammoth Rds.), 15–20 m of marked and groomed trails for beginner to expert on wide open meadows and rolling hills with High Sierra scenery; trail map available; instruction, guided tours, and rentals; snack bar at area. Mammoth Lakes, a full-service resort area, is accessible by Sierra Pacific Airlines and Greyhound bus. Touring information: Sierra Meadows Ski Touring Center, P.O. Box D-4, Mammoth Lakes, CA 93546. 714-934-6161. Accommodations: Mammoth Lake Chamber of Commerce, 714-934-2522. **Ernie's June Lake Ski Touring Center** (several m N), located in the Hartley Springs Area of the Inyo National Forest; novice to intermediate maintained trails on generally flat, heavily forested terrain with some rolling hills; trail map available; half- and full-day lessons; full-day guided tour with hot soup and wine; overnight tours to Bodie, Glass Meadows, and Devils Postpile including ski equipment, one lunch and dinner per day, community cook gear (some tents and packs available); winter survival and snow camping seminars; rentals and sales. Nearby June Lake downhill ski area has day lodge, cafeteria, bar, and lockers. Information: Ernie's June Lake Ski Touring Center, Box 36, June Lake, CA 93529. 714-648-7756. **Rock Creek Winter Lodge** (30 m S off US 395; halfway between Mammoth Lakes and Bishop; 8 m up Rock Creek Rd. from Tom's Place), 8 m of marked and maintained trails on glaciated valley terrain with surrounding peaks of over 13,000 ft, for beginners to advanced winter mountaineers; instruction and guided tours; rentals; accommodations in area lodge and cabins, family-style meals. Information: Mark Williams, Manager, Rock Creek Winter Lodge, RR, Tom's Place, Bishop, CA. 93514. 714-935-4464.

MT. SHASTA: Ski Shasta Nordic Tours (14 m NE via Everett Memorial Hwy.; off I-5, midway between Redding and Yreka), half- and full-day tours with instruction; 2-day overnight tours with lodging in rustic cabins; evening tours by arrangement; reservations required for rentals and instruction; downhill ski facilities with day lodge, cafeteria, bar. Accommodations, restaurants, and services in Mt. Shasta. Information: Ski Shasta, P.O. Box 271, Mt. Shasta, CA 96067. 916-926-2663.

PASADENA: Angeles National Forest, 650,000 acres of steep, rugged mountainous terrain N of the Los Angeles metropolitan area; popular trails for cross-country skiing include: **East Blue Ridge Rd.** (2 m SW of Big Pines on SR 2), 10 m of trail from Inspiration Pt. to Guffy Campground; excellent views from ridge top; primitive camping permitted, no snowmobiles; plowed parking area. Information: U.S. Forest Service, Big Pine Visitor Center, P.O. Box 1011, Wrightwood, CA 92397. 714-249-3504. **Charlton Picnic Area** (approx. 24 m NE on SR 2 from La Canada), 2 m of trails for beginners and intermediates on flat rolling mountaintop terrain with more wonderful views; snowmobiles permitted; limited parking. Information: U.S. Forest Service, Oak Grove Park, Flintridge, CA 91011. 213-796-5541. **Crystal Lake Ski Route** (on SR 39 at Crystal Lake Recreation Area), 200–300 acres for beginners to experts on mostly flat terrain surrounded by steep ridges; primitive winter camping permitted; no snowmobiles; snack bar; plowed parking area. Information: Ranger, U.S. Forest Service, Crystal Lake Ranger Station, Rt. 1, Azusa, CA 91702. 213-969-1012. Plans are proposed by the U.S. Forest Service to mark trails and maintain restroom facilities for the 3 above areas by 1984. Additional information: Forest Supervisor, U.S. Forest Service, 150 S. Los Robles Ave., Suite 300, Pasadena, CA 91101.

Mountain High Ski Area (on SR 2, 3 m NW of Wrightwood), cross-country ski lessons; downhill ski facilities, day lodge, cafeteria. Information: Mt. High Ski Area, Wrightwood, CA 92397.

Mt. Pinos Wintersports Area (90 m N via I-5; W of Gorman), many m of Forest Service trails suitable for cross-country skiing; toboggan and snowmobile areas, snow play area; rental equipment; snack bar. Accommodations in cabins (12). Information: Superintendent, Mt. Pinos Winter Sports Area, 9304 E. Ralph St., Rosemead, CA 91770. 213-280-5408.

SAN BERNARDINO: San Bernardino National Forest (621,000 acres N and E), cross-country skiing possible on existing trails where snow can be found; a popular area, **San Gorgonio Wilderness,** centering on a spine of mountains 10,000 ft high, has rugged terrain but maintained trails; access off SR 38 at Camp Angeles, Poopout Hill, and numerous other points; trails through pine, cedar, and white fir lead to and along the ridge, the view from the top encompasses a breathtaking 360-degree panorama; permit needed to enter wilderness (District Ranger, Mill Creek Ranger Station, Rt. 1, Box 264, Mentone, CA 92359. 714-794-1123).

Goldmine Ski Area (E off SR 38 at Big Bear Lake), primarily a downhill ski area, offers cross-country skiing; day lodge, cafeteria, restaurant, cocktail lounge; lodging, restaurants, and services in nearby Big Bear Lake. Information: Goldmine Ski Area, P.O. Box 1671, Big Bear Lake, CA 92315. 714-585-2517.

SEQUOIA and KINGS CANYON NATIONAL PARKS: 1300 sq m of park include groves of giant sequoias, 14,495-ft Mt. Whitney, peaks of the Sierra Nevada, 2 enormous canyons of the Kings River, lakes, waterfalls, wildlife, and vast mountain wilderness. **Sequoia National Park** (accessible via SR 198 from Visalia), Village of Giant Forest: Lodgepole Visitor Center (daily 9–5; 209-565-3364) offers 3-hour tours in the grove of giant sequoias for intermediate-level skiers, also 2-m compass course among the trees of Giant Forest with booklets and compasses for loan; information and maps for 7 marked trails include elevation, miles one way, and hours needed for round trip; accommodations and coffee shop at Giant Forest Lodge (reservations: Sequoia and Kings Canyon Hospitality Service, 209-565-3373); village general store; Wolverton Ski Bowl

(4 m N) has downhill ski facilities, snack bar, ski shop. **Kings Canyon National Park** (accessible via SR 180 from Fresno), Grant Grove: Grant Grove Visitor Center (daily 9–5; 209-335-2315) has information and maps for 5 marked cross-country ski trails; provides snowshoes for snowshoe walks, limited to 15 persons. Village service station has limited selection of groceries and light snacks. Accommodations at Wilsonia Lodge (209-335-2310). Additional information: Superintendent, Sequoia and Kings Canyon National Parks, Three Rivers, CA 93271.

Sequoia Ski Touring (next to Beetle Rock in Giant Forest, via SR 198 from Visalia), Nordic ski school certified by Professional Ski Instructors of America; beginner through advanced instruction, downhill lessons on cross-country skis, special children's lessons; guided tours into all areas of the park; 1-day and 4-day Winter Travel Courses cover snow camping, route finding, effects of cold, avalanche hazard, and rescue; overnight tours for new skiers with emphasis on snow camping, not distance, food and community equipment provided; Trans-Sierra Tours lead strong intermediate skiers across the Great Western Divide; moonlight tours; citizens' races; rentals for adults and children. Information: Sequoia Ski Touring, Sequoia National Park, CA 93262. 209-565-3308. **SEQUOIA NATIONAL FOREST**, in several sections, is part of the S end of the Sierra Nevada Range. **Big Meadows**, 10,000 acres surrounded by Sequoia and Kings Canyon National Parks, is a popular cross-country ski area (access via SR 180 to Grant Grove, 8–10 m E on Generals Hwy.); 20 m of Forest Service marked trails on generally rolling terrain for beginners to experts with most trails in the intermediate range; snowmobiles permitted in designated areas only; winter access and parking maintained, except snow removal can take time after a big storm (access information: 209-565-3351 or 209-336-1881). Additional information: Ranger, Pinehurst Ranger Station, U.S. Forest Service, Miramonte, CA 93641.

Montecito-Sequoia Nordic Ski Center (65 m E of Fresno via SR 180 to Kings Canyon National Park entrance station, continue 1.5 m to the "Y," turn right, then 8 m S), 52 m of marked and mapped trails meander over open meadows, wind along old logging roads and narrow bridle paths through groves of 3000-yr-old redwoods; trail maps marked with distance, difficulty, and vista points; professional instruction; guided half- and full-day tours; overnight camping trips by arrangement; rental ski equipment, ice skates, and snowshoes; retail shop. A self-contained Nordic center, lodge has 22 rooms with private bath, dining room, and recreation room, both with large stone fireplaces; family-style meals; rates include lodging, meals, and full use of recreation areas; special rates for 2-day stay and for children under 12. Information: Virginia C. Barnes, Montecito-Sequoia Lodge, 1485 Redwood Dr., Los Altos, CA 94022. 415-967-8612.

SODA SPRINGS: Royal Gorge Nordic Ski Resort (off I-80 at Donner Pass, then 1 m E on old SR 40; 3 hours from Bay Area) boasts the largest groomed trail system on the West Coast with 75 m of marked trails on 2300 acres of plateau region above the American River's Royal Gorge, unique for its rolling terrain on the crest of the Sierra; machine-groomed double-tracked trails for all abilities; full-time professional ski patrol on duty; trail fee ($3.50), map available; rentals; certified instructors offer group and private lessons (includes trail pass); warming huts with snack bars at 2 trailheads, plus 2 more warming huts en route; package weekend programs include 3-m sleigh ride from parking area to Wilderness Lodge, mulled wine and hors d'oeuvres on arrival, 2 nights' lodging, 5 meals (French cuisine and wine), trail passes, ski lessons and seminars, moonlight tours, hot tub and sauna, casual amusements; special 5-day ski-week programs; snow camping tours; midweek special with the **Soda Springs Hotel** (a great old place totally furnished with antiques, which are for sale) includes 5 nights' lodging, meals, rentals, instruction, and trail passes; guided tours to Yellowstone, Canada, Norway, and Argentina (in summer); annual series of Royal Gorge Cup Races, open to all skiers. Additional lodging and restaurants in Soda Springs area. Information: Royal Gorge Nordic Ski Resort, P.O. Box 178, Soda Springs, CA 95728. 916-426-3793. **Donner Ski Ranch** (3 m off I-80 at Soda Springs/ Norden exit), 300 acres open to cross-country skiing; no marked trails; primarily a downhill ski area; rentals and instruction; area lodge has accommodations, cafeteria, dining room, cocktail lounge, and ski shop. Information: Donner Ski Ranch, P.O. Box 66, Norden, CA 95724. 916-426-3578. Greyhound bus service to Soda Springs; Amtrak to Truckee (10 m E).

SONORA: Pinecrest Area of the **Stanislaus National Forest** (30 m E on SR 108), 4-m beginner loop with 2–6° grade, 15–20 m of intermediate trails with 5–10° grade; marked trails follow road beds and wind through conifer-forested slopes; elevations vary from 5600 to 7500 ft with snow lasting 3–4 months in the higher areas; trail map available; no snowmobiles allowed; winter camping permitted at Pinecrest Campground and in the forest; Pinecrest Lodge at area has dormitory facilities for youth groups, recreation room, and meals served family-style. Additional accommodations in Long Barn (10 m W); restaurants and services in Pinecrest and Strawberry. Information: District Ranger, Summit Ranger Station, Box 1295, Star Route, Sonora, CA 95370. 209-965-3434. Nearby **Dodge Ridge Ski Area** (32 m E on SR 108), with downhill ski facilities, has day lodge, cafeteria, snack bar, and babysitters. Information: Dodge Ridge Ski Area, P.O. Box 1035, Pinecrest, CA 95364. 209-965-3474. **Calaveras Big Trees State Park** (N via SR 49 & SR 4; 4 m NE of Arnold), 5994-acre park with Sierra redwood groves has marked trails suitable for cross-country skiers.

SOUTH LAKE TAHOE: Eldorado National Forest (S and W of Lake Tahoe), Forest Service offers a variety of free tours conducted by a local forest naturalist; tours vary from 3 to 6 hours, from easy level terrain to moderately strenuous terrain with climbs; starting point at intersection of Fallen Leaf Rd. and SR 89, ½ m N of Camp Richardson; tours include easy 3-hour tour through Taylor Creek Meadow; easy 4-hour tour to NE shore of Fallen Leaf Lake with lunch (bring your own) in Cathedral Meadow; more strenuous 5-hour tour with moderate climbing to Echo Lakes; 4-hour strenuous tour along the Pacific Crest to Benwood Meadows with spectacular views of Tahoe Basin en route. For complete list of tours and dates: U.S. Forest Service, Box 8465, South Lake Tahoe, CA 95731. 916-544-6420.

Sugar House West (5 m S via US 50 at Yank's Station in Meyers), no marked trails but maps and information available for unlimited touring in backcountry of Eldorado National Forest; certified ski school gives daily lessons for all skill levels at the Tahoe Paradise Golf Course, also classes for advanced downhill techniques; guided day tours into Sierra backcountry include instruction, map and compass use, avalanche recognition, and lunch if all-day tour; short evening tours end with a roaring campfire, steak, and wine; extended guided tours: from Echo Lakes to Squaw Valley (3 nights), into Mokelumne Wilderness (2 nights), along Pacific Crest South (2 nights); extended tour price includes all equipment, meals, and guides; easy overnight tours to a rustic cabin in Meiss Meadow off Carson Pass with steak dinner; orienteering and survival instruction;

snow camping; several scheduled team races; rental and retail ski and backpack shop; special youth group activities. Motel, restaurant, and lounge next door; additional lodging, restaurants, and services in South Lake Tahoe. Information: David A. Hamilton, Sugar House West, Box 8135, South Lake Tahoe, CA 95731. 916-541-6811.

TAHOE CITY: Squaw Valley Nordic Sports Center (5 m N off SR 89), site of 1960 Winter Olympic Games; certified instructors offer basic, intermediate, and advanced instruction: group and private lessons; guided half- and full-day tours, moonlight, and overnight tours; citizens' races; rental and retail shop. A major full-service resort area with extensive downhill ski facilities, budget to deluxe accommodations (package plans), numerous restaurants and lively night spots; Blyth Olympic Ice Arena (skating instruction available), heated swimming pool, saunas; nursery, general store, boutiques. Information: Squaw Valley Nordic Ctr., Box 2007, Olympic Valley, CA 95730. 916-583-6985. Reservations: 916-583-6966.
Big Chief Cross-Country Skiing (7 m N on SR 89), 20 m of marked trails; certified Nordic instructors offer lessons and guided tours; snow camping tours; races; rental and retail shop. Lodging in housekeeping cabins; restaurant. Information: Big Chief Cross-Country Skiing, P.O. Box 2427, Truckee, CA 95734. 916-587-4723.
    Sugar Pine Point State Park (10 m S on SR 89), 1975 forested acres on the shore of Lake Tahoe, has a trail suitable for cross-country skiing.

TRUCKEE: Northstar Nordic Center (on SR 267, 7½ m SE; 3½ hours from Bay Area), 50 km of marked and maintained trails on 2560 acres of open meadows and valleys and over old logging roads; trail donation ($1), map available; instruction and guided tours; scheduled overnight cabin and tent tours; rentals; downhill ski facilities, day lodge, cafeteria, restaurant, bar; nursery. A second-home family resort community with lodge and condominium accommodations for over 800; restaurant, bar, après-ski; deli, rental and retail shops. Information: Sam Medford, Director, Northstar Nordic Center, P.O. Box 129, Truckee, CA 95734. 916-562-0396.
Tahoe Donner Touring Center (in Truckee), 20 m of marked and maintained trails for beginners through advanced; small trail fee, trail map available; certified instructors; guided tours; rentals; area lodge serves snacks and dinners. Information: Rondi Thorwaldsen, Tahoe Donner Touring Center, P.O. Box 2462, Truckee,

CA 95734. 916-587-2496. **Tahoe Donner Ski Bowl** (2 m W on old SR 40, then 4 m N on Northwoods Blvd.), Nordic Center located at Northwoods Clubhouse; instruction, guided tours, and rentals; day lodge, cafeteria, bar, condominiums at base of down-hill ski area (3 m). Information: Tahoe Donner Ski Bowl, Drawer G, Truckee, CA 95734. Ski Bowl: 916-587-6046; Lodge: 916-587-2551. Accommodations, restaurants, and services in Truckee.

YOSEMITE NATIONAL PARK: Yosemite Mountaineering School (enter via SR 120 from Stockton, SR 140 from Merced and SR 41 from Fresno; school located in Curry Village), beautiful mountainous region with inspiring gorges, granite cliffs and waterfalls, groves of giant sequoias and forests of pine, fir, and oak, and meadows and lakes in the high country; Yosemite, the oldest touring school on the West Coast, offers an extensive teaching program: Touring I, a one-day course designed for those who have never skied, is an introduction to equipment and basic skills followed by a tour; Tour-ing II emphasizes learning and polishing skills for downhill tours and for techniques for tough terrain; Touring Survival teaches basics for what to do if you are caught out in the woods for a night or two; Advanced Instruction offers pointers on specific tech-niques; Overnight Tours for beginners to Mariposa Grove of Giant Sequoias include indoor bivouac at winter-closed Big Trees Lodge with dinner and breakfast; Snow Camping Tours are designed to teach and practice basics of winter camping and survival; 2- and 3-day tours to Glacier Point and Ostrander Lake ski huts in the beautiful High Sierra country are for advanced intermediates; for the advanced skier willing to carry own backpack gear and tent, trips to Mt. Hoffman and a 7-day tour into Tuolumne Meadows in the heart of the Sierra are scheduled; annual 13-km race and racing clinics; rentals available; other winter activities in the park include: ice skating (rentals), rock climbing, snow-cat rides, free Ranger-Naturalist-led snowshoe walks, guided valley bus tours. Accommodations at Ahwahnee Hotel, Yosemite Lodge and cabins, and a range of lodging in Curry Village; choice of restaurants; shops and services. Touring information; Yosemite Mountaineering, Yosemite Park & Curry Co., Yosemite National Park, CA 95389. 209-372-4611, ext. 244. Accommodations: Reservations Desk, Yosemite Park & Curry Co. 209-373-4171.

COLORADO

For additional information, contact the individual area or Colorado Visitors Bureau, 225 W. Colfax Ave., Denver, CO 80202.

ASPEN: Ashcroft Ski Touring Unlimited (W on SR 82 to Castle Creek Rd., ½ hour from Aspen), 30 km of marked and maintained trails, professionally groomed with Scandinavian tracksetters; daily trail fee ($4); 3 warming huts en route with potbellied stoves and complimentary hot beverages; certified instructors; rentals, waxing, repairs; ½-day beginner tours, all-day tours with picnic lunch at Kellogg Cabin, tours to Pine Creek Cookhouse for lunch featuring Hungarian and Swiss specialties with full complement of beer, wine, and spirits, or, with the help of a miner's head lamp and a guide, tours for evening dinner at the Cookhouse (reservations required a day in advance); overnight tours to Kellogg Cabin and to Toklat Chalet near the timberline at the gateway to Pearl Pass; touring center headquarters adjacent to parking area. Ashcroft courtesy bus leaves Rubey Park at the Mill Street Mall in Aspen 9:15 am and returns 4:30 pm daily. Reservations and information: Ashcroft Ski Touring Unlimited, Box 1572, Aspen, CO 81611. 303-925-1971.

    Aspen Mountain, Buttermilk, and Snowmass all offer instruction and guided tours for cross-country skiers; rentals available at shops in Aspen and at Snowmass; 8 km of maintained trails at Snowmass; Aspen boasts a cabin cafe that's only accessible by cross-country skiing. Aspen, a 3-mtn. (Aspen Mtn., Highlands, Buttermilk) full-service resort area has over 100 places to stay in and almost as many restaurants; old mining town atmosphere with Victorian-style hotels and Old West saloons; lots of night spots and live music. Snowmass (12 m W) with slopeside lodging, condominiums, and restaurants is a contemporary self-sustaining community at the base of an extensive downhill ski area. Both Snowmass and Aspen offer sleigh rides, wilderness dog sled rides, ice skating, heated outdoor swimming pools, saunas; nursery, boutiques, and movie theaters. Free shuttle service between all 4 ski areas and town of Aspen. Aspen touring information: Aspen Mtn. Ski School, P.O. Box 1248, Aspen, CO 81611. 303-925-1220. Reservations: Aspen

Reservations, Inc., P.O. Box 4546, Aspen, CO 81611. 303-925-4000. Toll free: 800-525-4014. Snowmass touring and reservation information: Snowmass Resort, P.O. Box 5566, Snowmass, CO 81615. 303-923-2000.

BRECKENRIDGE: Breckenridge Touring School (70 m from Denver via I-70 to exit 38, then S on SR 9), many m of marked and maintained trails; some meander past old mines and cabins dating back to the early 1800s; certified instructors offer class and private lessons for all skill levels, also advanced technique clinics on deep powder skiing and telemark turns; backcountry guided tours for beginners through experts; rentals; annual "Telemark Returns" festival features dual slalom and freestyle competition on touring skis and dress of the 1800s. Breckenridge, with extensive downhill ski facilities, is a major full-service resort area based in an old mining town with Victorian-era houses and shops; condominium, lodge, hotel, and dorm accommodations; full variety of restaurants, après-ski, shops, and services. Free shuttle bus meets westbound daylight hour buses at Frisco; shuttle service to Copper Mountain and Keystone. Information: Breckenridge Ski Corp., P.O. Box 1058, Breckenridge, CO 80424. 303-453-2368. Reservations: Breckenridge Resort Assoc., P.O. Box 1909. 303-453-2918. Snow report: 303-837-9907.

BOULDER: Ski Eldora (21 m W via SR 119 to Nederland, then 3 m W), 22 km of marked and groomed trails for beginner to advanced skiers on gentle rolling forested terrain; trail fee ($2), map available; instruction and rentals; guided tours on request; downhill ski facilities with base lodge, cafeteria, and nursery. Accommodations, restaurants, and services in Nederland and Boulder; bus service from Boulder. Information: Lake Eldora Corp., P.O. Box 430, Nederland, CO 80466. 303-447-8012. Snow report: 303-447-8013. Lodging reservations: Boulder Chamber of Commerce, 1001 Canyon Blvd., Boulder, CO 80302. 303-442-1044.

COLORADO SPRINGS: Pikes Peak Region Ski Touring Areas (NW via US 24), 5 areas recommended by El Paso County Parks & Rec. in cooperation with the Pike-San Isabel National Forests. **Saylor Park** (NW to Woodland Park via US 24, then N 3.5 m to Rampart Range Rd., proceed N on Rampart Range Rd. 8.3 m), sign and parking area at trailhead, parking permitted along roadway also; long open meadow with network of unmarked trails for all abilities; novice skiers should take care not to travel too far downhill; challenging terrain throughout the surrounding lodgepole pine forests for more experienced skiers. **Gove Creek Rd.** (US 24 to Woodland Park, then N to Rampart Range Rd., proceed 12.9 m from the end of the pavement N of Woodland Park to Gove Creek Rd.), nonmaintained portions of Gove Creek Rd., Rampart Range Rd., and surrounding area provide excellent opportunities for cross-country skiers; parking permitted along the roadside as long as the roadway is not blocked. **Rampart Reservoir** (US 24 to Woodland Park, then N about 4 m to Rampart Range Rd., proceed SE 2.4 m and park, or continue 1.4 m to entrance of the Rampart Recreation Area), varied terrain for all levels of skiers from gently rolling meadows to steep wooded hillsides; with enough snow, 13-m trail around the reservoir suitable for touring. **Crags Campground** (W on US 24 to Divide, then S on SR 67 for 4.2 m to Rocky Mtn. Mennonite Camp turnoff, from turnoff, road goes 1.5 m beyond to Crags Campground; road from highway may be impassable depending on snow conditions), great variety of terrain and generally good snow conditions make this a popular area for novice to advanced skiers. **Horsethief Park** (W on US 24 to Divide, then S on SR 67 for 9.1 m to the old railroad tunnel on the way to Cripple Creek), large mountain park which offers beautiful scenery to skiers willing to make the brisk uphill climb. Information: Pikes Peak District Ranger, Pike National Forest, 320 West Fillmore, Colorado Springs, CO 80907.

COPPER MOUNTAIN: Copper Mountain Ski Escape Ski Touring School (70 m from Denver via I-70), 35 km of marked and maintained trails on mountainous terrain surrounding Copper Mountain; certified instructors offer introductory lessons with morning class in basic technique followed by a gentle and scenic afternoon tour; intermediate and advanced clinics for honing skills in flat track and downhill technique including telemark turns; private and group instruction; guided tours include moonlight tours with picnic supper prepared by guide over a campfire, Historical Cabin Dinner Tour to rustic Wheeler Guard Station for an old American family-style dinner with kerosene lamps and a wood-burning stove re-creating a "first settler" atmosphere; certified mountain touring guides available for backcountry full-day powder tours and overnight trips into the Vail Pass Area; Tour the Summit program offers all-day guided tours with lunch and shuttle transportation to nearby Breckenridge and Keystone; rentals at touring center; lift ticket exchange program entitles skier to rental equipment and a discounted ski touring lesson followed by a short tour; Nastar cross-country races every Sat. Copper Mountain, a large downhill ski area, has a complete village with condominium accommodations, restaurants, lounges, shops, and services. Free shuttle meets Continental Trailways bus at Dillon/Frisco (9 m); free village shuttle; shuttle to Breckenridge and Keystone. Information: Copper Mountain Ski Escape Ski Touring School, Box 1, Copper Mountain, CO 80443. 303-668-2882.

CRESTED BUTTE: Crested Butte Mountain Resort (from Denver via US 285, US 50, and SR 135; 30 m N of Gunnison via SR 135), 12 km of marked and groomed trails; trail fee; Nordic pass ($2) on Keystone chair good for 2 chairlift rides; private and group instruction; guided half-day and day tours, overnight tours to Elkton ($60), Irwin ($80), and Aspen ($100); rentals; extensive downhill ski facilities, base lodge, cafeteria, dining room, lounge; nursery, health club, heated swimming pools; snowshoeing, ice fishing, snowmobiling. A modern ski village and old mining town of Crested Butte (2½ m) combine to make a full-service resort area with lodging for 2500; variety of restaurants, bars, après-ski; shops, services, and convention facilities. Air and Continental Trailways bus service into gateway Gunnison. Information: Crested Butte Mountain Resort, P.O. Box 528, Crested Butte, CO. 81224. 303-349-6611. Snow report: 303-349-5327.

DURANGO: San Juan National Forest (2 million acres N and E), extensive trail system for cross-country touring; access to the forest via US 160 and US 550; avalanche danger exists above 9000 ft. Information: Supervisor, San Juan National Forest, U.S. Forest Service, 701 Camino Del Rio, Durango, CO 81301. 303-247-4874. Located in the forest, **Purgatory Ski Area** (25 m N via US 550) has 45 m of trails, 20 m of which are maintained and groomed with tracks prepared every other day; no trail fee; rolling hills and lots of snow for beginners to experts; altitude ranges from 8500 ft to 11,000 ft; certified instructors, private and group lessons; rentals; major downhill ski area with base lodge, cafeteria, restaurant, bar, nursery. Lodge and condominium accommodations at area;

deli, drugstore, liquor store. **Tamarron Resort** (8 m S of Purgatory) offers rentals and instruction; has lodge and townhouse accommodations, gourmet dining, après-ski, heated pool, indoor tennis, sleigh rides, tobogganing. Ski instruction and rentals also available in **Durango** as well as a wide variety of lodging, restaurants, and services. Touring information for Purgatory, Tamarron, and Durango: Purgatory Ski Area, Durango Ski Corp., P.O. Box 666, Durango, CO 81301. 303-259-1490 or 259-1485. Lodging reservations: Chamber of Commerce Reservation Service, P.O. Box 1311, Durango, CO 81301. 303-247-3838.

ESTES PARK: Rocky Mountain National Park (E via US 34 or SR 66), 410-sq-m park in the Rockies' Front Range with towering peaks over 14,000 ft; east side of the park receives much less snow and more winds and has generally more rugged terrain; west side of the park has more snow, less wind, but colder temperatures. Cross-country skiing in this park might more aptly be described as ski mountaineering since numerous hazards exist in the rugged, high-country terrain; all skiers should tour with caution, especially beginners. All overnight tourers must obtain a Backcountry Use Permit (Park Headquarters near Estes Park, 303-586-2371, or West Unit near Grand Lake, 303-627-3471). Most popular trips on the east side include: **Bear Lake to Hallowell Park,** trailhead marked with red plastic arrowheads, begins at Bear Lake parking lot; 4.5-m one-way trip takes 3 to 5 hours; has short steep climb, lots of downhill and some level terrain; recommended for advanced beginners; leave a car at Hallowell Park on your way to Bear Lake. **Glacier Gorge Junction to Loch Vale,** from parking lot ½ m below Bear Lake, trail leads to Loch Vale and Alberta Falls; allow 4 to 6 hours for round trip. **Glacier Gorge Junction to Glacier Gorge,** follow the above route to the Loch Vale-Glacier Gorge trail jct, then several hundred yds up the Loch Vale drainage, turn left across the wooden bridge; summer trail leads to Glacier Gorge and Lake Mills with some steep climbs and descents en route, not recommended for beginners; about a 4-to-6-hour round trip. **Nymph, Dream, and Emerald Lakes,** from Bear Lake trail to Nymph Lake, is easy 1–2-hour round trip tour; from W shore of Nymph Lake, an easy climb leads to Dream Lake ½ m farther; then up the valley 1 m more is Emerald Lake; tour to Dream and Emerald Lakes for experienced skiers. **Bear Lake to Fern Lake and Moraine Park,** 10 m, 1- or 2-day tour, for experienced ski mountaineers in excellent condition; topographic map and compass will be needed; be prepared for severe wind and low temperatures. **Wild Basin,** follow road from Copeland Lake (S on SR 7) to Wild Basin Trailhead; summer trail leads to Ouzel Falls, 3 m, and to Thunder Lake, 7 m (one-way); lower Wild Basin offers level terrain and few avalanche hazards, above treeline, precipitous slopes present many slide paths. Rangers, often on duty at Bear Lake on weekends, will assist skiers and provide winter information. Brochure with detailed tour suggestions as well as information about terrain, equipment, weather, safety, avalanches, and park policies concerning winter travel in the park is available at the Park Headquarters near the Beaver Meadows Entrance or the West District Office near Grand Lake.

Popular tours on the west side of the park include: **East Inlet** (from Grand Lake via US 34 and SR 278), follow the "tunnel road" to its end near the eastern shore of Grand Lake, ski E ½ m up past Adams Falls into the first meadow; from here, ski out across the meadow or along the frozen river into the second meadow; after first 2 m, trail steepens; rated intermediate to advanced. **North Inlet** (from "tunnel road" N of Grand Lake, turn right at water works bldg., proceed to Summerland Park), first 1½ m shared with snowmobilers, beyond Summerland, foot travel only; 3½ m to Cascade Falls; for beginners to advanced. **Tonahutu Creek Trail** (park at West Unit Visitor Center), head E for easy 2-m tour to Grand Lake; or continue to Big Meadows, 4 m from the Visitor Center and a climb of 700 ft. **Green Mountain Trail** (trailhead 3 m N of Visitor Center), shortest route to Big Meadows, 2 m; all-day loop possible by combining this trail with Tonahutu Creek Trail. **Onahu Creek Trail** (N of Visitor Center, trailhead at Onahu Creek picnic area), half- to full-day loop back to Green Mtn. Trail for advanced skiers; difficult area between Big Meadows and Onahu Creek; topographical map necessary. **Valley Loop Trail** (8 m N of Visitor Center, at Timber Creek Campground), park near the amphitheater; follow markers N and E across frozen beaver ponds and elk meadows, then S down the Kawuneeche Valley to the old Holzwarth Homestead; trail continues back up the east side of the Colorado River to trailhead; 2-m loop for beginner to intermediate skiers. **Colorado River Trail** (park at the end of plowed road; US 34 closed in the winter), ski off the road to the left and follow markers directly N along the river; en route are ruins of miner cabins (2 m) and former boom town, Lulu City (2 m); at this point, trail steepens and leads to La Poudre Pass at 10,000 ft and to other skiing opportunities involving overnight camp. Pamphlet describing touring opportunities on the west side of the park is available at the Park Visitor Center, 2 m N of Grand Lake on US 34. Additional information: Superintendent, Rocky Mountain National Park, Estes Park, CO 80517.

Hidden Valley (on US 34, 10 m W), a good jumping-off point for tours in Rocky Mtn. National Park; downhill ski area with base lodge, cafeteria, and nursery on weekends; popular family area. Information: P.O. Box 98, Estes Park, CO 80517. 303-586-4887.

Rocky Mountain Ski Tours, Inc. (in Estes Park), staff of certified instructors offer 1-day introductory class, 3-day course in basic technique, and 5-day course covering waxing, flat-track, up and downhill, poling, trail skills, and wilderness skills; guided tours on 100 m of trails throughout Rocky Mountain National Park; tours tailored to individual or group; rentals and repairs; group rates for instruction, tours, and rentals. Information: Rocky Mountain Ski Tours, Inc., Box 413, Estes Park, CO 80517. Instruction center: 303-586-3553. Ski rental center: 303-586-2114. Accommodations, restaurants, and services in Estes Park. Information: Estes Park Chamber of Commerce, P.O. Box 3050, Estes Park, CO 80517. 303-586-4431.

FRASER: Devil's Thumb Ranch Cross-Country Center (just off US 40, 3 m N; 7 m N of Winter Park), 50 km of professionally designed trails on a gently rolling valley bordering the Arapahoe National Forest, directly below the Continental Divide; 15-km race course designed to F.I.S. standards; staff of professional instructors; all trails carefully groomed; trail fee ($2) for non-guests; lodge accommodations with both economical and deluxe rooms, fine hearty mountain fare, exercise room, Jacuzzi and sauna; ski store, rentals, skis waxed free of charge for daily snow conditions. Complimentary transportation to Winter Park; combination tickets available for downhill and cross-country skiing. Devil's Thumb, official Rocky Mountain training site for the U.S. Cross-Country Ski Team, is directed by Dick Taylor, former U.S. Olympic Team Captain. Information: Devil's Thumb Ranch Cross-Country Center, Fraser, CO 80442. 303-726-8155 or 726-8298.

GRANBY: C Lazy U Ranch (7 m N of Granby off SR 125), many m of marked and groomed trails on 5000-acre ranch; rolling meadows and forested foothills provide every type of terrain for beginner through advanced skiers; rentals, instruction, and guided tours available; sledding, tubing, ice skating, and sleigh rides; lodge accommodations include some suites with fireplace; package plans include all facilities, services, and activities of the ranch, 3 meals daily, fresh basket of fruit daily in each room, cross-country ski instruction, and courtesy transportation to Granby and Winter Park (a major downhill ski area). Continental Trailways bus from Denver stops in Granby. Information: P.O. Box 378, Granby, CO 80446. 303-887-3344. **Snow Mountain Ranch** (off US 40, 7 m from Granby; 75 m from Denver), operated by the YMCA, offers many m of trails suitable for cross-country skiing on 3000 acres; tubing hill, ice skating, snowmobiling, sleigh rides; downhill skiing at nearby Winter Park; wide range of accommodations for families, youth groups, and large adult groups; extensive conference facilities. Information: YMCA Snow Mountain Ranch, Box 558, Granby, CO 80446. 303-887-3332. In Denver: 303-861-8300.

GRAND JUNCTION: Mesa Lakes Resort (45 m E; 14 m S of Mesa on SR 65), 33 m of trails on the Grand Mesa, largest flat-top mountain in the world; terrain is rolling and in some places rugged; snow conditions usually excellent because of 10,000- to 11,000-ft altitude, minimum avalanche danger due to flatness; some trails groomed, trail fee requested; instruction, rentals, and guided tours available; trail map grades 8 trails from beginner through advanced, and length varies from ½ m to 5 m; West-Branch Trail leads to Powderhorn; ice skating, ice fishing, and snowmobiling (in certain areas); accommodations in heated cabins, lodge restaurant serves 3 meals daily and will pack a box lunch; package plans available. Information: Mesa Lakes Resort, Box 230, Mesa, CO 81643. 303-268-5467.

    Powderhorn (40 m E via I-70 and SR 65), located on the N slope of the Grand Mesa, offers ideal terrain for cross-country skiers with panoramic views of mesas and canyons; downhill ski area with base lodge, cafeteria. Information: Powderhorn Ski Area, P.O. Box 1826, Grand Junction, CO 81501. 303-268-5482 or 242-5637.

GUNNISON: Curecanti National Recreation Area (W of Gunnison), area extending 40 m along the Gunnison River with Blue Mesa,

Morrow Point, and Crystal Lakes; 4 unplowed roads popular with cross-country skiers wind through sagebrush mesas and into timbered slopes of higher elevations. **Dry Creek Rd.** (15 m W on US 50), 12-m tour is a strenuous trip from 7600 to 10,500 ft, first 4 m easy. **East Elk Creek Rd.** (17 m W on US 50), easy 4-m tour along a stream from 7600 to 8000 ft. **Red Creek Rd.** (20 m W on US 50), moderate 10-m grade from 7600 to 10,200 ft. **Soap Creek Rd.** (26 m W on US 50, then 2 m W on SR 92), 17-m tour rated easy to moderate climbs from 7600 to 8000 ft. No snowmobiles permitted. Information: Superintendent, Curecanti National Recreation Area, P.O. Box 1040, Gunnison, CO 81230. 303-641-2337.

KEYSTONE: Keystone (68 m W of Denver via I-70; 6 m E of Dillon on US 6), 20 m of marked and maintained trails for beginners to advanced; 5-m practice loop groomed daily; trails over mountainous meadows and rolling valleys with old mining cabins en route; free trail map; instruction, guided tours, and rentals available; extensive downhill ski facilities; ice skating, sleigh rides, dogsled rides, swimming pool, saunas, indoor tennis; nursery; a contemporary full-service resort village with lodge (Keystone Lodge rated AAA 4-star) and condominium accommodations, cafeteria, restaurants, après-ski, shops. Additional lodging and services in Dillon and Frisco. Free shuttle meets Continental Trailways bus service to Frisco (10 m); shuttle service to Breckenridge and Copper Mountain. Information: Keystone Resort Association, P.O. Box 38, Keystone, CO 80435. 303-468-2316.

    Ski Tip Touring Center (on Montezuma Rd., just beyond Keystone), instruction at all levels by certified Nordic instructor; guided tours throughout Summit Country and moonlight tours, weather and moon permitting; full-day tours include refinements on technique, waxing, and mountain safety, minimum 2 persons; rentals. Information: Barry Dow, Ski Tip Lodge, Montezuma Rd., Dillon, CO 80435. 303-468-9928.

IDAHO SPRINGS: Berthoud Pass (57 m NW of Denver on US 40), pass straddles Continental Divide in the Arapahoe National Forest; roughly marked trails on mountainous terrain recommended for intermediate to advanced skiers; trail map and rentals available; downhill ski facilities; accommodations at area lodge (11,314 ft elevation), 3 meals served daily. Continental Trailways bus from Denver stops on request. Additional accommodations, restaurants, and services in Winter Park (10 m W). Information: Berthoud Pass Ski Area, Box 520, Idaho Springs, CO 80452. 303-572-8014.

LEADVILLE: Ski Cooper (10 m N via US 24; 110 m SW of Denver via I-70, SR 91, and US 24), 8 m plus of marked and maintained trails for beginner to expert skiers in the San Isabel National Forest; high elevation assures great snow conditions; trail map available; no rentals or instruction; downhill ski facilities with base lodge, cafeteria, and nursery; accommodations at area lodge. Additional lodging, restaurants, and services in historic Leadville. Information: Ski Cooper, P.O. Box 973, Leadville, CO 80461. 303-486-2277.

LYONS: Peaceful Valley Ski Touring Center (18 m W via SR 7 and SR 72; 45 minutes from Boulder), many m of marked trails in the Front Range of surrounding Roosevelt National Forest; area immediately N of the lodge has snow-making equipment to guarantee good snow conditions for lessons; PSIA-certified instructors offer private and group classes; guided tours; rentals; year-round resort offers lodge and chalet accommodations, informal dining with homestyle cooking; heated pool, whirlpool bath, sauna, game room; extensive conference facilities; all-inclusive cross-country ski touring vacation rates. Information: Karl E. Boehm, Director, Peaceful Valley Lodge, Star Rt., Lyons, CO 80540. 303-747-2582.

STEAMBOAT SPRINGS: Steamboat Ski Touring Center (at Steamboat Village Golf Course), 20 km of groomed trails for beginners through advanced, 2-km practice loop; small trail fee; unlimited touring possibilities in over a million acres of surrounding **Routt National Forest;** professionally staffed ski school offers instruction; guided half-day tours to Fish Creek Falls, all-day tours including lunch, to Rabbit Ears Pass or Hot Springs (24-hour reservation and minimum of 4 persons for all tours); retail and rental shop; warming area and locker facilities, restaurant and bar; shuttle service between touring center and Steamboat Village Inn, and Rockies and West Condos. Steamboat, a full-service resort area, has extensive downhill ski facilities on Mt. Werner; lodge and condominium accommodations; restaurants, bars, après-ski; nursery; swimming, sleigh rides, saunas. More accommodations, restaurants, night spots, and plenty of friendly Western atmosphere in town of Steamboat Springs (2 m); bus service available to and from the ski area. Touring information: Steamboat Ski Touring

Center, P.O. Box 1178, Steamboat Springs, CO 80477. 303-879-2220, ext. 2295. Reservations: Steamboat Springs Chamber Resort Assoc., P.O. Box L, Steamboat Springs, CO 80477. 303-879-0740.

Bear Pole Ranch (5 m N), over 50 m of marked trails on gently rolling beautiful terrain bordering Routt National Forest; professional instruction for basic touring technique, waxing, backpack skiing, and winter camping; guided half-day, full-day, moonlight, and overnight tours; rentals; accommodations in rustic mountain cabins or dormitory units; buffet-style meals; sauna; recreation facilities in the "barn"; package plans available; complimentary transportation to Steamboat ski area. Information: Bear Pole Ranch, Steamboat Springs, CO 80477. 303-879-0576. **Mountaincraft Inc.** (in Steamboat Springs), certified instructors offer half-day and full-day lessons and guided tours tailored to the ability of the group; special rates and tours available for large groups; rentals; reservations required for group tours. Information: Mountaincraft Inc., P.O. Box 359, Steamboat Springs, CO 80477. 303-879-2368. **Glen Eden Ranch** (18 m NW On County Rd. 129 in Clark), 600 acres with 25 m of marked and groomed trails on open meadows and through stands of pine and aspen on the gradual hills of the Elk River Valley; small trail fee; group instruction and rentals; guides, special tours, wine and cheese parties by advance reservation; lodging in private mountain cabins with housekeeping facilities, electric heat, stone fireplace; main lodge has full restaurant; continental breakfast, brunch, sandwiches, and homemade soups served in Fireside Lounge and on sundeck overlooking Sand Mtn.; live music on weekends; banquet and meeting room facilities. Information: Frank E. Leonard, Glen Eden Ranch, Box 867, Clark, CO 80428. 303-879-3906. **Vista Verde Ranch** (25 m NE on Seedhouse Rd.), 8–10 m of marked and groomed trails on 600-acre ranch in a valley between Hinman and Colton Creeks; access to wilderness skiing in surrounding Routt National Forest; instruction and guided tours; seasonal highlight is an overnight tour to a log cabin at the base of Mt. Zirkel Wilderness Area; ice fishing at nearby Steamboat Lake, sleigh rides, wine and cheese parties; accommodations in cozy housekeeping log cabins with fireplace and sweeping views; no meals served in the main lodge during winter months, but special luncheons and dinners may be arranged. Information: Vista Verde Guest Ranch, Box 465, Steamboat Springs, CO 80477. 303-879-3858.

VAIL: Ski Touring School at Vail (100 m W of Denver via I-70; 140 m NE of Grand Junction via I-70), qualified ski touring instructors offer lessons and tours for beginner through experienced skiers; private lessons by advance reservation; choice of 20 different touring trips in the Vail area of the White River National Forest; extended tours and special powder excursions can be arranged for experienced skiers; rentals and repairs. Vail, one of the largest single mountain ski resorts in the country, is a complete full-service village at the base of the alpine slopes; lodge, condominium, and motel accommodations; over 70 restaurants and bars, après-ski; over 100 shops and services; ice skating, swimming pools, saunas, indoor tennis, movie theater. Free shuttle bus in village area. Bus service from Denver and Grand Junction; air service to Eagle County Airport. Ski touring information: Ski School at Vail, Box 819, Vail, CO 81657. 303-476-5601, ext. 3268. For reservations: Vail Resort Assoc., P.O. Box 1368, Vail, CO 81657. 303-476-5677.

WINTER PARK: Beaver Village Cross-Country and Touring Program (2 m W; 60 m NW of Denver on US 40), 10–12 m of maintained and groomed trails; terrain varies from flat meadow to steep wide trails; trail fee ($2); instruction including downhill and telemark technique; guided tours for the family, moonlight tours to a campfire with refreshments, powder tours into the Berthoud Pass area; winter camping and touring packages; accommodations at area. Additional accommodations, restaurants, and services in Winter Park. Information: Beaver Village, P.O. Box 43, Winter Park, CO 80482. 303-726-5741. **Tour Ski Idlewild** (W on US 40 in Hideaway Park; 70 m NW of Denver), 30 km of marked and groomed trails on a wide variety of terrain; easy beginner trail meanders along the Fraser River, advanced trails have fast challenging downhill descents winding through the trees, South Fork Loop has good lunch sites along the creek; Nordic ski school, rentals, and shop located in the Touring Barn; guided photography tours and overnight trips available; downhill ski facilities with warming house, cafeteria, cocktail lounge, rentals, ski shop, nursery; accommodations at Idlewild Lodge, modified American plan; heated outdoor pool, steam bath, game room. Information: Ski Idlewild, Box 3, Winter Park, CO 80482. 303-726-5562. See also Fraser.

CONNECTICUT

For additional information, contact the individual area or State of Connecticut, Dept. of Commerce, 210 Washington St., Hartford, CT 06106.

CORNWALL: Mohawk Ski Area (off SR 4, 2 m E of US 7), many m of marked and maintained trails in Mohawk State Forest; group and private instruction; rentals; downhill ski facilities with day lodge, restaurant, ice skating. Accommodations, restaurants, and services nearby. Information: Manager, Mohawk Mountain Ski Area, Cornwall, CT 06753. 203-627-6100.

DERBY: Osbornedale State Park (main entrance on Chatfield Rd.; N off SR 34 or SR 8), several interconnecting marked trails on rolling fields and through woods suitable for novice skiers; ice skating on Picketts Pond; snowmobiles prohibited; map available; parking area and restroom. Information: Recreation Specialist, Connecticut Dept. of Environmental Protection, 251 Judd Hill Rd., Middlebury, CT 06762. 203-934-9301.

EAST HARTLAND: Tunxis State Forest (in Hartland Co.), 8000 wooded acres with many m of marked trails and unplowed Forest Service roads suitable for novice to advanced skiers; trail map available; **Hartland Hollow Block** (W of SR 179, S of East Hartland) has 500 acres with marked trails and roads for novice and intermediates; no snowmobiles. Information: Recreation Specialist, Connecticut Dept. of Environmental Protection, P.O. Box 161, Pleasant Valley, CT 06063. 203-379-0771. **Pine Mountain Ski Touring Center** (SR 179, S of East Hartland), adjacent to Tunxis State Forest, offers instruction and rentals. Information: 203-653-4174.

FALLS VILLAGE: Riverrun Ski Touring Center (on SR 126 in Falls Village, 1 m E of US 7 intersection), 30-m trail system winds through protected woodlands and along the Housatonic River; marked and groomed trails for beginner to advanced skiers; no trail fee, but donation appreciated; instruction; moonlight tours and citizens' races; rentals, repairs, waxing, retail shop with equipment, clothing, and accessories; warming room, snack bar. Bonanza Bus Lines from NYC. Information: Riverrun Ski Touring Center, Falls Village, CT 06031. 203-824-5579.

FARMINGTON: Winding Trails Recreation Area (off SR 4, 1 m W of Farmington Center), 350 acres with 8 novice to intermediate marked and groomed interconnecting trails; mostly flat terrain with several hillocks, ponds, wooded areas, and lake; trail fee ($1), complimentary trail map; group and private lessons; rentals; extensive program of cross-country events includes orientation and waxing clinic, Moonlight Tours with Wine & Cheese Party, Nature Tours, Candy Tours for children, Family Relay Race, Annual Winding Trails Derby, and Bill Koch League Special Events (advance registration required for all events); heated Ski Hut with restroom, Coke machine, refreshment stand, and tables for brown-bag lunches; outdoor shelters with tables and fireplaces; no snowmobiles. Lodging, restaurants, services in Farmington. Information: Winding Trails Inc., Farmington Town Hall, Farmington, CT 06032. Main office: 203-673-3271, ext. 22; Ski Hut: 203-678-1758.

GRANBY: McLean Sanctuary (on Barndoor Hill Rd., S of Granby), 3400-acre area with many marked trails and unplowed roads on wooded terrain suitable for novice and intermediate skiers; snowmobiles prohibited. Information: Forester, McLean Sanctuary, Granby, CT 06035.

LIME ROCK: Lime Rock Ski Touring Center (off SR 112, E of US 7), 400 acres in the Berkshire foothills with many m of groomed trails through forest and open sloping fields for novice to advanced skiers; trail fee ($3); group instruction with individual attention and tour; day lodge has rental and retail shop including waxes and accessories, warming area with fireplace; scheduled activities and competitive events; lodging can be arranged at nearby White Hart Inn (Salisbury) and Interlaken Inn (Lakeville). Information: Lime Rock Ski Touring Center, c/o The Village Store, Salisbury, CT 06068. 203-435-2814 or 435-9459.

LITCHFIELD: White Memorial Foundation (2.5 m W off US 202), 35 m of woods roads and trails on 4000-acre preserve with fields, woods, streams, and lakes; mostly flat terrain with some hills suit-

able for beginner and intermediate skiers; no trail fee, excellent
map (50¢) shows mileage and natural features of trails; no snowmobiles; instruction and rentals available at Wilderness Shop in
Litchfield. Map and information at Nature Center and Museum
(Tues.–Sat., 9 am–5 pm) or Robert H. Shropshire, Superintendent,
White Memorial Foundation, Inc., Box 368, Litchfield, CT 06759.
203-567-8217. **Topsmead Forest** (E on Old East Litchfield Rd. to
Buell Rd., then ¼ m S to forest entrance), 3 marked interconnecting
trails on 550 acres of open fields and woods; varied gentle terrain
for beginners and intermediates; map available; plowed parking
area. Information: Recreation Specialist, Connecticut Dept. of
Environmental Protection, P.O. Box 161, Pleasant Valley, CT
06063. 203-379-0771. Accommodations, restaurants, and services in
Litchfield.

MIDDLEFIELD: Powder Ridge Ski Area (on Powder Hill Rd. off
SR 147 W of Middlefield: SE of Meriden), 5 m of trails on both
open and wooded terrain, only primitive trails for expert skiers are
marked; new cross-country trail with snowmaking and night lighting;
class instruction on weekends; rentals available; winter camping on
Mattabesett Trail; downhill ski facilities with day lodge, cafeteria
(health foods available), nursery; ice skating, tobogganing; area
accommodations at Powder Ridge Inn (package plans), restaurant,
cocktail lounge, discotheque. Additional lodging, restaurants, and
services in Meriden (4 m). Information: Powder Ridge Ski Area,
Middlefield, CT 06455. 203-349-3454. Toll-free from CT:
1-800-622-3321; from NY, NJ, MA, RI, NH: 1-800-243-3760.

NORFOLK: Blackberry River Ski Touring Center (on US 44, 2½
m W of Norfolk), 25 m of well-marked and groomed trails on
1000 acres; trails wind through pine and birch forest with occasional
clearings offering beautiful views of the Berkshire foothills; trail
fee ($2.50); group and private lessons; Friday night tour includes
rental, guide, wine and cheese (reservations by 6 pm); Ladies' Day
Package includes lesson, rental, and luncheon; retail and rental
shop; operates Wed.-Sun., hols., hol. wks., 8:30 am-5:00 pm; after
ski warm-up in the "Ice House" with hot spiced wine and fireplace;
lodging and hearty cuisine at Blackberry River Inn. Information:
Rick Mansfield, Blackberry River Ski Touring Center, Rt. 44,
Norfolk, CT 06058. 203-542-5614. Lodging: 203-542-5100.

PHOENIXVILLE: Natchaug State Forest (SE off SR 198), many m of old logging roads and hiking trails suitable for cross-country skiers; gentle to moderate grades; snowmobiles permitted; 2 parking areas near forest hq; map available. Information: Recreation Specialist, Connecticut Dept. of Environmental Protection, State Forest Nursery, RFD 1, Voluntown, CT 06384. 203-376-2513.

SIMSBURY: Great Pond Forest (SR 10 S, then SR 309 W to intersection of Farms Rd., then N on Farms Rd. to Great Pond Rd., turn right to forest entrance), several m of interconnecting well-defined trails and wood roads on 280 acres of white pine, hemlock, and hardwood; gentle novice terrain; abundant wildlife; map available; parking area at trailhead. Information: Recreation Specialist, Connecticut Dept. of Environmental Protection, P.O. Box 161, Pleasant Valley, CT 06063. 203-379-0771.

TORRINGTON: Sunnybrook State Park (3 m N on west side of Newfield Rd.), 444 acres of gentle rolling meadows in long narrow valley of flood control area; novice terrain, no map available; no snowmobiles. **Minetto State Park** (SR 4 W to SR 272, then N on SR 272 about 5 m), marked trails and unplowed roads on 150 acres of meadows and woods in flood control area; gentle beginner terrain, map available; no snowmobiles; parking area. Information: Recreation Specialist, Connecticut Dept. of Environmental Protection, P.O. Box 161, Pleasant Valley, CT 06063. 203-379-0771.

UNION: Nipmuck State Forest (1.5 m E off SR 197), numerous foot trails and old logging roads through evergreen woodlands; some steep grades; map available; snowmobiles permitted; parking area at adjacent Bigelow Hollow State Park. Information: Recreation Specialist, Connecticut Dept. of Environmental Protection, State Forest Nursery, RFD 1, Voluntown, CT 06384. 203-376-2513.

VOLUNTOWN: Pachaug State Forest (in several sections surrounding Voluntown), largest forest in the state system with 24,000 acres; **H. H. Chapman Area** (accessible from forest hq off SR 49 N of Voluntown) has many m of unplowed forest roads and interconnecting foot trails; beginner to intermediate terrain with easy grades; parts of Nehantic, Castle, Quinnebaug, and Pachaug Trails pass through the area; connecting trail to **Green Falls Area** (S of SR 138) where Nehantic Trail joins Narraganset Trail; the latter trail connects to the Rhode Island **Yellow-dot** trail system; trail maps available for both areas; snowmobiles permitted. Information: Recreation Specialist, Connecticut Dept. of Environmental Protection, State Forest Nursery, RFD 1, Voluntown, CT 06384. 203-376-2513.

WOODBURY: Woodbury Ski & Racquet (on SR 47, 4 m N of Woodbury), 30 m of trails on 2000 acres; flat to hilly terrain for beginner to expert skiers in Shepaug River Area; no trail fee, map available; instruction and rentals; no snowmobiles; downhill ski facilities with day lodge, snack bar; tennis. Lodging nearby at The Inn on Lake Waramaug, New Preston, CT (203-868-2168) and The Mayflower Inn, Washington, CT (203-868-0515). Information: Woodbury Ski & Racquet, Rt. 47, Woodbury, CT 06798. 203-263-2203.

STATE PARKS AND FORESTS: In addition to the parks and forests mentioned above, the following are recommended as offering suitable terrain for cross-country skiing: **Seth Low Pierrepont State Park** (N of Ridgefield off SR 116), marked trails around the lake and through wooded areas; beginner terrain. **Wadsworth Falls State Park** (N of Middlefield off SR 157), marked trails and unplowed roads through open and wooded areas for beginners. **State Bridle Trail** (from Southbury to Waterbury), over 10-m trail on nearly level terrain; snowmobiles prohibited, but when light snow cover, horseback riders may be on trail. **Meshomasic State Forest** (NE of Portland), unplowed forest roads and trails over moderately steep wooded terrain; Shenipsit Blue Trail runs N from Cobalt (on SR 66) by pretty Great Hill Pond to the Massachusetts line (with breaks); no snowmobiles. **Nathan Hale State Forest** (W of Coventry off SR 31), marked horse trails on wooded terrain suitable for novice skiers; no snowmobiles. Hunting permitted in most state forests; snowmobiles prohibited in all state parks, all state fish and game areas, and permitted in some state forests on specially designated trails. Information: Connecticut Dept. of Environmental Protection, State Office Building, Hartford, CT 06115.

ue on level and downhill terrain; special package of 4 con-
e Sat. or Sun. of lessons for basic skills through more ad-
d techniques and also for familiarizing skiers with snow
ions and touring areas; Powder Hounding Tours for overnight
country excursions, pre-trip clinic included, advance reserva-
required; skis and backpacking equipment rentals available.
tooth Mountaineering, Inc. publishes a nifty little guide with
ils and maps of 9 trails in the Boise Basin, printed on specially
ted moistureproof paper; also contains tips on winter and auto-
bile survival, list of distress signals, and list of useful local
one nos. Information: Lou Florence, Sr., Sawtooth Mountaineer-
g, Inc., 401 S. 8th St., Boise, ID 83706. 208-336-8950.

For additional information on maintained trails in the Boise
National Forest: District Forest Ranger, Idaho City Ranger District, U.S. Forest Service, Idaho City, ID 83631. 208-392-4421.

COEUR D'ALENE: Coeur d'Alene National Forest (725,000-
acre forest N and E) has several trail areas open and plans to
develop additional trails for the next few years to meet demand.
Cedar Creek Ski Area (E on I-90), eastern end access from Fourth
of July Summit; parking area just E of the Summit at Mullan Tree,
then walk 400 yds along the shoulder of I-90 to where Rd. #614
begins, continue .2 m down Rd. #614 to trailhead at beginning of
Rd. #3016; western end access from milepost 93.9 on US 95A, take
Rd. #438 for .3 m to jct of Rd. #1575, which is ski route, parking
area at trailhead; trail is 13.6 m long and marked with blue diamond
signs; from E to W, there is a downgrade on good road, then an
easy climbing grade to a generally level segment on a wide, brush-
free road, and finally a downgrade steep enough for a good ride on
fast snow; trail periodically compacted and tracks set; entire trail
should be attempted by experienced, well-conditioned skiers only.
English Point Ski Trails (6 m N on US 95 to Rimrock Rd., then 3.6
m E to jct of English Point Rd.), trailhead and parking area at the
logging road about 150 ft S of jct; 3 interconnecting loops of .6 m,
1.5 m, and 3.1 m, marked with color-coded blue, green, and yellow
diamond signs; generally level or easy grades except for a moderately
steep downgrade and upgrade on a section of the longest trail;
snow compacted and tracks set. For trail maps and information on
both areas: District Ranger, Fernan Ranger District, P.O. Box 1649,
Coeur d' Alene, ID 83814. 208-667-2561.

IDAHO

technic
secutiv
vance
condi
back
tion
Sav
det
tre
m
p
ir

For additional information, contact the individua
Division of Tourism & Industrial Development, Ca
Boise, ID 83720. 208-384-2470.

ARCO: Craters of the Moon National Monument (20 m
26, 20, 93A), 83 sq m of volcanic craters, cones, lava t
caves; 7-m loop road, closed to vehicular traffic in the wi
popular touring trail with just one steep section; backcountr
permitted in the 43,000-acre wilderness area, although there
designated trails; visitor center open year round contains exh
administrative offices, and restrooms. Information: Superintenc
Craters of the Moon National Monument, P.O. Box 29, Arco,
83213.

BURLEY: Broad Hollow Area (Albion-Declo exit off I-80, 13 m S
on SR 77 to Pomerelle turnoff, then 7 m W on Pomerelle Rd. to
trailhead), located in the **Sawtooth National Forest;** 7–9 m of marked
scenic trails through stands of Douglas fir and quaking aspen;
numerous open areas for downhill runs; terrain suited for beginner
to intermediate skiers; plowed parking area at trailhead. **Pomerelle
Ski Area** (proceed to Pomerelle turnoff as above, then 9 m W on
Pomerelle Rd.), 3 m of marked beginner to intermediate trails on
mountainside and open flat terrain (area closed to snowmobiles);
trail map available; rentals ($7 per day); downhill ski facilities with
day lodge and cafeteria. Winter camping permitted, mandatory
check-out and check-in with Forest Service. Information: District Ranger, Burley Ranger District, 2621 S. Overland Ave., Burley,
ID 83318. 208-678-0439. Snow report: 208-678-2991 or 3000.

BOISE: Sawtooth Mountaineering, Inc. (in Boise) offers guided
tours on about 50 m of marked and maintained trails in the Boise
Basin of the **Boise National Forest;** has beginner instruction program
designed to teach basic skills of touring and an appreciation of
winter in 2 half-day sessions; intermediate classes designed to further

IDAHO FALLS: Kelly Canyon Ski Area (17 m NW via US 26), located in **Targhee National Forest;** no developed trails, but cross-country skiers head up the canyon from base lodge or ride the lift to the top and start their tour from there; a significant number of roads in the vicinity are totally snowed in during winter months and are excellent for ski tours and snowshoeing; winter camping permitted, but it is advisable to notify **Palisades Ranger District** (Idaho Falls, ID 83401) in case an emergency should arise; snowmobiles permitted, but closures may be in effect in certain areas; ski area facilities include day lodge, food service, plowed parking area; rentals, accommodations, and restaurants in Idaho Falls. Information: Manager, Kelly Canyon Ski Area, Idaho Falls, ID 83401. 208-538-6261. Snow report: 208-523-7474.

KETCHUM: Busterback Ranch (40 m N on US 93), 20 m of manicured trails on 2500 acres of private pastures and woodlands, plus unlimited skiing on thousands of acres of adjacent Sawtooth National Recreation Area where the lower glacial moraines offer excellent terrain for telemark turns and downhill techniques; rentals and instruction; small trail use fee; accommodations for 16 guests, abundance of tasty ranch-type food; hot lunches twice a week at one of Busterback's wagons; 5-m guided tours down the valley to the ranch house for a lamb dinner (minimum of 4); family and group discounts available. Information: Busterback Ranch, Star Route, Ketchum, ID 83340. 208-774-2217.

Galena Lodge (24 m N on US 93), located within the Sawtooth National Recreation Area; 30 m of marked trails over rolling meadows, wooded ridges, and open slopes; most of trail system groomed with double tracks; trails for all skill levels including powder terrain for advanced skiers; daily trail usage fee ($2) includes wax room, lodge facilities, first aid, parking, trail map, and free bowl of hot soup; USSA-certified instructors and guides teach basic and advanced touring technique, freestyle powder skiing, telemark turns, and backpack skiing; guided half-day, day, moonlight, and overnight tours; rentals available; Thunderpaws Express, a Siberian husky sled team, is available for a ride through the foothills of the Boulder Mtns. (reservations at the lodge); accommodations in rustic mountain cabins; Galena Lodge open daily for breakfast (9 am) and lunch, freshly baked sweets and box trail lunches a specialty; dinner is served in the log lodge with kerosene lighting and a warm fire; variety of cuisines served with a choice of beer, wine, hot drinks, and freshly ground coffee; 48-hour advance reservation and deposit required for groups of 10 or more. Information: Galena Lodge Touring Center, Star Route, Ketchum, ID 83340. 208-726-4010.

POCATELLO: Caribou National Forest (E and S), over 1-million-acre forest made up of several sections of north-south towering mountain ranges with peaks over 8000 ft, divided by broad valleys; 1066 m of recreation trails and roads are used by cross-country skiers in developed areas as well as remote backcountry; marked trails specifically for skiers are in the planning stage; variable terrain from rolling hills to very steep rocky ridges and drainages; snowshoeing and winter camping permitted, snowmobiling with some restrictions; numerous plowed parking areas on and adjacent to the forest. Specific information at District Ranger Stations in Idaho Falls, Malad, Montpelier, Pocatello, Soda Springs, and in Freedom, WY. Food, lodging, and services in the above cities plus in the Bear Lake area. Additional information: Forest Supervisor, Caribou National Forest, P.O. Box 4189, Pocatello, ID 83201. 208-232-1142.

    Skyline Ski Area (off I-15, 15 m SE), downhill ski area from which some cross-country skiing originates; trails in Caribou National Forest; area facilities include day lodge, cafeteria, and cocktail lounge. Information: Manager, Skyline Ski Area, 398 Hyde Ave., Pocatello, ID 83201. 208-775-3744.

ST. ANTHONY: Targhee National Forest (1½ million acres, partly in WY), many miles of riding and hiking trails into remote backcountry areas suitable for cross-country skiing. **Teton Basin Ranger District,** 75,000-acre area including west slope of the Tetons and the Big Hole Range, has no marked trails to date, but several planned; caution advised for backcountry skiing on hazardous west slope of Tetons due to avalanche danger. Information: Forest Supervisor, Targhee National Forest, St. Anthony, ID 83445. Or: Forest Ranger, Teton Basin Ranger District, Driggs, ID 83422. 208-354-2312.

    Bear Gulch Ski Basin (17 m NE on SR 47), downhill ski area in **Targhee National Forest;** cross-country equipment rentals; day lodge, snack bar. Information: Manager, Bear Gulch Ski Basin, St. Anthony, ID 83445. 208-624-3981. (See also Grand Targhee Resort, Jackson, WY.)

SALMON: Salmon National Forest (1¾-million-acre forest surrounding the town of Salmon); the Forest Service does not furnish information for cross-country skiers at this time; however, they recommend **Wilderness River Outfitters,** a guide service for tours into the Salmon River Country; variety of tours includes 2- or 3-day trips to hut camps (warm shelters) and a 5-day ski camp package with lodging, meals, instruction, a day trip, and an overnight tour with all gear except personal clothing. Information: Wilderness River Outfitters, P.O. Box 871, Salmon, ID 83467. 208-756-3935.

SANDPOINT: Chipmunk Rapids Ski Trails (SW via US 2 to Priest River, then N on SR 57 about 22.3 m to entrance road for State Gravel Pit No. 057-022), trailhead and parking area about .2 m SE of SR 57 at the gravel pit; several m of interconnecting old roads lying between the Priest River and SR 57; snow compacted and tracks set periodically; trail map available. Information: District Ranger, Priest Lake Ranger District, U.S. Forest Service, P.O. Box 490, Sandpoint, ID 83864.

SAWTOOTH NATIONAL FOREST: 1,800,000 acres of spectacular rugged country with glacial-sculptured 12,000-ft mountain peaks; northern division contains **Sawtooth Recreation Area,** and within the recreation area is **Sawtooth Wilderness,** 216,000 acres of toothlike mountains, glacial basins, waterfalls, hundreds of lakes, timbered slopes, and open meadows; abundant wildlife. Popular trails on the E side of the Sawtooth Range include: **Big Wood Cross-Country Trail** (3 m N of Ketchum on US 93), 4-m marked trail on gentle rolling terrain, suited for beginners and intermediates; trail groomed and machine-tracked; plowed parking area. **Prairie Creek** (16 m N of Ketchum via US 93), marked 6-m beginner loop; at trailhead is registration box, bulletin board, toilet, and garbage can; area marked with cross-country skier sign adjacent to hwy; plowed parking area; closed to snowmobiles. **Owl Creek** (18 m N of Ketchum via US 93), 3-m round-trip trail for intermediate to advanced skiers with good open slopes for downhill; trail not marked; trailhead and plowed parking area marked by cross-country skier sign. **North and South Cherry Creeks, Senate and Gladiator Creeks, Westernhome Gulch, and Horse Creek** (22 m N of Ketchum on US 93), a series of interconnecting logging roads, offers tours of many m on a variety of terrain from flat track in valley bottoms to downhill powder runs on side slopes; those trails originating from

US 93 have plowed parking areas and are marked by cross-country skier signs; some of the trails in this area are marked and groomed by **Galena Lodge** (see Ketchum). **Salmon River Headwaters** (30 m N of Ketchum on US 93), 8-m to 10-m round trip, suited for beginners through advanced; trail not marked; plowed parking at the "Chain-Up Area" at base of Galena Summit, near Frenchman Creek bridge. **Alturas Lake** (25 m S of Stanley), 4- to 5-m interesting and scenic route along the Alturas Lake Creek; trail not marked; plowed parking area adjacent to US 93. **Pettit Lake** (22 m S of Stanley on US 93), 4-m to 5-m round trip on road to the lake; plowed parking off US 93. **Redfish Lake** (5 m S of Stanley on US 93), road to the lake is also used by snowmobiles; other routes follow along top of glacial moraine or Redfish Creek; 6-m round trip, routes unmarked; plowed parking off US 93. **Iron Creek** (2.5 m W of Stanley on SR 21), 9-m round trip for beginner through advanced on unmarked Forest Service Trail, main road used by snowmobiles; plowed parking area adjacent to hwy. **Stanley Lake Trail** (5.5 m W of Stanley on SR 21), 6-m round trip; road used by snowmobiles but other side routes possible; plowed parking adjacent to hwy. Where registration boxes are provided, please register your party. Permits required for tours in the Sawtooth Wilderness between Nov. 15 and May 15.

Information for trails around Ketchum: Ketchum Ranger District, U.S. Forest Service, Box 656, Ketchum, ID 83340. 208-622-5371. Information for **Wood River Zone** (just N of Ketchum): Sawtooth National Recreation Area, U.S. Forest Service, Star Route, Ketchum, ID 83340. 208-726-8291. Information for **Stanley Zone:** Sawtooth National Recreation Area, Stanley, ID 83278. 208-774-3511. For guide service see: Boise, Ketchum, Stanley, and Sun Valley. For trail suggestions in the Twin Falls and Burley Ranger Districts, see Burley. Additional information and maps: Visitor Information, Sawtooth National Forest, 1525 Addison Ave. E, Twin Falls, ID 83301.

STANLEY: Leonard Expeditions (in Stanley), developers of the Sawtooth Hut system, offer guided tours for 1 to 5 nights; each tour, tailored to group ability and time, utilizes one or more huts on the 38-m trail system; distance between huts ranges from 5 to 11 m with numerous side-trip possibilities; terrain varies from flat open meadows good for beginners to 1500-ft powder bowls perfect for learning the advanced telemark turns; roomy huts for 8 have comfortable bunks, wood/cooking stoves and spectacular panoramas of the Sawtooth Mountains; Gourmet Tour includes food, guide, and sherpa, you carry your sleeping bag and personal gear; Helper Tour includes food and guide; Do It Yourself Package includes use of hut and cooking and eating utensils; also offered are day trips with lunch, tent camping expedition to Castle Peak in the White Cloud Range, tours into the Challis National Forest, and a Youth Wilderness Camp during Christmas and spring vacations; transportation provided to and from Stanley. Guides are licensed by the State and recognized by the U.S. Forest Service. Information: Joe and Sheila Leonard, Leonard Expeditions, Box 98, Stanley, ID 83278. 208-774-3325.

SUN VALLEY: Sun Valley Nordic Ski Touring Center (in Sun Valley at the Golf Pro Shop), founded and directed by Leif Odmark; many miles of marked and maintained trails in and around Sun Valley, trails groomed daily on the Sun Valley Golf Course; daily guided tours (by bus) to Prairie Creek, Cherry Creek, Senate Creek, North Fork, Baker Creek, Westernhome, and Emma Gulch in the Sawtooth National Forest; helicopter tours to backcountry, cabins for overnighters; special tours include: tour to Devil's Bedstead Guest Ranch for lunch and helicopter back, Ski the Tiki Lighted Course to Trail Creek Cabin for dinner, or to Lostin Foundry for dinner and dancing; group and private lessons; complete rental department; beginning and intermediate races; alpine lift and lesson tickets exchangeable for Nordic equipment and lessons. Sun Valley is a major full-service year-round resort area with extensive downhill ski facilities; sleigh rides, indoor and outdoor ice skating, 2 swimming pools, 2 saunas, Jacuzzi; 2 hotels and a wide variety of condominium accommodations; restaurants ranging from cafeteria-style to French cuisine; cocktail lounges, live entertainment, discotheques; Playschool with supervised play, hot lunches, ski lessons, and ice skating. Free shuttle bus in Sun Valley; bus service to Ketchum (50¢). Air service to Hailey (20 minutes from Sun Valley). Information and reservations: Sun Valley Nordic Ski Touring Center, Box 272, Sun Valley, ID 83353. 208-622-4111, ext: 2250 or 2251. Toll-free (Sun Valley Company, Inc.): 800-635-8261.

ILLINOIS

All state parks are open for cross-country skiing. The parks listed below are recommended because they have designated trails and terrain suited to skiing. Also, all Cook (312-839-5617) and DuPage (312-629-5700) County Forest Preserves and Evanston City Parks (312-328-4280) encourage cross-country skiing.

For additional information, contact the individual area or Illinois Department of Conservation, 605 William G. Stratton Bldg., Springfield, IL 62706.

AURORA: Silver Springs State Park (14 m S; 5 m W of Yorkville on River Rd.), 2 m of marked trails; easy to intermediate terrain with several beaver dams en route; plowed parking area at trailhead; snowmobiles permitted. Information: Superintendent, Silver Springs State Park, RR1, Box 318, Yorkville, IL 60560. 312-553-6297.

CHICAGO: Moraine Hills State Park (N of Chicago; 3 m S of McHenry off River Rd.), 1668-acre park with glacial topography including natural glacial lake, lowland marsh areas, rolling hills and forested uplands; 3 loops totaling 11 m; difficulty ranges from flat beginner trails to more challenging terrain for experienced skiers; trails marked with mileage and directional signs, trail map available; park office serves as warming house, food concession in lower level; rentals; ski clinics (check park office for schedules); ice skating and sledding on Lake Defiance; no snowmobiles or winter camping permitted; plowed parking area at trailhead. Accommodations and restaurants in Crystal Lake. Information: Superintendent, Moraine Hills State Park, 914 South River Rd., McHenry, IL 60050. 815-385-1624. **Chain O'Lakes State Park** (44 m NW via US 12), 2450-acre park with Illinois's largest concentration of natural lakes; 2.25- and 4.5-m marked trails of slight to moderate difficulty on gently sloping hills and ravines; trail map available; ice skating, ice fishing, winter camping ($5 per night) permitted; plowed parking area and warming house at trailhead; no snowmobiles. Accommodations and restaurants in Fox Lake. Information: Superintendent, Chain O'Lakes State Park, 729 E. State Park Rd., Spring Grove, IL

60081. 312-587-5512. **Illinois Prairie Path,** 40-m trail spanning Du-Page and Kane Counties, beginning at Elmhurst and continuing through Wheaton. Information: P.O. Box 1086, Wheaton, IL 60187. 312-665-5310.

Norge Ski Club (40 m NW via US 14; ½ m N of intersection of US 14 and SR 22 on Ski Hill Rd. in Fox River Grove), 10 km of marked, maintained and groomed trails; beginner to advanced intermediate rated trails through marshes and wooded rolling hills with overlooks of the Fox River; lighted area for night skiing, Tues. and Thurs. 7–10 pm; no trail fee, but donation appreciated; clubhouse with large stone fireplace and kitchen facilities (available to groups with advance special request); ski shop has a shelter area with soft drinks and snacks; rentals, sales, repairs; lessons and clinics by U.S. Ski Assn.-Central Div.-certified instructors; competition programs, club trips and activities; junior and senior Nordic and ski jumping programs, co-sponsored by the Chicago Metropolitan Ski Council. Founded in 1905, Norge claims to be the oldest continuous ski club in the US. Information: Manager, Norge Ski Club, 100 Ski Hill Rd., Fox River Grove, IL 60021. 312-639-5955.

DIXON: White Pines State Park (12 m N between Polo and Oregon on White Pines Blacktop), 385 acres with 5.5 m of marked trails on rolling hills; beginner to intermediate terrain; trail map available; lodge closed during winter months; snowshoeing and winter camping permitted; no snowmobiles; plowed parking area at trailhead. Information: Superintendent, White Pines State Park, RR1, Mt. Morris, IL 61054. 815-946-3717.

FREEPORT: Lake Le-Aqua-Na State Park (15 m NW; 3 m N of Lena off SR 73), 715-acre park with 7 m of interconnecting marked trails on rolling hills around the lake; terrain recommended for intermediate skiers; snowshoeing and ice skating; free trail map; no snowmobiles; tent and trailer camping with permit; concession. Information: Superintendent, Lake Le-Aqua-Na State Park, RR2, Lena, IL 61048. 815-369-4282.

Plum Tree Ski Area (SW on SR 72 and SR 73), long trail for cross-country skiers; downhill ski facilities with lodge, restaurant, cocktail lounge, locker rooms and showers. Accommodation referral service. Information: Manager, Plum Tree Ski Area, Shannon, IL 61078. 815-493-2881.

GALENA: The Galena Territory (5 m E on US 20), 7000-acre recreational community with rolling hills, lake, golf course, and heavily wooded areas open to cross-country skiers; some marked trails; no trail fee; skiers asked to register at lodge; limited rental equipment ($4.50 per hour); snowshoeing and snowmobiles permitted; lodge at trailhead has 50 rooms, full food and beverage service. Restaurants and 300 rooms in Galena. Information: B. Elton, Manager, The Galena Territory, Box 1000, Galena, IL 61036. 815-777-2800.

KANKAKEE: Kankakee River State Park (on SR 102 in Bourbonnais), nearly 3 m of marked and maintained bicycle trails reserved for cross-country skiers; mostly flat trail with a few hilly spots, follows the river; free trail map; no lodge, but a heated restroom building; winter tent and trailer camping with permit; snowmobiles on designated trails. Information: Superintendent, Kankakee River State Park, Rt. 1, Bourbonnais, IL 60914. 815-933-1383.

KEWANEE: Johnson Sauk-Trail State Park (5 m N off SR 78; 6 m S of I-80), 6 to 8 m of moderately difficult trails over rolling hills and open fields and through pine and hardwood forest; marked trails, trail map available; winter camping and snowmobiles permitted; warming house and plowed parking area at trailhead. Information: Superintendent, Johnson Sauk-Trail State Park, RFD 3, Kewanee, IL 61443. 309-853-5589.

MACOMB: Argyle Lake State Park (8 m E via US 136; 1 m N of Colchester), 6 m of trails on difficult, rough terrain; cross-country skiing permitted, but not encouraged; winter camping and snowmobiles permitted; no trail map; no plowed parking area. Information: Superintendent, Argyle Lake State Park, Colchester, IL 62326. 309-776-3422.

MONMOUTH: Big River State Forest (25 m NW), 3000-acre forest along the Mississippi River; many m of skiing on old logging roads and firebreaks that interlace the pine forest; area maps available; snowshoeing, winter camping, and snowmobiles permitted; plowed parking and warming center at trailhead. Information: Ranger, Big River State Forest, Keithsburg, IL 61442. 309-374-2496.

MORRIS: Illinois & Michigan Canal State Trail (passes through Morris), 2 sections of canal trail open to skiers: 15 m of trail from **Channahon to Morris** are shared with snowmobiles; Channahon access has parking area and restrooms; additional restrooms, parking and camping areas en route; 10-m **Morris to Seneca** section for cross-country skiing only; Morris access, from Canal Headquarters in **Gebhard Woods State Park,** has shelter, restrooms, plowed parking area; tent camping permitted. Entire trail, flat and easy, follows towpath of the historic canal past locks and aqueducts; map available. Information: David Carr, Superintendent, Illinois & Michigan Canal State Trail, P.O. Box 272, Morris, IL 60450. 815-942-0796.

PEORIA: Jubilee State Park (10 m W via I-74 to exit 82, then follow signs 4 m N), 3200-acre park with 2 interconnecting marked loops totaling 10 m; moderately difficult trails over rolling hills of hardwood forest; snow compacted after each snowfall, track set periodically; free trail map; snowshoeing and winter camping permitted; no snowmobiles; plowed parking area, no shelter. Information: Superintendent, Jubilee State Park, RR 2, Brimfield, IL 61517. 309-243-7683. **Spring Lake Conservation Area** (about 20 m SW; E of Manito), 3 to 4 m of marked trails for cross-country skiers. Information: Superintendent, Spring Lake Conservation Area, RR 2, Manito, IL 61546. 309-968-6197.

ROCKFORD: Rock Cut State Park (5 m N on Harlem Rd.), 3 interconnecting trails of 1.5 m, 2.4 m, and 7.1 m, rated easy to semi-rugged, passing over marshy areas and old farm fields and through pine plantings and hardwood forest; the 7-m trail loops around Pierce Lake; abundant wildlife; a 4th trail from the Visitor Center, 1 m long, is recommended for advanced skiers; marked trails plus maps at various points on trail serve as reference points; concession stand; rentals on weekends ($2 per hour, $6 per day); limited winter camping; separate 200-acre area for snowmobiles. Accommodations, restaurants in Loves Park and Rockford. Information: Superintendent, Rock Cut State Park, RR 1, Box A-49, Caledonia, IL 61011. 815-885-3311.

ROCK ISLAND: Black Hawk State Park (off SR 2, just E of US 67, in Rock Island), 207-acre park bordering the Rock River; 3 m of interconnecting, marked trails on gentle, wooded rolling terrain with several steep areas; rated moderate to difficult; 7-acre beginner area lighted until 10 pm for night skiing; free trail map; ice skating, ice fishing, sledding; no snowmobiles; winter camping permitted for youth groups. Information: James P. Wieser, Park Superintendent, Black Hawk State Park, Rock Island, IL 61201. 309-788-9536.

SAVANNA: Mississippi Palisades State Park (3 m N off SR 84), 7.5 m of intermediate to expert trails through woods and prairies and over rolling ridge tops with scenic overlooks of the Mississippi River; trails marked and maintained; free trail map; free instruction and guided tours by reservation at park office; warming house and plowed parking area at trailhead; winter camping by permit; separate snowmobile trails. Motel and restaurants adjacent to park. Information: Superintendent, Mississippi Palisades State Park, RR 1, Box 160, Savanna, IL 61074. 815-273-2731.

INDIANA

For additional information, contact the individual area or Indiana Tourism Development Division, 336 State House, Indianapolis, IN 46204.

ANGOLA: Pokagon State Park (5 m N off I-69), 1200-acre park on the shores of Lake James; 1-m easy-to-moderate trail with some slopes and curves runs through wooded areas and past animal pens where deer and elk may be seen; 2.5-m one-way loop with some steep and rugged terrain offers advanced skiers lake views and an opportunity to see wildlife; trails marked, color-coded, and maintained; trail map available; no snowmobiles permitted; additional winter activities include rink and lake ice skating, sledding, ice fishing, ice boating, 1700-ft double lane toboggan slide (no private sleds permitted); ski rentals on weekends and holidays 9-5 ($1 per hour, 25¢ each quarter hour thereafter); park gate fee ($1.25 per car or 25¢ per person on bus); camping facilities open year round with modern restrooms and showers; Potawatomi Inn (80 rooms), European Plan; dining room also open to non-guests. Information: Pokagon State Park, RR 2, Box 29C, Angola, IN 46703. 219-833-2012.

INDIANAPOLIS: Eagle Creek Park (exit from I-65 or I-465 onto 71st St. W), 3000-acre park with 1300-acre reservoir in NW part of city; 8 m of marked trails and old fire lanes on varied wooded terrain recommended for intermediate skiers; whitetail deer abundant; ranger station and plowed parking area at trailhead; park entrance fee ($1.25 per car, weekends only); free trail maps; no snowmobiles. Information: Superintendent, Eagle Creek Park, 5901 Delong Rd., Indianapolis, IN 46254. 317-293-4827.

MICHIGAN CITY: Indiana Dunes National Lakeshore (S off I-94, then N on SR 49 to US 12, E on US 12 to Visitor Center on Kemil Rd.), 8000 acres of beautiful dunes, bogs, and marshes along Lake Michigan's southern shore; entire park open to skiers except where posted "No Skiing"; 3 areas recommended for skiers are: **Horse Trail** (in Furnessville-Tremont Area of park), 3.5-m marked trail on level to slightly rolling wooded terrain and wetlands; parking lot at trailhead on Schoolhouse Rd. N of US 20. **Calumet Bike-Hike Trail,** 9.2-m trail parallels US 12 and South Shore Railroad tracks from Mineral Springs Rd. near Dune Acres to the Mount Baldy area near Michigan City; flat easy trail; 5 parking areas along the way; trail passes through Indiana Dunes State Park (no park entrance fee for use of this trail). **Bailly Trail,** 1.75-m trail begins at Chellberg Farm parking lot (off Mineral Springs Rd.), continues to Bailly Homestead (dating to 1822) and returns via Bailly Cemetery and Chellberg Farm; mostly level trail except for an extremely steep ravine on the section returning to Chellberg Farm. No snowmobiles permitted on National Lakeshore. Visitor Center open 8-4:30 daily; scheduled winter ecology and ski tours on weekends. Information: Superintendent, Indiana Dunes National Lakeshore, RR 2, Box 139 A, Chesterton, IN 46304. 219-926-7561. **Indiana Dunes State Park** (S off I-94 on SR 49; within the boundaries of the National Lakeshore), marked trails over dunes and through inland wooded areas; park entrance fee ($1.25 per car); free trail map; winter camping permitted; no snowmobiles; parking area at Information Center. Information: Property Manager, Indiana Dunes State Park, Box 322, Chesterton, IN 46304. 219-926-1215.

SOUTH BEND: Bendix Woods County Park (12 m W on SR 2, Western Ave.), 192-acre park with 6 m of marked and groomed trails; rolling to very hilly terrain for novice to advanced skiers; lighted trails for night touring; rentals, instruction, and guided tours; small trail fee, free map; downhill ski area, lighted ice-skating pond, tubing; heated shelter with large fireplace, restrooms, snack bar; no snowmobiles. Information: Carl Baumgras, Manager, Bendix Woods County Park, RR 2, Box 72-A, New Carlisle, IN 46552. 219-654-3155. **Potato Creek State Recreation Area** (7 m S on US 31, then 6 m W on SR 4), easy .8-m loop on open fields; moderate 2-m trail with some short grades through both open and wooded areas; 3-m trail for advanced skiers with rugged sections of short, steep slopes and curves; 5.5-m loop with variety of terrain for all skill levels, view of the lake, 2 skis-off park road crossings; trails marked and color-coded for difficulty; free trail maps; rentals ($1 per hour, 25¢ each quarter hour thereafter); ice skating weather permitting; shelter, restrooms. Information: Potato Creek State Recreation Area, 65601 Pine Rd., North Liberty, Indiana 46554. 219-656-3490.

WINAMAC: Tippecanoe River State Park (6 m N on US 35), 2700-acre park with about 15 m of marked and maintained trails for novice to intermediate skiers; flat to gently rolling terrain, some small sand dunes and ridges; free trail maps; plowed parking area and large shelter house with 3 fireplaces at trailhead; no rentals or food service; winter camping permitted; no snowmobiles. Information: John Bergman, Property Manager, Tippecanoe River State Park, Winamac, IN 46996. 219-946-3213. **Winamac State Fish and Wildlife Area** (5 m N on US 35, then follow signs), 4592 acres open to skiers; no marked or maintained trails; therefore, range of difficulty depends on snow depth and condition; property map available; terrain for all skill levels includes open flat fields, low brushy swamp areas, oak woods laced with sand ridges and knolls; whitetail deer, rabbit, fox, pheasant, and waterfowl native to area; skiing not recommended until after hunting season; plowed parking area, no shelter; no snowmobiles. Information: Bill Bean, Property Manager, RR 4, Box 62, Winamac, IN 46996. 219-946-4422.

IOWA

For additional information, contact the individual area or Tourism and Travel Division, Iowa Development Commission, 250 Jewett Bldg., Des Moines, IA 50309.

CHARITON: Stephens State Forest (in 6 separate sections E and W of town), 9182 acres of hills and valleys with hardwood and conifer plantations; **Backpacking Trail Area** (access via US 34 to Lucas, then S 4 m on US 65, then W on County Rd. M for 3½ m, turn S for ½ m and then W ¾ m on graveled lane), 4 marked and maintained interconnecting trails along ridges and streams and over fields of corn or hay planted specifically to provide winter food and cover for abundant area wildlife; 5 campsites en route, winter camping permitted; map with trail descriptions available; snowmobiles permitted throughout forest. Information: District Forester, Iowa Conservation Commission, Rt. 3, Box 31, Chariton, IA 50049. 515-774-5581. **Red Haw Lake State Park** (1 m E off US 34), terrain suitable for cross-country skiing. Information: Park Ranger, Red Haw Lake State Park, Chariton, IA 50049. 515-774-5632. **The Cinder Path** (between Chariton and Derby), 13-m trail utilizing old cinder railroad bed; begins at SW edge of Chariton on old Hwy. 34 and ends at W edge of Derby; access also from any of several intersecting county roads; trail, heavily lined with trees, winds along the Chariton River part of the way, features a covered bridge, lookout tower, and rest areas; snowmobiles permitted. Information: Lucas County Conservation Board, Chariton, IA 50049.

FORT MADISON: Shimek State Forest (25 m W on SR 2; 1 m E of Farmington), 8500 acres of slightly rolling forested terrain with intermittent open glades, some steep slopes, and numerous ponds; entire forest open to cross-country skiers; however, many marked trails at present limited to snowmobiles; winter camping permitted; no trail map available; plowed parking area. Accommodations, restaurants, services in Donnellson (10 m). Information: Area Forester, Shimek State Forest Headquarters, Farmington, IA 52626.

319-878-3811. **Lacey-Keosauqua State Park** (37 m W via SR 2, then N on SR 1 toward Keosauqua), 1600 acres of wooded hills, gorges, and meadows along Des Moines River; marked foot trails around lake and along the river suitable for cross-country skiing. Information: Park Ranger, Lacey-Keosauqua State Park, Keosauqua, IA 52565. 319-293-3502.

McGREGOR: Yellow River State Forest (9 m NW on SR 364 or SR 76; hq off SR 76), 3500 acres with backpack trails and camping areas along streams and bluffs with overlooks. Information: District Forester, Yellow River State Forest Headquarters, McGregor, IA 52157. 319-586-2254. **Pikes Peak State Park** (3 m SE on SR 340), marked and maintained foot trails, camping areas on 500-ft bluff along the Mississippi River. Information: Park Ranger, Pikes Peak State Park, McGregor, IA 52157. 319-873-2341.

STATE PARKS: 42 parks are recommended as having suitable trails and terrain for cross-country skiing. For list of names, locations, and telephone numbers, contact Iowa Conservation Commission, Wallace State Office Bldg., Des Moines, IA 50319.

KENTUCKY

For additional information contact Kentucky Dept. of Public Information, Capitol Annex Bldg., Frankfort, KY 40601.

ASHLAND: Greenbo Lake State Resort Park (14 m W via US 23 and SR 207), marked trails including one to 19th-C. blast furnace ruins, on hilly wooded terrain with rock outcrops; cross-country ski clinic with basic ski technique and care of equipment; accommodations at Greenbo Lake Lodge, restaurant. For clinic dates, equipment rental information, and reservations: Greenbo Lake State Resort Park, Greenup, KY 41144. 606-473-7324.

MAINE

For additional information, contact the individual area or Maine State Development Office, Executive Dept., 193 State St., Augusta, ME 04333.

ACADIA NATIONAL PARK (16 m S of Ellsworth via SR 3), beautiful rugged coastal area with spectacular views of mountains, lakes, ocean, and offshore islands; over 30 m of winding carriage paths on the eastern side of **Mt. Desert Island** designated for cross-country skiing; separate trails for snowmobiles. Instruction, rentals, repairs, sales; accommodations, restaurants, and services in Bar Harbor. Information: Superintendent, Acadia National Park, Rt. 1, Bar Harbor, ME 04609. 207-288-3338.

ANDOVER: Akers Ski Center (on Pine St. in Andover; 12 m NW of Rumford), 6 m of marked and maintained trails starting from Akers Ski Shop; main trail is gentle with no steep hills and 2-way traffic, a lean-to shelter about 1 m out is for use of ski tourers; other more difficult trails, at times used for racing, wind over rolling wooded terrain with excellent views of the valley and surrounding mountains; trail donation appreciated, map available; Aikers rustic log cabin, heated with woodbox stove, is available for rental by 5 intermediate or better skiers (6-m tour) willing to backpack sleeping bags and food (wood, dishes, 5 foam mattresses, 2-burner gas stove, and gas lanterns furnished; water available from stream); rentals; waxing room; instruction by arrangement; warming area with fireplace in rental section; luncheonette next door. Accommodations, restaurants, and services 20 minutes away. Information: Akers Ski, Inc., Andover, ME 04216. 207-392-4582.

AUBURN: Lost Valley Ski Area (exit 12 off Maine Turnpike; in W Auburn), 4 m of marked, maintained, and groomed trails for novice to expert skiers; trail fee ($1.50); trail map available; certified instructors offer group and private lessons; guided tours; rentals; downhill ski facilities with day lodge, snack bar, cocktail lounge; supervised playroom. Information: Manager, Lost Valley Ski Area, P.O. Box 260, Auburn, ME 04210. 207-784-1561.

BETHEL: Sunday River Ski Touring Center (2 m E via US 2, SR 5 & 26, then left at Sunday River Ski Area turn, continue 3 m to Inn), 25 m of marked and maintained trails, 15 m of which are machine-groomed; many novice and intermediate trails follow old logging roads, originally built with gradual climbs for horses; access to 100 m of unmarked logging roads in the Mahoosic Mountain Range; trail fee ($2; no charge for guests of the Inn), trail map available; group and private instruction; guided tours, plus Friday night tour by kerosene lamplight; rental and retail shop; waxing and warming room; coffee shop. Sunday River Inn, family-oriented, has small comfortable rooms (no private baths) and a dormitory (bring your own sleeping bag); hearty family fare with homemade breads and desserts; game room; modified American plan (breakfast and dinner); group rates available. Information: Steve & Peggy Wight, Innkeepers, Sunday River Inn Ski Touring Center, RFD 2, Box 141, Bethel, ME 04217. 207-824-2410. **Mt. Abrams Ski Slopes** (5 m S via SR 26 in Locke Mills) has a 2-m cross-country trail; rental and retail shop; downhill ski facilities with day lodge, cafeteria, snack bar, cocktail lounge, 2 sundecks. Information: Manager, Mt. Abrams Ski Area, Locke Mills, ME 04255. 207-875-2601. Numerous accommodations, restaurants, services in Bethel.

BRIDGTON: Pleasant Mountain Ski Area (6 m W off US 302), 5 m of cross-country ski trails wind through Long Lake-Bridgton region; rentals; downhill ski facilities with 2 day lodges, 2 cafeterias, lounge and night club. Numerous accommodations (package plans available), restaurants, and services in Bridgton area. Information: Manager, Pleasant Mountain Ski Area, Bridgton, ME 04009. 207-647-2022.

CAMDEN: Camden Snow Bowl (1 m NW; 3 m off US 1 at Ragged Mtn.), 30 m of marked and maintained trails for beginners to experts; scenic views of Penobscot Bay area; no trail fee, map available (50¢); group instruction and guided tours; rentals; downhill ski facilities with day lodge, cafeteria. Information: Mr. Ken Hardy, Snow Bowl, P.O. Box 456, Camden, ME 04843. 207-236-3438. Snow report: 207-236-4418. **Camden Hill State Park** (N off SR 172 at Lincolnville) has 6 m of roads and trails for novice skiers; great views of the coast. Accommodations, restaurants, and services in Camden.

CARRABASSETT VALLEY: Carrabassett Valley Touring Center (N of Kingfield via SR 16 & 27), one of the largest ski touring facilities in New England, has 50 m of marked and numbered trails on varying terrain from easy, rolling logging roads and old railroad beds to expert wilderness areas near the Bigelow Preserve; trails machine-groomed with packers and track setter; trail information center updates trail conditions daily and will assist skiers in planning tours; trail fee ($2 adult, $1 child 13 or younger); trail map ($1.25); EPSTI-certified instructors offer group and private lessons, half- and full-day guided tours (reservation required, minimum of 4 persons); waxed and waxless rental skis; full retail shop with equipment, clothing, and accessories; touring center, a town-owned facility, has cafeteria, two-way fireplace, ski shop, warming room, spacious sundeck with outside barbecue. Package plan accommodations available at a number of area inns, lodges, motels, and condominiums (Sugarloaf Area Association, Kingfield, ME 04947. 207-237-2861). Touring information: Jack Lufkin, Director, Carrabassett Valley Touring Center, Box 518, Carrabassett Valley, ME 04947. 207-237-2205. Adjacent **Sugarloaf/USA** alpine ski area is a full-service resort with condominiums, restaurants, pub, country store, laundromat, shops, nursery. Information: 207-237-2000.

FARMINGTON: Titcomb Mt. Ski Area (1.5 m off US 2 at Farmington), 15 km of marked trails on 200 acres; some trails groomed; access to another 20–30 km of marked trails on surrounding property; beginner to expert terrain; trail fee ($1), trail map available; instruction and guided tours by appointment; group rates; rentals at Northern Lights, 1 m from center; trailhead lodge with lunch counter. Lodging, restaurants, and services in Farmington. Information: Manager, Titcomb Mt. Ski Area, Farmington Ski Club, Farmington, ME 04938. 207-778-9384.

FRYEBURG: Evergreen Valley (N off SR 5 at E. Stoneham), access to unlimited touring in White Mountain National Forest; some maintained and groomed trails; downhill ski facilities with day lodge, restaurant, cafeteria, cocktail lounge, fireside lounge, sundeck; a family resort with lodging in large modern inn and condominiums. Information: Evergreen Valley Resort, Inc., E. Stoneham, ME 04231. 207-928-3300.

GREENVILLE: Squaw Mountain (off SR 15 & 6, N of Greenville),

25 m of maintained trails for beginners through experts; unlimited touring possibilities on abandoned logging roads and trails throughout Moosehead Lake area; fly-in ski trips can be arranged into the Allagash Region and the Maine Northwoods; rentals; downhill ski facilities; full-service resort overlooking scenic Moosehead Lake has 56-room hotel, cafeteria, restaurant, cocktail lounge, heated indoor pool, saunas; nursery. Information: Squaw Mountain at Moosehead Resort, Greenville, ME 04441. 207-695-2272.

KINGFIELD: Deer Farm Ski Touring Center (N off SR 27; 14 m S of Sugarloaf/USA), 26 m of marked and maintained trails for novice to expert on old logging roads and hunting trails through rolling forested terrain; scenic views of the lovely Carrabassett Valley and the Longfellow Range; 80% of trails groomed; trail fee ($2), trail map (35¢); group and private instruction; guided tours, luncheon and moonlight tours; workshops; Ski Barn has rentals, waxing facilities (assistance provided), waxes and accessories for sale; warming hut; accommodations in rustic heated log cabins with showers; traditional New England meals served family-style in the main lodge; package plans available, modified American plan. Information: Larry Minnehan, Deer Farm Ski Touring Center, Kingfield, ME 04947. 207-265-2241. **Sugarloaf KOA Campground & Ski Touring Center** (4 m N on Tufts Pond Rd.), 25 km of marked and groomed trails for all skill levels; instruction; guided tours, moonlight tours, workshops, races; rentals; touring center lodge has ski shop, waxing facility, wood-heated lounge, recreation room, laundry, hot showers, store with camping supplies. Information: Sugarloaf KOA Campground, Kingfield, ME 04947. 207-265-2222.

MILLINOCKET: Baxter State Park (22 m NW), over 200,000 acres of beautiful wilderness area with mountains and lakes dominated by Mt. Katahdin, highest point in Maine; 50-m perimeter road, not plowed in the winter, is excellent for touring, and connects to a network of roads designated by the park as ski touring trails; snowmobiles prohibited; no trail maps, but maps of the park available free; trails recommended for intermediate to expert skiers only; **Appalachian Trail** starts on Mt. Katahdin (ends in Chattahoochee National Forest in Georgia); winter camping with special use permit only (applications must be submitted to the Millinocket Park office at least 4 weeks in advance). Information:

Supervisor, Baxter State Park Authority, 64 Balsam Dr., Millinocket, ME 04462. 207-723-5140. **Katahdin Lake Wilderness Camps** (located outside SE corner of Baxter State Park; drive NW from Millinocket, leave car at Togue Pond Gate, then ski 10 m to Camp via Roaring Brook Rd.), 50 m of marked and maintained trails for intermediate to expert skiers on quiet rolling hills near Katahdin Lake with beautiful views of Mt. Katahdin, Turner and Barnard Mtns.; guided tours if requested; access to Baxter State Park; accommodations in wood-heated log cabins (sleep 1–10 persons), linen furnished; home-cooked family-style meals served in main cabin; no telephone or auto access. By reservation only: Katahdin Lake Wilderness Camps, Alfred J. Cooper III, Box 398, Millinocket, ME 04462.

RANGELEY: Saddleback Mountain Ski Area (off SR 4, 7 m E; Maine Turnpike exit 12), 10 m of beginner to expert marked trails in scenic Rangeley Lakes area; average annual snowfall over 200 inches; trail map available; instruction and guided tours; rentals; downhill ski facilities with modern base lodge, cafeteria, 2 fireplaces, sundeck, lounge, rental and retail shop, nursery (2 years old and up). Condominium accommodations at area; additional lodging, restaurants, and services in Rangeley. Information: Saddleback Kingdom, Inc., Box 490, Rangeley, ME 04970. 207-864-3380. Lodging: Rangeley Chamber of Commerce, Box 317, Rangeley, ME 04970. 207-864-5571.

RUMFORD: Chisholm Winter Park (on Black Mountain, 4 m from Rumford), 7 m of cross-country trails for beginners and intermediates; downhill ski facilities with day lodge, sundeck, snack bar, lounge. Accommodations, restaurants, and services in Rumford and Mexico area. Information: Manager, Chisholm Winter Park, Rumford, ME 04276. 207-364-8977.

MARYLAND

For additional information, contact the individual area or Maryland Department of Economic & Community Development, 2525 Riva Rd., Annapolis, MD 21401.

GAITHERSBURG: Trails East, Ltd. (16698 Oakmont Ave.), operating out of Hudson Bay Outfitters, Ltd., offer 3 types of cross-country ski programs: Full Day Clinics include classroom session on how to choose ski equipment, basic technique, and waxing, then a full day of skiing at an area with suitable snow conditions, rental and lunch part of the package; Overnight Cross-Country Class includes evening classroom session and full weekend on snow with rentals, deluxe cabin accommodations at Blackwater Falls State Park (Davis, WV) and meals; Cross-Country Ski Lessons include 3 hours of waxing and ski technique instruction at New Germany State Park; also available, 6 days of ski touring in Vermont package with transportation, lodging, meals, trail fees, tips, and taxes. Information: Trails East, Ltd., 16698 Oakmont Ave., Gaithersburg, MD 20760. 301-840-0650.

GRANTSVILLE: New Germany State Park (5 m S off US 40), 5.1 m of marked trails on varied terrain; novice trails marked with green follow a wooded stream; more difficult trails marked with blue have steep spots and one ¾-m downhill run; intersections are marked and arrows show suggested direction of travel; color-coded map available; parking area at trailhead. Information: Superintendent, New Germany State Park, Rt. 2, Grantsville, MD 21536. 301-895-5453 or 895-5940.

OAKLAND: Herrington Manor State Park (5 m NW on County Rd. 20), 427-acre park with 2.7 m and 1.5 m of interconnecting marked trails partly along Herrington Lake and through pine plantations; relatively mild terrain suitable for novice skiers; trail map available; trailheads at day-use parking area. Winterized camping available at adjacent **Swallow Falls State Park.** Information: Superindentent, Herrington Manor State Park, Rt. 5, Box 122, Oakland, MD 21550. 301-334-9180.

SHARPSBURG: Chesapeake & Ohio Canal National Historical Park (hq SW off SR 34), park follows route of the 184-m canal along the Potomac River from Washington to Cumberland; maintained towpath has bumpy and hilly spots, but with snow cover is suitable for cross-country skiing; campsites located every 5 m from Cumberland to Seneca, winter use permitted; no snowmobiles; map available. Information: Superintendent, C & O Canal National Historical Park, P.O. Box 4, Sharpsburg, MD 21782.

301-432-2231 or 948-5641. **Antietam National Battlefield Site (**N off SR 65; 12 m S of Hagerstown), site where Gen. Robert E. Lee's first invasion of the North failed in a bloody battle; 800-acre park of open rolling country side bisected by stone and barbed-wire fencing; suitable for cross-country skiing when snow conditions allow; no snowmobiles; winter camping for organized groups only. Information: Superintendent, Antietam National Battlefield Site, P.O. Box 158, Sharpsburg, MD 21782. 301-432-5124.

THURMONT: Catoctin Mountain Park (3 m W on SR 77), 5768-acre park with beautiful forested ridges, sparkling streams, and panoramic vistas of the Monocacy Valley; 12 m of foot trails and 12 m of bridle trails suitable for beginner to advanced skiers; intersections marked on foot trails, orange blazes mark bridle paths; parking areas at Visitor Center and trailheads, parking in undesignated areas not permitted; no snowmobiles; Camp David, the Presidential retreat, is located within the park; trail map available. Information: Superintendent, Catoctin Mountain Park, Thurmont, MD 21788. 301-271-7447 or 824-2574.

MASSACHUSETTS

For additional information, contact the individual area or Massachusetts Dept. of Commerce & Development, Division of Tourism, State Office Building, 100 Cambridge St., Boston, MA 02202. For more information on state parks and forests, contact Massachusetts Dept. of Environmental Management, Division of Forest and Parks, Leverett Saltonstall Bldg., 100 Cambridge St., Boston, MA 02202.

ATHOL: Otter River State Forest and **Lake Dennison State Park** (7 m NE via US 202), hilly wooded terrain with many m of hiking trails and forest roads suitable for cross-country skiers. **Federated Women's Clubs State Forest** (7 m SW off SR 122), trails along wooded shoreline of Quabbin Reservoir. **Erving, Northfield,** and **Mt. Grace State Forests** (8 m W on SR 2; adjoin going N to state line), unlimited touring possibilities of many m of forest roads and hiking trails.

BERKSHIRES: See Great Barrington, Lenox, Pittsfield, and North Adams. For additional information on Berkshire ski areas, calendar of winter events and help with reservations contact Berkshire Vacation Bureau (division of Berkshire Hills Conference), 20 Elm St., Pittsfield, MA 01201. 413-443-9186. For up-to-date snow condition report: 413-499-0700; toll-free (from NY, NJ, CT, RI, NH, VT) 800-628-5030.

BOSTON: Blue Hills Reservation (S between SR 28 & SR 138, N of SR 128), many acres with hiking and nature trails, ponds. **Wompatuck State Park** (14 m SE, S off SR 3A in Hingham), nature and hiking trails suitable for novice and intermediate skiers. N of Boston: **Middlesex Fells Reservation** (between Medford and Stoneham; bisected by I-93 and SR 28), 3500 acres with trails and ponds; wooded rolling terrain; snowmobiles permitted.

CHARLEMONT: Berkshire East Ski Area (off SR 2 on South River Rd.), trails for cross-country skiers; downhill ski facilities, 2-day lodges, cafeteria, restaurant, cocktail lounge, live entertainment; nursery; accommodations, restaurants, and services in Greenfield (17 m E). Information: Berkshire East Ski Area, Charlemont, MA 01339. 413-339-6617.

CUMMINGTON: Cummington Farm Ski Touring Center (on South Rd. off SR 9; W of Northampton), 40 km of well-marked and groomed trails on 700 beautiful acres of rolling meadows with woods of spruce, fir, and maple, frozen ponds and a beaver bog; night skiing on 3 km of lighted trails; trail fee ($3, children under 12, $2); EPSTI instruction; scheduled events include: Full Moon Night Tours, Annual Hare & Hound Race (for anyone 17 and under), Cummington Farm Citizen Race; Instructor Training Courses sponsored by EPSTI (advance registration required); rental and retail shop; lodging in rustic cabins with wood stoves (baggage sent to cabin, but you ski; you supply own bedding), dormitory facilities for groups; restaurant serves hearty food family style and homemade breads, full bar; package plans; no snowmobiles. Information: Cummington Farm Ski Touring Center, South Rd., Cummington, MA 01026. 413-634-2111.

FALL RIVER: Freetown State Forest (NE), gently wooded terrain with trails and forest roads suitable for cross-country skiers; heavy snowmobile use.

FITCHBURG: Leominster State Forest (3 m S on SR 31), hiking trails on wooded, hilly terrain with ponds. **Wachusett Mtn. State Reservation** (SW off SR 140), marked trails suitable for novice and intermediate skiers; wooded terrain with pretty views. **Pearl Hill State Park** and **Willard Brook State Forest** (5 m N on SR 31), adjoining areas offer many m of trails and forest roads for cross-country skiers; woods, ponds, waterfall. **Pheasant Run Ski Area** (E in Leominster; on Exchange St., 1.5 m off SR 2 & SR 12), cross-country ski trail; downhill ski facilities, day lodge, snack bar, sitter service. Lodging, restaurants, and services in Leominster and Fitchburg. Information: Pheasant Run Ski Area, Leominster, MA 01453. 617-537-9293.

GREAT BARRINGTON: Beartown State Forest (E on SR 23 between Great Barrington and Monterey; S access from SR 23 via Blue Hill Rd.; N access from SR 102 in South Lee via Beartown Mountain Rd.), about 11 m of red-blazed bridle trails and blue-blazed hiking trails around pretty Benedict Pond and through rolling wooded terrain, suitable for intermediate to advanced skiers; skiers permitted on orange-blazed snowmobile trails and unplowed forest roads (use is heavy); trailhead and plowed parking area at Benedict Pond; free trail map at forest hq on Blue Hill Rd. Information: Forest Supervisor, Beartown State Forest, Blue Hill Rd., Monterey, MA 01245. 413-528-0904. Nearby **Butternut Ski Touring** (E of town on SR 23) operates out of a rustic warming hut located at the base of **Butternut** downhill ski area; 7 km of groomed novice and intermediate trails begin here, loop around a pond, and meander over rolling meadows; a more difficult 10-km wilderness trail traverses the alpine slopes and continues into adj East Mountain State Forest; trail maps available for both Butternut and Beartown State Forest; EPSTI-certified instructors offer group and private classes for all skill levels, plus special downhill instruction and advanced racing technique; child-care center, ski shop, beautiful big new day lodge with cafeteria. Information: Butternut Ski Touring, Great Barrington, MA 01230. 413-528-0610. **Oak n' Spruce** (NE via US 7 & SR 102 in South Lee), 440 acres with many m of woodland trails, unplowed country roads, and open rolling meadows, plus access to trails in adjoining Beartown State Forest; instruction and rentals; downhill ski slopes, tobogganing, ice skating; year-round resort with accommodations for 200, dining room, cocktail lounge, nightclub; indoor pool, whirlpool, saunas;

Learn-to-Ski Packages. Information: Oak n' Spruce Resort, South Lee, MA 01260. 413-243-3500. Toll-free outside MA: 800-628-5072.

Otis State Forest (15 m E on SR 23; access via Nash Rd. in West Otis), over 3800 acres with about 15 m of hiking trails and woods roads along Upper and Lower Spectacle Ponds, and on parts of the Knox Trail (old historic Boston to Albany road). State Forest trails connect to **Otis Ridge Ski Touring** (off SR 23 between West Otis and Otis Center; access via Judd Rd.), 4 m of interconnecting groomed trails for beginner to advanced skiers; trail fee ($2 adult, $1 children 12 or under), trail map available; adult and junior rentals; group and private instruction; one-hour Beginner Special includes lesson and rentals; All-Day Learn-to-Ski program includes rental, morning lesson, lunch, afternoon guided tour followed by wine and cheese; downhill ski facilities with day lodge, cafeteria; adj Grouse House, a cozy inn, offers fine dining, cocktail lounge and overnight lodging. Information: Otis Ridge Ski Touring, Rt. 23, Otis MA 01253. 413-269-4444. **Sandisfield State Forest** (E on SR 23 and SR 57 to New Marlboro, then 3 m S on SR 183), 2-m marked hiking trail around York Lake, plus about 5 m of unplowed forest roads suitable for novice to advanced skiers on 4300 acres of rolling wooded terrain; snowmobiles permitted; trailhead at York Lake picnic area. Information and map: Forest Supervisor, Sandisfield State Forest, West Street, Sandisfield, MA 01255. 413-258-4774. **Flying Cloud Inn** (12 m E off SR 57 at New Marlboro), 200 acres with 5-m beginner to intermediate trail through woods and open fields; the inn, originally a farm home built in 1771, offers good food and wine, comfortable rooms for 20 guests furnished in Early American style, and a warm hearth; ski equipment and use of trails reserved for inn guests; reservations required. Information: The Flying Cloud Inn, Box 143, Star Route, New Marlboro, MA 01230. 413-229-2113. **Red Fox Ski Touring Center** (E on SR 23 and SR 57; at New Marlboro), 15 km of marked beginner to expert trails with access to Sandisfield State Forest; Nordic ski patrol; trail fee ($1.50); instruction available; area barn houses rental shop and food concession; open weekends and holidays. Information: Red Fox Ski Touring Center, New Marlboro, MA 01230. 413-229-7790. **Riverrun North** (2 m S on US 7), scenic novice trail along the Housatonic River; close proximity to area trail systems; group and private instruction; moonlight tours; citizens' races; warming hut, rental and retail shop, beverage bar, babysitting arrangements. Information: River-run North, Rt. 7, Sheffield, MA 01257. 413-528-1100. **Bartholomew's Cobble** (S off US 7 in Ashley Falls), nature center with limestone outcrops over the Housatonic River and access to open meadows, pleasant for cross-country skiing.

Mt. Washington State Forest and **Mt. Everett Reservation** (14 m SW via SR 23 and SR 41; in SW corner of state), many m of un-plowed forest roads and hiking trails, several on ridge tops with beautiful overlooks into 3 states; trails are sparsely marked in these 2 areas and a topographical map should be used; parking at forest hq, S through Mt. Washington village on East St.; Mt. Everett, 1 m N of forest hq. Information: Forest Supervisor, Mt. Washington State Forest, Mt. Washington, MA, c/o RD, Copake Falls, NY 12517. 413-528-0330. **Jug End** (W off SR 23 near NY state border), 1200 acres with many m of cross-country trails on rolling terrain of the southern Berkshires; downhill ski facilities, ice skating, tobogganing; indoor tennis, indoor pool; year-round resort with lodging, dining room, cocktail lounge, entertainment. Information: Jug End Resort, South Egremont, MA 01258. 413-528-0434. **Egremont Inn** (W on SR 23 at South Egremont), trails, rentals and instruction available at the inn, plus access to many m of area trails; old country inn with comfortable lodging, fine dining, lounge, and warm fireplaces. Information: Egremont Inn, South Egremont, MA 01258. 413-528-2111. **Egremont Country Club Ski Touring Center** (W on SR 23 at South Egremont), 300 acres with groomed trails and open golf course areas, brooks and picnic spots; trail fee ($2); rentals; group and private instruction by appointment; fondue and hot drinks served in lounge with fireplace. Information: Egremont Country Club, South Egremont, MA 01258. 413-528-4222. The southern Berkshire area has an abundance of accommodations ranging from modern motels to old country inns, many offering low winter rates, and a wide choice of fine restaurants.

GROTON: Groton Hills Ski Area (on Martins Pond Rd.), 150 acres with about 10 m of marked trails for beginner to expert skiers; varied terrain with pine groves, orchard area, open fields, and wooded ridges; trails maintained and groomed with track setter; trail fee ($2), map available; rentals and instruction; downhill ski facilities, hang gliding, snowshoeing; day lodge, snack bar; self-contained camping trailers permitted; no snowmobiles. Lodging, restaurants, and services in Ayer, Lowell, and Nashua (NH). Information: Groton Hills Ski Area, Groton, MA 01450. 617-448-5951. **Indian Head Ski Area** (N in East Pepperell on SR 111), trails for cross-country skiers; downhill ski facilities, day lodge, snack bar. Information: Indian Head Ski Area, East Pepperell, MA 01437. 617-433-2249.

IPSWICH: All Year Round, Inc. (on SR 1A in town), ski touring center with access to 50 to 100 m of trails in nearby Bradley Palmer State Park, Willowdale State Forest, Ipswich Wildlife Sanctuary, and Cranes Castle area on ocean; center offers guided tours, moonlight tours, citizens' races; rentals and instruction; snowmobiles permitted in Bradley Palmer State Park. Information: All Year Round, Inc., Rt. 1A, Ipswich, MA 01938. 617-356-0131.

LENOX: Pleasant Valley Wildlife Sanctuary (N off US 7 on West Mountain Rd.), owned and operated by Massachusetts Audubon Society; 14 m of marked, interconnecting trails on over a square m of woodlands and meadows with a trout stream and a series of beaver ponds; color-coded markers indicate trail direction to and from parking area and cross trails; mostly beginner and intermediate terrain; a strenuous advanced trail leads to a firetower and a breathtaking view of the valley; small trail donation; trail map available; ski clinics and winter nature programs; snowshoeing permitted; no snowmobiles; warming room, restrooms; plowed parking area. Information: Pleasant Valley Wildlife Sanctuary, West Mountain Rd., Lenox, MA 01240. 413-637-0320. **John Drummond Kennedy Park** (in Lenox; adjoins Pleasant Valley on the N): **Main Trail,** marked with white triangles, begins at the entrance to the Church-on-the-Hill (SR 7A) and leads to the reservoir on Reservoir Rd.; **Lookout Trail,** marked with red diamonds, begins at a public parking area (on SR 7A just before N jct with US 7), and leads to Pleasant Valley Sanctuary with several overlooks and a pond en route, intersects the Main Trail twice; other unmarked trails; hilly wooded terrain for beginner to advanced skiers, some steep spots; some snowmobile use. Information: John D. Kennedy Park Restoration Committee, Lenox Town Hall, 6 Walker St., Lenox, MA 01240. 413-637-3010. **October Mountain State Forest** (E of Lenox), state's largest forest with 14,000 acres; several hiking trails around Felton Lake and Half-Way Pond and along Roaring Brook used by cross-country skiers; **Appalachian Trail** passes N to S through forest; many m of forest roads and trails, but most receive very heavy snowmobile use. Information: Regional Forest Supervisor, Cascade St., Pittsfield, MA 01201. 413-442-8992. **Foxhollow** (S off US 7), many m of beautiful trails on property; instruction and rentals available; year-round resort with lodging, gourmet dining, lounge. Information: Foxhollow Resort, Rt. 7, Lenox, MA 01240. 413-637-2000.

LITTLETON: Hartwell Hill Ski Area (on Hartwell Ave.), 6 m of marked and groomed trails on gentle wooded terrain; trail fee ($3); downhill ski facilities, day lodge with fireplace, snack bar; snowshoeing and winter camping permitted; no snowmobiles. Lodging, restaurants, and services within 2 m. Information: Hartwell Ski Area, 46 Hartwell Ave., Littleton, MA 01460. 617-486-4546.

METHUEN: Merrimac Valley Ski Area (on Hampshire Rd., 2 m W of Pelham St. exit off I-93), trails for cross-country skiers; downhill ski facilities, day lodge, cafeteria. Information: Merrimac Valley Ski Area, Methuen, MA 01844. 617-686-6021.

NORTH ADAMS: Savoy Mountain State Forest (SE off SR 2), 11,000-acre forest with 15 m of designated cross-country trails, plus many unplowed roads suitable for skiers; some novice terrain, but mostly intermediate to advanced on wooded mountain uplands with lakes, streams, and pretty Tannery Falls (80-ft drop); trails marked, maintained, and some groomed; trail map available; abundant wildlife; 3 log cabins, reservations accepted and advised (4 persons per cabin; $8 per night), outhouse, winter camping gear needed; snowmobiles in designated areas; plowed parking area at North Pond near forest hq. Information: Ranger, Savoy Mtn. State Forest, RFD 2, North Adams, MA 01247. 413-663-8469. **Mt. Greylock State Reservation** (S off SR 2 or E off US 7 at Lanesboro), many m of hiking trails and old logging roads; **Bellows Pipe Trail** is popular with skiers; intermediate to advanced mountainous terrain with Mt. Greylock (3491 ft), highest point in the state; trail map available; Appalachian Trail passes N to S through reservation with several lean-to shelters en route; area receives heavy snowmobile use. Information: Supervisor, Mt. Greylock State Reservation, Box 138, Lanesboro, MA 01237. 413-499-4263. **Taconic Crest Trail** (W of North Adams; runs N to S paralleling MA/NY state line), about 30 m long, runs from VT state line S, crosses SR 2 at Petersburg Pass, continues S through Pittsfield State Forest to US 20 in

Lebanon Valley (NY); recommended for intermediate to advanced skiers; parts of trail receive heavy snowmobile use. **Clarksburg State Park** (6 m N off SR 8 on Middle Rd. in Clarksburg), 317-acre park with hiking trails on forested mountain uplands with streams and Mauserts Pond; parking area at pond. Information: Supervisor, Clarksburg State Park, Clarksburg, MA 01247.

NORTH ANDOVER: Boston Hill Ski Area (on SR 114; 19 m N of Boston via I-93), trails for cross-country skiers; downhill ski facilities, day lodge, cafeteria. Information: Boston Hill Ski Area, North Andover, MA 01845. 617-683-2733.

NORTHFIELD: Northfield Mountain Ski Touring Center (on SR 63, 10 minutes E of I-91 exit 27), 3000 acres with 26 m of marked and groomed (daily) trails for beginner to advanced skiers; rolling forested terrain with views; Nordic Ski Patrol; all skiers must register, sign in and sign out; trail fee ($2 adult, $1 children 7–14); certified instruction; ski and snowshoe rentals, ski repairs and waxing; 6 m of separate snowshoe trails (no trail fee); heated lounge and picnic lunchroom; snacks, hot chocolate, coffee and tea available in small shelter at trail intersection 8; trail maps; no snowmobiles. Lodging, restaurants in Millers Falls (2 m). Information: Northfield Mountain Ski Touring Center, Rt. 63, Northfield, MA 01360. 413-659-3713.

PITTSFIELD: Pittsfield State Forest (W of town off West St.), large, well-marked trail system for beginner to advanced skiers; trail map available; heavy use by Pittsfield students; picnic area, snowmobiles permitted; trail connects to Taconic Crest Trail. Information: Forest Supervisor, Cascade Street, Pittsfield, MA 01201. 413-442-8992. **Canoe Meadows** (in SE part of town off Holmes Rd. and Williams St.), about 5 m of marked beginner trails on wooded and open farmlands; ski clinics and winter nature programs; no snowmobiles. Information: Massachusetts Audubon Society, West Mt. Rd., Lenox, MA 01240. 413-637-0320. **Notchview Reservation** (E on SR 9 in Windsor), 3000-acre preserve with 25 m of marked, interconnecting trails for beginner to expert skiers, warming and waxing room at Visitor Center; trail map available; snowmobiles on separate trails. Supervisor, Notchview Reservation, Windsor, MA 01270. **Bucksteep Manor Ski Touring Center** (S on Washington Mt. Rd., 15 minutes from Pittsfield), 15 m of marked and groomed trails on 300 acres; adjoins October Mtn. State Forest (see Lenox); color-coded marked trails for beginner to expert skiers; small trail fee, map available; guided moonlight tours; rentals; touring center located in old rustic barn with huge fireplace, overstuffed sandwiches and soup served, full bar; entertainment and dancing Fri.–Sun. nights. Information: Bucksteep Manor, Washington Mt. Rd., Washington, MA 01223. 413-623-5535.

PLYMOUTH: Myles Standish State Forest (S), 13,000 acres of wooded rolling terrain with hiking trails and forest roads suitable for cross-country skiing; snowmobiles permitted.

SPRINGFIELD: Wilder Ski Track (on Veterans Golf Course, S. Branch Pkwy.), 10 km of beginner to intermediate marked and groomed trails on rolling open terrain and through wooded areas with brooks and waterfall; trail fee ($1); EPSTI-certified group and private instruction; moonlight and nature tours, citizens' races, waxing clinics, equipment demonstrations and film programs; full rental and retail shop; group rates; light lunch and hot drinks available in golf course clubhouse; city bus service .75 m away. Information: Wilder Ski Track, Veterans Golf Course, South Branch Pkwy., Springfield, MA 01119. 413-783-4411.

MICHIGAN

Michigan Department of Natural Resources, U.S. Forest Service, U.S. National Park Service, Huron-Clinton Metropolitan Authority, and local governments have designated thousands of acres of public land as Winter Quiet Areas where motorized use is prohibited. Trails in these areas are marked with triangular Pathway markers. State Game Areas are managed primarily for wildlife and hunting; skiers are welcome but should note hunting seasons.

For additional information, contact the individual area or Michigan Tourist Council, Commerce Center Building, 300 S. Capitol Ave., Lansing, MI 48926.

ALPENA: Norway Ridge Pathway (on Werth Rd. 4½ m SW of

Alpena), several loops totaling 5.5 m; map available; hike-in camping permitted. **Chippewa Hills Pathway** (S of Alpena, 11 m W of South Ossineke on Nicholson Rd.), 3 loops of 1.3 m, 2.5 m, 4.5 m; marked trails through a cedar grove and along a pine-filled valley; map available; hike-in camping permitted. **Besser Natural Area** (14½ m N off US 23 on County Rd. 406), 1-m trail along Lake Huron shoreline; 86 acres closed to motorized vehicles. Above 3 trails are located in designated Winter Quiet Areas of the Alpena and Thunder Bay River State Forests. For maps and information: Dept. of Natural Resources, Area Forester, Alpena, MI 49707. 517-354-2209.

ANN ARBOR: Pinckney Recreation Area (14 m NW of Ann Arbor via Dexter), 5-m Crooked Lake Trail, 2-m Silver Lake Trail, 17-m Potawatomi Trail on 3900 acres; maps available. Information: 313-426-4913. Adjacent **Waterloo Recreation Area** (18 m NW of Ann Arbor off I-94 and SR 52), established trails on 5700 acres of hilly forested terrain. Information: 313-475-8307. **Park Washtenaw of Lyndon** (5 N of Chelsea, E of SR 52, on N. Territorial Rd.), 5 m of looped trails. Information: 313-994-2575. See also **Hudson Mills Metropark** (Detroit). All Winter Quiet Area trails.

BATTLE CREEK: Binder Park (5 m S of Battle Creek on 6½ Mile Rd.), cross-country skiing; 1 hill for sledding and tobogganing, 1 hill for skiing. Open weekends (weather permitting) 9–4; fee: 50¢ per car, 10¢ per person per busload. Information: 7500 Division Dr., Battle Creek, MI 49016. 616-962-0424. **Fort Custer Recreation Area** (between Battle Creek and Kalamazoo, N of I-94 on Dickman Rd.), 12 m of marked trails on 3000 acres; Winter Quiet Area. Information: 616-731-4200.

BAY CITY: Bay Valley Inn (off I-75 at Saginaw Rd. exit), 25 m of marked trails on 500-acre Bay Valley property; rental equipment available. Outdoor skating rink, 6 indoor tennis courts. Year-round luxury resort, motor inn accommodations, restaurant, bar, swimming pool, sauna. Information: 2470 Old Bridge Rd., Bay City, MI 48706. 517-686-3500, toll free: 1-800-292-5028.

BENTON HARBOR: Warren Dunes State Park (off I-94, 20 m S), 1350 acres of dunes and forest along Lake Michigan; Winter Quiet Area. Information: 616-426-4013. **Warren Woods** (23 m S off I-94), 312 acres of forested terrain in Winter Quiet Area. **Van Buren**

State Park (18 m N on I-196), over 300 acres on Lake Michigan with cross-country ski area. Information: 616-637-2788.

BOYNE FALLS: Warner Creek Pathway (S of Boyne Falls, 1½ m E of US 131 on SR 32), 3.8-m marked trail through rolling hardwood forest and along O'briens Pond and Warner Creek; map available. **Spring Brook Pathway** (7½ m NE of Boyne Falls via Country Rd. 626, then Slashing Rd.), 2 loops of 5 m and 4 m; trail partially along old railroad grade; map available. Information: 616-582-6681. Both Pathways in Winter Quiet Areas of the Jordan River State Forest.

Boyne Mountain (1 m off US 131 at Boyne Falls), marked trails on 4000-acre property; rentals and instruction. Year-round resort with extensive downhill ski facilities; base lodge, cafeteria, restaurant, nursery, babysitters; 3 lodges (package plans), condominiums, chalets, cocktail lounges, après-ski; heated outdoor pool, ice-skating rink, general store, 4200-ft paved airstrip. Information: Boyne Mountain Lodge, Boyne Falls, MI 49713. 616-549-2441. **Thunder Mountain** (5 m NE off Thumb Lake Rd.), marked cross-country trails. Primarily a downhill ski area, open weekends; clubhouse with cafeteria and bar. Chalet rentals at area. Information: Thunder Mountain Ski Area, Boyne Falls, MI 49713. 616-549-2441. **Walloon Hills** (4 m E of Wallon Lake jct of US 131 and SR 75), cross-country and snowshoe trails through beautiful hardwood forest. Downhill ski area with redwood lodge, cafeteria, bar, ski and rental shop. A-frame housekeeping cottages at area. Information: Walloon Hills Ski Area, Boyne Falls, MI 49713. 616-549-2441.

CADILLAC: Caberfae Ski Area (15 m W off SR 55), 2-m and 5-m marked and groomed trails; instruction, 600 sets of rental equipment available. Base lodge, cafeteria, snack bar, cocktail lounge, nursery; accommodations at area (package plans); après-ski. Information: RR 4, Cadillac, MI 49601. 616-862-3300. **MacKenzie Trail** (at Caberfae Ski Area), 4 loops totaling 8¼ m; marked and maintained trails start at Caberfae parking lot, free trail map; novice and intermediate terrain with hardwood areas, pine plantation, meandering stream, bridge crossing; Winter Quiet Area in Manistee National Forest. Nearby **Olga Lake Ski Trail** (9 m W on SR 55), 11¾ m of novice and intermediate marked trails through forested areas. Plowed parking lot; toilet facilities at both extremities. Snowshoeing, backpacking. Information: U.S. Forest Service,

P.O. Box 409, Cadillac, MI 49601. 616-775-8539. **Lost Pines Lodge** (3 m from Caberfae on W. 38 Mile Rd.) borders Manistee National Forest and maintains connecting trail to Caberfae and other marked trails; caters to snowmobilers. Rentals; 1 rope tow, sleigh rides, ski jouring; accommodations, restaurant, bar, après-ski. Information: Harrietta, MI 49638. 616-389-2222.

Timberlane Ski Touring Lodge (25 m W off SR 55), 20 m of marked and groomed trails in Manistee National Forest. CSIA-certified instructors; rental equipment; weekend and week-long tours. Individual and group lodging and meals at area. Information: Irons, MI 49644. 616-266-5376. **Enchanted Acres Campground** (W of Cadillac, on Brooks Rd., ½ m S of Irons), marked trails of 1 to 3 m, 3 to 5 m, 7 to 10 m. Information: Brooks Rd., Box 7, Irons, MI 49644. 616-266-5102.

Cool X-Country Ski Trails (S of Cadillac, W of US 131 on LeRoy Rd.), novice to expert groomed trails; individual or group instruction; sales and rentals. Daily trail fee; Ladies Day every Tues. and Thurs., with half-price rental and trail fee. Moonlight tours. Information: LeRoy Rd., LeRoy, MI 49655. 616-768-4624. **Vocational Training School Trail** (on E. 36 Mile Rd., in Wexford County), 12-m trail for experienced skiers beginning at school's main parking lot. Information 616-775-8505.

CHARLEVOIX: Bell's Bay Trail (2 m SW via US 31 to Bell's Bay Rd.), 2-m marked loop along Lake Michigan; designated Winter Quiet Area in the Jordan River State Forest. Information: 616-582-6681. For map: Dept. of Natural Resources, Information Services Center, Box 30028, Lansing, MI 48909.

CHEBOYGAN: Cheboygan-Black Lake Trail (at Cheboygan), 46-m trail; start at either Alpena St. Rd. on the northern end, or at Black Lake on the southern end; tavern and restroom facilities en route. Camping areas at Cheboygan State Park and Onaway State Park as well as forest service campground on Black Lake beaches. Information: Dept. of Natural Resources, 120 A St., Cheboygan, MI 49721. 616-627-4547.

CLARE: Green Pine Lake Pathway (14 m NW of Clare on SR 115 at Lake Station Rd.), 3 loops of 2.5 m, 5 m, 7 m; marked trails start at Pine Lake State Forest Campground; map available; shelter and restroom facilities on trail. A Winter Quiet Area in the Chippewa

River State Forest. Information: Dept. of Natural Resources, Area Forester, Paris, MI 49338. 616-832-2281.

CRYSTAL FALLS: Lake Mary Plains Pathway (1 m S off SR 69, 6 m E of Crystal Falls), 2 marked loops of 3.4 m and 6.2 m; parking and trailhead at Glidden Lake State Forest Campground; map available. Winter Quiet Area in the Iron Range State Forest. Information: Dept. of Natural Resources, Information Services Center, Box 30028, Lansing, MI 48909.

DETROIT: Kensington Metropark (35 m NW of Detroit at exits 151 or 153 off I-96), 3 beginner to intermediate marked trails of 4.5 m, 2.56 m, 4 m through wooded areas and along Kent Lake shoreline. Adjacent golf course area offers 3 beginner loops of 1.28 m, 1.08 m, .57 m; trail maps available. Ski rentals at golf course ski center building; instruction on weekends. Tobogganing, sledding, skating, ice fishing; heated building with snack bar at skating area. Park office: 2240 W. Buno Rd., Milford, MI 48042; 313-685-1561; Ski Center: 685-1408. **Stony Creek Metropark** (6 m N of Utica off SR 53, on 26 Mile Rd.), 3 loops totaling 6 m of beginner to advanced trails; rentals at Ski Touring Center, Eastwood Beach; instruction available. Information: 313-961-5865. **Hudson Mills Metropark** (12.5 m NW of Ann Arbor off US 23 on N. Territorial Rd.), 600 scenic acres with a 3-m trail. Information: 313-426-8211. **Willow Metropark** (7 m NW of Flat Rock, off I-275, on Willow Rd.), looped trails on 1500 acres along Huron River. Information: 313-697-9181. Adjacent **Oakwoods Metropark** (entrance on Willow Rd.) open to cross-country skiers. **Lower Huron Metropark** (2 m W of Romulus on Hannan Rd., ¼ m S off I-94 at Haggerty Rd. exit), 1200 acres with trails along Huron River. Information: 313-697-9181. The above parks are designated Winter Quiet Areas. For maps and additional information: Huron-Clinton Metropolitan Authority, 3050 Penobscot Building, Detroit, MI 48226. **Belle Isle** (in Detroit River, via MacArthur Bridge off Jefferson Ave.), skiing permitted.

    Proud Lake Recreation Area (off I-96 or SR 59, 2 m SE of Milford via Wixom Rd.), 1100 acres with established trails. Information: 313-685-2433. **Highland Recreation Area** (off SR 59, 2 m E of Highland), trails through 1400 acres. Information: 313-887-5135. Both are Winter Quiet Areas.

    Heavener Ski Center (6 m N of I-96 Wixom exit, follow Proud Lake Rec. Area signs, then left on Garden Rd.), trails in Proud

Lake Recreation Area (see above); rentals with 2-hour minimum, instruction, guided twilight and night tours; special weekday and group rates. Information: 2775 Garden Rd., Milford, MI 48042. 313-685-2379.

Mt. Grampian Ski Area (14 m N of Pontiac, 2 m E of Oxford on Lakeville Rd. off SR 24), 4.5 m trail for cross-country skiers; downhill ski facilities include rentals, ski shop, lodge, restaurant. Information: Lakeville Rd., Oxford, MI 48051. 313-628-2450.

ESCANABA: Cedar River Pathway (S of Escanaba on Cedar River Rd., 7½ m N of Cedar River), 4 marked interconnecting loops of 2 m, 3.5 m, 5 m, 7 m; trails along the Cedar River with campground en route; map available; parking area at trailhead. Information: 906-753-6317. **Days River Pathway** (5½ m NW of Gladstone via US 2 and County Rd. 446), 3 interconnecting marked loops of 2.2 m, 6.5 m, 9.2 m; parking area; trail map available. Information: 906-786-2351. Both pathways in designated Winter Quiet Areas of the Menominee and Bay de Noc State Forests.

FLINT: Holloway Reservoir Regional Park (E of Flint, off SR 21, on Coldwater Rd. W of Elba Rd.), skiing on 800 acres with 4–5-m trail; restroom on trail. Information: Genesee County Parks & Rec. Commission, G-5055 Branch, Flint, MI 48503. 313-736-7100. **Ortonville Recreation Area** (between Flint and Pontiac at Ortonville, Bloomer #3 Park Unit), 3-m trail; restroom and shelter at area; hike-in camping permitted. Information: Roger Bailey, 5779 Hadley Rd., Ortonville, MI 48462. 313-627-3828. **Metamora-Hadley State Recreation Area** (E of Flint via US 21 and SR 24, on Hurd Rd., 3 m W of Metamora), short trails in park; shelter, restrooms, campground. Information: Metamora, MI 48455. 313-797-4439.

GAYLORD: Pine Barren Pathway (6 m SW of Gaylord via Old Alba Rd. and Lone Pine Rd.), 4 interconnecting loops of about 2 m each, outside loop totals 6.25 m; map available; marked trails in the Otsego State Forest. Information: 517-732-4154. **Shingle Mill Pathway** (11 m E of Vanderbilt on Sturgeon Valley Rd.), .75 m- and 1.25-m novice loops, 6-m intermediate loop, 10-m and 11-m loops with numerous steep slopes recommended for experienced skiers; trailhead and parking at Pigeon Bridge State Forest Campground; several lakes, Pigeon River, overlook, and campsites on route. Pathway connects to High Country Pathway at Sturgeon Valley

Rd. on the southern end and just over Grass Lake Rd. on the northern end. Information: Area Forester, Pigeon River Country S.F., 9966 Twin Lakes Rd., Vanderbilt, MI 49795. 517-983-4101. **High Country Pathway** (access from Vanderbilt: via Sturgeon Valley Rd. at Pigeon Bridge State Forest Campground), very long pathway looping through 3 state forests; see listing under Onaway. Above pathways in designated Winter Quiet Areas.

Ken-Mar on the Hill (4 m S of Gaylord on Old 27), 100 wooded acres with over 20 km of marked, groomed trails for novice to advanced skiers; rentals including children's equipment; lessons free; small trail fee for non-guests; rentals and trail fee less on Ladies Day (Tues.); warming hut with sandwiches and beverages available. Family-style resort; motel accommodations. Information: Mr. and Mrs. John H. Forshew, Rt. 3, Box 679, Gaylord, MI 49735. 517-732-4950. **Michaywè Slopes** (7 m S of Gaylord off Old 27), 10 m of marked, groomed and tracked trails through dense forest and over rolling meadows; rentals and instruction available. Downhill skiers share day lodge, snack bar, cocktail lounge. Accommodations, restaurants in Gaylord. Information: Rt. 3, Box 632, Gaylord, MI 49735. 517-939-8800. **Sylvan Knob** (5 m E of Gaylord on County Rd. F-44), cross-country ski trail and rental equipment; family ski area, downhill ski facilities, warming house, snack bar. Information: RR 1, Box 237B, Gaylord, MI 49735. 517-732-4733.

GRAND RAPIDS: Grand Rapids City Parks (in Grand Rapids), Aman, Comstock-Riverside, John Ball, Huff, and Ken-O-Sha Parks open to cross-country skiers. Egypt Valley X-Country Trail (begins at Two Mile Rd. and Honeycreek Ave. in Seidman Park, NE Grand Rapids) has 15 m of trails connecting with Cannonsburg State Game Area. Information: 616-454-9242. **Cannonsburg State Game Area** (5 m NE via Four Mile Rd.), several marked loops totaling 7 m; Winter Quiet Area. Information: 616-456-5071. **Yankee Springs Recreation Area** (SE off US 131 and SR 37, 12 m W of Hastings), 3 loops of 4 m, 5 m, and 10 m on 1200 acres of woods, hills, glades, and scenic lakes; Winter Quiet Area. Information: 616-795-9081.

Cannonsburg Ski Area (10 m NE of Grand Rapids; 4 m E off US 131 on Cannonsburg Rd.), 3 groomed beginner to intermediate wooded trails of 1 km, 3 km, and 5 km; instruction, guided tours; 200 pair of rental skis; trail fee, package plans for rentals and lessons, group rates. Major downhill ski area; base lodge, 4 cafeterias, cocktail lounge, ski shop. Numerous accommodations, restaurants in Grand Rapids area. Information: Box 14, Cannonsburg, MI 49317. 616-874-6711; toll free (IN, OH, IL), 1-800-253-8748. **Double RR Ranch** (4424 Whites Bridge Rd. in Smyrna, 20 m NE of Grand Rapids), miles of trails on 400 acres; connects to nearby State Trail; skiing and snowmobiling by request or reservation only. Information: 4424 Whites Bridge Rd., Smyrna, MI 48887. 616-794-0520. **Sandy Pines** (10 m W of Dorr at Lake Monterey Golf Course), 7 m of groomed, marked trails; small daily trail fee. Information: P.O. Box 135, Burnips, MI 49314. 616-896-8311.

GRAYLING: Rasmus Hanson Recreation Area (off SR 72 and SR 93, 1½ m W), 10 trails totaling 32 miles; rentals, instruction, and maps available. Municipally operated area; downhill ski facilities, warming lodge, fireplace, snack bar; ice skating, sledding; annual Winter Sports Festival, cross-country races. **Hartwick Pines State Park** (6 m N on SR 93), 3 marked loops totaling 15 m on 5000 acres; campground, restroom facilities. Above trails in designated Winter Quiet Areas. For maps and information: Grayling Regional Chamber of Commerce, P.O. Box 406, Grayling, MI 49738. 517-348-3336.

HARRISVILLE: Reid Lake Ski Trails (19 m W on SR 72, 3 m E of SR 65), 3 marked loops totaling 5 m; shelter, restrooms; hike-in camping permitted. Winter Quiet Area in the Huron National Forest. Information: Huron Shores Chamber of Commerce, Box 151, Harrisville, MI 48740. 517-739-8783.

Mt. Maria (at Spruce, at S end of Hubbard Lake), 26 m of marked trails; downhill ski area, rustic day lodge, cafeteria, cocktail lounge. Breathtaking views of Hubbard Lake. Information: Mt. Maria Ski Lodge, Spruce, MI 48762. 517-736-8377.

HOUGHTON: Mount Ripley Ski Area (½ m E of bridge on SR 26), downhill ski area with trails for cross-country skiers; chalet snack bar. Lodging, restaurants in Houghton-Hancock area; university town atmosphere. Information: Houghton, MI 49931. 906-487-2340.

IRON MOUNTAIN: Pine Mountain Ski Area (2½ m N off US 2 and 141), competition-length cross-country trail (qualifies to national specifications); downhill ski facilities, cafeteria, restaurant.

World's highest artificial ski jump. Accommodations for 120 at Pine Mountain Lodge, heated indoor-outdoor pool, après-ski, Rathskeller. Information: Pine Mountain Corp., 1126 Bay Shore Drive, Iron Mountain 49801. 906-774-2747.

IRON RIVER: Ge-Che Ski Trail System (1 m W on US 2, then S on SR 73 for 1 m, turn W on Forest Rd. 101 for 4 m; turnoff well signed), 3.4 m of marked and maintained interconnecting trails on rolling terrain suitable for beginners to intermediates; trail map available; parking area, toilet and telephone at trailhead. Information: District Ranger, Iron River District, Ottawa National Forest, Iron River, MI 49935. 906-265-5139. **Brule Mountain Ski Area** (7 m SW between SR 189 and SR 73, along Brule River), groomed and tracked cross-country trails; instruction and guided tours available. Primarily a downhill ski area; chalet, snack bar, cocktail lounge, evening dining; picnic shelter; ski shop. Rental chalets and camper hook-ups at area. Information: Iron River, MI 49935. 906-265-4957; toll free (Nov.-Mar.), 1-800-338-7174.

IRONWOOD: Indianhead Mountain (2 m N off US 2 between Wakefield and Bessemer), trails, rentals and instruction for cross-country skiers; extensive downhill ski facilities; base lodge, mountain-top lodge, restaurants, cafeteria, bars, après-ski; nursery, ski shop. Lodge accommodations, rental chalets at area; saunas, heated outdoor pool. Information: Wakefield, MI 49968. 906-229-5181; toll free (Oct. 15–Apr. 1), 800-338-1240.

ISHPEMING: Al Quaal Recreation Area (in Ishpeming) maintains 3 cross-country trials of 1 to 7 m in length; downhill ski facilities, junior jumping hills, toboggan run; snack bar. Also in Ishpeming, National Ski Hall of Fame and National Ski Museum (Wed.-Sun., 1–4; daily 10–4 in summer). **Suicide Ski Bowl** (2 m E from Al Quaal Recreation Area), 4 loops of 1.7 m, 3.5 m, 5 m, 7 m; 5 jumping hills. **Black River Pathway** (10 m SW of Ishpeming off County Rd. 581), 2.5-m marked loop on slightly hilly terrain; trailhead at parking area adjacent to campground and Black River Falls; map available; Winter Quiet Area in the Michigamme State Forest. Information for above areas: Ishpeming Chamber of Commerce, Ishpeming, MI 49849. 906-486-4841.

Craig Lake State Park (W of Ishpeming, 4 m N of Three Lakes, off US 41), 5700 acres with numerous abandoned logging roads available to cross-country skiers; Winter Quiet Area. Information: Department of Natural Resources, District Headquarters, Baraga, MI 49908.

KALAMAZOO: Al Sabo Land Preserve (9th St. near Kalamazoo Community College), marked trails on 800 acres owned by the City of Kalamazoo Water Dept.; maps available at trailhead or from the Water Dept. Information: 616-375-8149. **Maple Glen Park** (in Cooper Township), variety of trails with a slightly steeper terrain, just minutes from downtown. City Parks information: 616-385-8193. **Coldbrook County Park** (MN Ave. E of 40th St.), marked trails in 275-acre park with Portage Lake and Blue Lake. Information: Kalamazoo County Parks and Recreation Dept. 616-383-8776.

Kleinstuck Preserve (accessible from Maple Street YMCA), quiet deep-woods trails; state-owned area in the city. **Allegan State Game Area** (25 m NW of Kalamazoo; 5 m NW of Allegan off 118th Ave.), 26 m of marked trails on 12,000 acres of unspoiled wilderness. Free trail map from Allegan Area Development Assoc., Allegan, MI 49010. Information: 616-673-2430. **Barry State Game Area** (30 m NW, Bradley-Hopkins exit off US 131), marked trails; map available. Information: 1805 S. Yankee Springs Road, Middleville, MI 49333. 616-795-3280.

Timber Ridge Ski Area (13 m NW of Kalamazoo via US 131, then D Ave. or I-94 to SR 40, then E at Gobles), 5 m of groomed trails, small daily fee; downhill ski facilities, chalet, cafeteria, 2 cocktail lounges; ski shop. Information: RR 2, Gobles, MI 49055. 616-694-9449.

LANSING: Fitzgerald Park (5 m E via SR 43 at Grand Ledge), 1½-m trail for cross-country skiers. Information: Grand Ledge, MI 48837. 517-627-2383.

LUDINGTON: Sheep Ranch Pathway (E of Ludington; 2 m E of Baldwin on US 10), 1 river loop of 2.3 m with overlook and 1 lake loop of 1 m with 2 campgrounds on route; pathways totaling 4.5 m in Pere Marquette State Forest; parking at trailhead; trail map available. Information: 616-745-4651. **Bowman Lake Foot Travel Area** (E of Ludington; 10 m SW of Baldwin off Carrs Rd.), 6 m of marked trails in Manistee National Forest. Information: 616-745-4631. **Silver Lake State Park** (S of Ludington; 10 m SW of Hart), marked trails on 640-acre park bordering Lake Michigan, sand dunes. Information: 616-873-3083. Above trails in designated Winter Quiet Areas. **Ludington State Park** (7 m N), 18 m of marked trails for novice to advanced skiers. Information: 616-843-8671.

Ward Hills Ski Area (6½ m N of Branch, between Ludington and Baldwin), 3 marked trails, longest 14 m; rental equipment; downhill ski facilities, warming house, snack bar. Family area. **YMCA Camp Martin Johnson** (just N of Ward Hills Ski Area); 300 wooded acres for cross-country skiers to enjoy in Manistee National Forest; rental equipment; lodging with family-style cooking; group rates. Both above areas operated by YMCA of metropolitan Chicago; Information: YMCA Camp Martin Johnson, RR 1, Irons, MI 49644. 616-266-5202. **Barothy Lodge** (E of Ludington; 2 m S, then 1 m E of Walhalla), 300 acres available with marked trails from resort on Pere Marquette River. Information: P.O. Box 165, Walhalla, MI 49458. 616-898-2340. **Whiskey Creek Recreations** (28 m SE of Ludington), 30 m of marked trails in Manistee National Forest; small daily fee. Year-round camping resort with toboggan run, rope tow, snowmobile race track; lodge, light dining, cocktail lounge, heated indoor pool, sauna; laundromat, store. Information: P.O. Box 624, Pentwater, MI 49449. 616-869-8671.

MACKINAW CITY: Wilderness State Park (15 m W), 2400 acres on Lake Michigan; many miles of established trails along rocky shoreline and through evergreen forest; camping and picnic areas; maps available; Winter Quiet Area. Information: 616-436-5381.

MANCELONA: Mt. Mancelona (½ m NE on US 131), cross-country trails; downhill ski facilities; day lodge, snack bar, fireside lounge; winter trailer park area. Information: Mancelona, MI 49659. 616-587-8631. **Schuss Mt.** (6 m W on SR 88), 5 miles of marked trails; daily fee; rentals and instruction; downhill ski facilities; restaurant, cafeteria, cocktail lounge; lodge, condominium and chalet accommodations for 400 at area (children under 12 ski and sleep free midweek), heated outdoor pool, après-ski. Information: Mancelona, MI 49659. 616-587-9162. **Chain O'Lakes KOA Campground** (NW on SR 88 between Mancelona and Bellaire), 125 wooded acres with marked and groomed trails. Information: P.O. Box 484, Bellaire, MI 49615. 616-533-8432. **Shanty Creek Lodge** (2 m S of Bellaire off SR 88), several miles of marked trails; rentals and instruction; downhill ski facilities; restaurant, cafeteria, cocktail lounge; year-round resort, lodge accommodates 300;

nursery; heated outdoor pool, saunas, ice skating, snowmobiles. Package plans. Information: Bellaire, MI 49615. 616-533-8621.

MANISTIQUE: Ashford Lake Pathway (16 m N on SR 94), 3 interconnecting, marked loops of 3 m, 6 m, and 9 m; map available; parking area at trailhead; Winter Quiet Area in the Manistique River State Forest. Information: 906-341-2518.

MARQUETTE: Presque Isle Park (on Lake Superior), 2-m trail on wooded peninsula; scenic shoreline. **Park Cemetery** (in Marquette), 2-m loop. Information: City of Marquette, Recreation Dept. Marquette, MI 49855. 906-228-8200.

Blueberry Ridge Pathway (6 m S of Marquette at jct of County Rd. 480 and County Rd. 553), 3 interconnecting marked loops of a 2.5-m level trail and 2 hilly trails of 5 m and 8.5 m; trailhead at parking area; map available; adjacent snowmobile trail but pathway designated Winter Quiet Area in the Michigamme State Forest. **Anderson Lake Pathway** (just S of Gwinn off County Rd. 557), 2.5-m beginner trail, 3.5-m intermediate trail, and 4.3-m advanced trail interconnect to form 3 loops; 4 lakes plus Anderson Lake Campground; trailhead at parking area; map available. Winter Quiet Area in the Escanaba River State Forest. Information: Dept. of Natural Resources, Information Services Center, Box 30028, Lansing, MI 48909.

Cliffs Ridge Ski Area (in Marquette), 4-m cross-country trail maintained; downhill ski facilities, base lodge, cafeteria, cocktail lounge; picnic shelters; ski shop. Information: Box 487, Marquette, MI 49855. 906-225-0486.

MIO: Cross State Trail (E and W through Mio), shelter, restroom, and camping facilities along route. Information: Mio Chamber of Commerce, Mio, MI 48647.

Hinchman Acres Resort (N of city limits on SR 33), marked and groomed trails in Huron National Forest area; rentals and instruction available; warming hut with fireplace and snack bar; guest cottages accommodate 60; snowmobiling, ice fishing, ice skating. Information: Box 146, Mio, MI 48647. 517-826-3991. **Shibui Fun Valley** (on Lewiston Rd., N of Mio), 2 m of trails on 160 acres; shelter, restrooms, and lodging available. Information: Box 544, Rt. #1, Mio, MI 48647. 517-848-2250.

MUNISING: Pictured Rocks National Lakeshore (NE on Lake Superior), one of Michigan's most scenic areas with sandstone cliffs, dunes, inland lakes, waterfalls, marshes, hardwood and coniferous forests, abundant wildlife; cross-country ski trails maintained at both east and west ends of park: **Munising Ski Trail** (accessible from East City Limits Rd. or Park Headquarters at Sand Point), 5 m of marked, interconnecting trails on easy to moderately difficult hilly terrain. **Grand Marais Ski Trail** (accessible from Park Information Station off SR 77, W of Grand Marais), 3.1-m beginner to intermediate trail through wooded areas along the Sable Creek and near Sable Falls; trail marked with red tape, map available with compass readings for use during periods of poor visibility. Winter camping permitted at designated campsites throughout park; snowmobiles not permitted on ski trails. For maps and information: Superintendent, Pictured Rocks National Lakeshore, P.O. Box 40, Munising, MI 49862. 906-387-4859.

Munising Area Cross-Country Trails. There are endless touring possibilities in the beautiful rugged country of Hiawatha National Forest and the State Forests surrounding Munising. Information: Parks and Recreation Director, Munising; or Chamber of Commerce, Munising, MI 49862. 906-387-2138.

MUSKEGON: Muskegon State Park (5 m W on SR 213), interconnecting trails on 1200 acres of forested dunes along Lake Michigan; Winter Quiet Area. Information: 616-744-3480.

NEWAYGO: Manistee Hiking Trail (N of Newaygo; trail starts 5 m S of White Cloud and ends at Highbanks Lake near Lilley), 30-m marked trail in Manistee National Forest. Information: 616-689-1592. **Newaygo Winter Park** (4 m N off SR 37), established trails on 60 acres, with connecting trail to Manistee Hiking Trail. Information: Box 420E, RR 4, Newaygo, MI 49337. 616-652-9191.

Woods & Waters Campground (5 m NE; 5 m S of White Cloud off SR 37), groomed trails connecting with many miles of wilderness trails; snowmobile area; winter camping facilities, recreation center, lodge, snack bar, heated indoor pool, saunas. Information: RR 1, White Cloud, MI 49349. 616-689-6701.

NEWBERRY: Tahquamenon Falls State Park/Natural Area Pathway (on SR 123, 23 m NE of Newberry; 14 m W of Paradise), 13-m interconnecting trail system; beautiful wilderness terrain with bog lakes, muskeg, pine-forested sand ridges, broad open spaces, forest of beech and hemlock; beginners' loop at Upper Falls trailhead; Wolf Lake to Lily Pond not recommended for novice skiers; foundations of a late 1800s logging camp on the Wilderness Loop; Pathway mile markers, trail map available. Pathway travels through the Old Trail Natural Area Preserve (2176 acres) and the Betsy Lake Natural Area (15,000 acres in Lake Superior State Forest); Winter Quiet Area. Parking areas and trailheads at Upper Falls and Lower Falls. Information: Tahquamenon Falls State Park, 906-492-3415; or Area Forester, Department of Natural Resources District Headquarters, Newberry, MI 49868. 906-293-5131.

Canada Lakes Pathway (5½ m SE of Newberry via SR 28 and County Rd. 403), 2 marked loops of 3.5 m and 5 m; trailhead at parking area; map available; Winter Quiet Area in Tahquamenon River State Forest. Information: (above address), 906-293-5131.

ONAWAY: Sinks Hole Area (13.5 m S via SR 33 and Tomahawk Lake Rd., E of Shoepac Lake Campground), marked trails through 2600 acres of Black Lake State Forest. Information: 517-733-8722. **High Country Pathway** (access from SR 33 on the E at Shoepac Lake, Tomahawk Lake, or Clear Lake State Park Campgrounds; from the W via Sturgeon Valley Rd. at Pigeon Bridge State Forest Campground), very long marked pathway looping through Black Lake State Forest, Thunder Bay River State Forest, and Pigeon River State Forest; 3 smaller connecting pathway systems (including Sink Holes Area) and 10 State Forest Campgrounds en route; designated Winter Quiet Area. Maps and information: Department of Natural Resources, Information Services Center, Box 30028, Lansing, MI 48909.

ONTONAGON: Porcupine Mountains Wilderness State Park (off SR 107, 17 m W of Ontonagon) maintains 3 cross-country trails of 4 m, 7 m, 9 m; rental equipment and repair service; downhill ski facilities; base chalet with fireplace, cafeteria, ski shop, first-aid room. Most of the 55,000-acre park open to snowmobiling, but cross-country trails are in designated Winter Quiet Area. Information: Area Forester, Dept. of Natural Resources District Headquarters, Ontonagon, MI 49953. 906-885-5798; or Ontonagon County Tourist Assoc., Ontonagon, MI 49953. Ski Hill: 906-885-5170. **Old Grade Ski Trail** (E on SR 38; 7 m W of Nisula at jct of SR 38 and Forest Rd No. 203 leading to Courtney Lake Recrea-

tion Area), 500-acre area with 3.9 m of marked interconnecting trails; trails marked with orange triangles; gently rolling novice terrain with 2 lakes; trail map available; snowmobiles not permitted on ski trails. Information: District Ranger, Ontonagon Ranger District, Ottawa National Forest, Ontonagon, MI 49953. 906-884-2411.
Gogebic Ridge-West Ski Trail (S on SR 64; trailhead: 3 m N of Bergland on SR 64, and 3 m W of Bergland on SR 28 at jct of Forest Rd No. 798), 5.5 m of marked trails plus unlimited skiing on surrounding acres; rolling timbered terrain with some steep grades, difficult to climb on skis, recommended for expert skiers; overlook of Lake Gogebic en route; trail map available; snowmobiles not permitted on ski trail. Information: District Ranger, Bergland Ranger District, Ottawa National Forest, Bergland, MI 49910. 906-575-3441.

PETOSKEY: Petoskey State Park (3 m N off SR 131), marked trails in 295-acre park; Winter Quiet Area. Information: 616-347-2311. **Wildwood Hills Pathway** (on Wildwood Rd., 12 m E of Petoskey), 3 marked interconnecting loops of 3 m, 6 m, and 8.75 m; map available; 2 parking areas; Winter Quiet Area in Hardwood State Forest. Information: 616-238-9313.

Boyne Highlands (8 m W off SR 131), many miles of marked, groomed trails; daily fee; rentals and instruction available; extensive downhill ski facilities; dining room, cafeteria, cocktail lounge; nursery, babysitters; year-round resort with lodging for 500 (package plans); heated outdoor pool, saunas; ice skating; après-ski. Information: Harbor Springs, MI 49740. 616-526-2171. **Nub's Nob** (NW via US 31 and SR 131; 5 m NE of Harbor Springs on Pleasant View Rd.), 3-m marked trail; rentals and instruction available; downhill ski facilities; year-round resort with accommodations for 75 (package plans); dining room, cafeteria, cocktail lounge; heated indoor pool. Information: Harbor Springs, MI 49740. 616-526-2131.

ROGERS CITY: Ocqueoc Falls Bicentennial Pathway (11.5 m W via SR 68 at the Ocqueoc Falls Scenic Site), 3 interconnecting loops along the Ocqueoc River of 3 m, 4 m, and 6.5 m; falls and trailhead at parking area; campground adjacent; Winter Quiet Area; map available. Information: 517-733-8722. **Silver Creek Trail** (W via SR 68; on Walker Rd., E of Millersburg), 36-m trail through Black Lake State Forest to Lake Huron; campground and restrooms en route. Information: Dept. of Natural Resources 120 A St., Cheboygan, MI 49721. 616-627-4547.

ROSCOMMON: Tisdale Triangle Pathway (Gardner Rd., NE corner city limits and off Main St., .75 m from town center), 5 interconnecting loops totaling 10.3 m; pathway and intersection markers; parking at both starting points. **Nokomis Pathway** (3.5 m S of Houghton Lake on County Rd. 400), .75-m loop interconnecting with a 1.5-m loop; map available with suggested direction of travel; parking area at trailhead. Both pathways designated Winter Quiet Areas. Maps and information: Area Forester, Houghton Lake State Forest, Houghton Lake, MI 48629. 517-422-5522.

    Cross Country Ski Headquarters Trail (9475 N. Cut Rd., Higgins Lake), 3-m and 6-m trails; hike-in camping. Information: Rt. #2, Box 394, Higgins Lake, Roscommon, MI 48653. 517-821-6661. **Pioneer Hill** (Coor ISD, central office parking lot), 5-m marked trail; shelter, hike-in camping. Information: Coor ISD, Pioneer Hills, Roscommon, MI 48653. 517-275-5137.

SAGINAW: Bintz Apple Mountain Ski Area (5 m NW off SR 47, center of Tri-City area near Freeland), 1-m and 3-m trails through the apple orchard; rentals and instruction. Downhill ski area with base lodge, restaurant, snack bar, cocktail lounge, après-ski; accommodations within 5 m. Information: Bintz Apple Mtn. Ski Lodge, 4535 N. River Rd., Freeland, MI 48623. 517-781-0170 or 517-781-0030.

SAULT STE. MARIE: Pine Bowl Pathway (S off I-79, 2 m E of Kincheloe Air Force Base via SR 129 and Wilson Rd.), 3 interconnecting, marked loops of 2 m, 5.4 m, and 9.5 m; map available; parking area at trailhead. Winter Quiet Area in Munuscong State Forest. Information: 906-635-5281; or Dept. of Natural Resources, Information Services Center, Box 30028, Lansing, MI 48909.

TAWAS CITY: Corsair Cross-Country Ski Trails (8 m NW of East Tawas on Monument Rd.), 4 interconnecting loops totaling 11 m; hilly terrain along the Silver Creek drainage, recommended for intermediate skiers; one section of trail joins Michigan Shore-to-Shore Trail; map available. **Highbanks Trail** (15 m NW of East Tawas; follow Monument Rd. N to River Rd., then W 3 m to Iargo

Springs), 6-m marked trail for beginner to intermediate skiers; hilly terrain along the banks of Au Sable River and through the historic Lumberman's Monument Area. Above trails marked and maintained; plowed parking areas; designated Winter Quiet Areas in the Huron National Forest. Information: Tawas District Ranger, U.S. Forest Service, Box 472 Federal Building, East Tawas, MI 48730. 517-362-4477.

Michigan Shore-to-Shore Trail is a 210-m trail across the Northern Lower Peninsula from Tawas City on the east to Elberta or Empire on the west. Information: Chamber of Commerce, 402 Lake St., Tawas City, MI 48763. Maps and information for about 100 m of trail across the Huron National Forest from above Tawas District Ranger address. **Tawas Point State Park** (4 m E of East Tawas off US 23), 80 acres with lovely trails on peninsula in Lake Huron. Information: 517-362-5041.

TRAVERSE CITY: Sand Lakes Quiet Area (5 m SE of Williamsburg; E of Traverse City), winter parking and access path from SR 72 via Broomhead Rd.; many miles of trails on 2800 acres of rolling forested land with numerous small lakes and a wide range of animal life; Shore-to-Shore Riding-Hiking Trail intersects trails on the southern edge of area; camping permitted in area with drinking water and toilet facilities at Sand Lakes No. 1. Information: 616-258-9471. **Muncie Lake Pathway** (6 m NE of Mayfield via Garfield Rd., Hobbs Rd. and Ranch Rudolf Rd.; SE of Traverse City), 4 interconnecting loops of 2 m, 6 m, 8 m, and 9 m; variety of novice to intermediate terrain along the Boardman River and Dollar and Muncie Lakes. Information: 616-946-4940. **Lost Lake Nature Pathway** (2.5 m NW of Interlochen Corners via US 31 and Wildwood Rd.; S of Traverse City), 3 interconnecting loops of 2.5 m, 4.5 m, and 5.5 m in Fife Lake State Forest. Information: 616-946-4920. **Chain-O-Lakes Pathway** (2 m SW of Lake Ann via Almira and Reynolds Rds.; W of Traverse City), 2 interconnecting loops of 1.5 m and 2 m in Betsie River State Forest. Information: 616-325-4611. All above trails in designated Winter Quiet Area. For maps, contact: Dept. of Natural Resources, Information Services Center, Box 30028, Lansing, MI 48909. **Sleeping Bear Dunes National Lakeshore** (30 m W via US 31, SR 72, and SR 22) stretches 30 m along Lake Michigan shoreline and contains some 60,000 acres of rolling sand dunes, hardwood ridges, cedar and hemlock swamps; entire park open to skiing with over 30 m of marked trails in 3 locations: **Alligator Hill Trails** (trailhead off SR 109, opposite D. H. Day Campground), 3 interconnecting trails of 3.5 m, 2.1 m and 4.6 m; hilly terrain with 3 overlooks. **Schauger Hill-Windy Moraine Trails** (trailhead at Visitor Center, intersection of SR 109 and Welch Rd.), 3 interconnecting trails of 1.5 m, 3 m, and 5.1 m; all trails very hilly. **Platte Plains** (access from Platte River Campground or off SR 22 at Esch Rd.), about 12 m of interconnecting trails; mostly flat terrain with 3 small lakes, 2 overlooks and Jack Pine Campground (use permit required) en route. D. H. Day and Platte River Campgrounds are open during winter months. Information, permits and maps at Park Ranger Stations or Sleeping Bear Dunes National Lakeshore, Park Headquarters, 400 Main Street, Frankfort, MI 49635. 616-352-9611.

Ranch Rudolf (12 m SE), 2 m, 4 m, 9 m, and 11 m of marked and groomed interconnecting trails along the Boardman River in over 100,000 acres of forested hills of Fife Lake State Forest; no trail fee; ski jouring behind trained sled dogs; night skiing; rentals and instruction; snowmobiling. Year-round resort with cozy lodging (package plans, children under 12 sleep and ski free midweek when sharing parents' room), western-style restaurant, saloon; general store (Boardman Valley Outfitting Co.). Information: P.O. Box 587, Traverse City, MI 49684. 616-946-5410. **Traverse City Holiday** (5 m E on US 31 N), 5 to 8 m of marked trails; rentals; downhill ski facilities; base lodge, snack bar. Information: Box 305, Traverse City, MI 49684. 616-938-1360. **Yogi Bear's Jellystone Campground** (4050 Hammond Rd., just E of 5-mile Rd.), 2.5-m and 5-m marked trails; access to South Boardman, Fife Lake, and Kalkaska State Forest trails; rentals available; snowmobiling. Year-round campground, heated recreation lounge, restrooms, snack bar, store. Information: 4050 Hammond Rd., Traverse City MI 49684. 616-947-2770. **L'Da Du Resort** (10 m SE on Spider Lake), cross-country skiing; snowmobiling; food, lodging. Information: Box 273, RR 4, Traverse City, MI 49684. 616-946-8999. **Crystal Mountain** (6 m E of US 31 on SR 115, near Thompsonville; SW of Traverse City), 2.5-m marked and groomed trail system; daily fee; rentals available; downhill ski facilities; dining room, cafeteria, 3 cocktail lounges; après-ski. Heated outdoor pool; ice-skating rink, ski shop; year-round resort with lodge and chalet accommodations (package plans). Information: Box 60, Thompsonville, MI 49683. 616-378-2911.

NE of Traverse City in Leelanau County: **Schill-Haus** (on SR

High-country ski touring, Vail, Colorado. PETER RUNYON

Great Smoky Mountains National Park, North Carolina.
N.C. TRAVEL AND TOURISM DIVISION/JOEL ARRINGTON

Vail, Colorado. PETER RUNYON

A Telemark turn. BRECKENRIDGE SKI CORP., COLORADO

Stowe, Vermont. VERMONT DEVELOPMENT AGENCY

In the Montana wilderness.
TRAVEL PROMOTION UNIT, MONTANA DEPT. OF HIGHWAYS

Crossing a footbridge in Aspen, Colorado.

22 at Glen Lake Narrows), old logging roads and access trails to Sleeping Bear Dunes National Park; rentals available. Empire, MI 49630. 616-334-3252. **Sugar Loaf Mountain Resort** (18 m NW near Cedar), over 13 m of marked, wooded trails; small trail fee; rentals and instruction available; downhill ski facilities; year-round resort with variety of slopeside accommodations, dining room, cafeteria, 2 cocktail lounges, après-ski; nursery; indoor tennis, heated outdoor pool, hang-gliding. 4300-ft year-round landing strip. Information: Rt. 1, Cedar, MI 49621. 616-228-5461. **The Homestead Resort** (2 m N of Glen Arbor on SR 22), 30 m of marked trails; rentals, instruction, and guided tours; maps provided. Information: Glen Arbor, MI 49636. 616-334-3041.

WATERSMEET: Land O'Lakes Ski Trail (W of town and S of US 2), 15 m of marked trails for novice and intermediate skiers on 21,000-acre Sylvania Recreation Area; flat, gently rolling terrain with many lakes; trail map available; no snowmobiles permitted; trailhead at **Sylvania Outfitters** (3 m W on US 2), trail also connects to Land O'Lakes, WI; instruction and rentals; ski shop and lounge; cabin rentals. Information: Bob Zelinski, Sylvania Outfitters, West US 2, Watersmeet, MI 49969. 906-358-4766. Additional information: District Ranger, Watersmeet Ranger District, Ottawa National Forest, Watersmeet, MI 49969. 906-358-4551.

WEST BRANCH: Greenwood Campground (between West Branch and Alger on Greenwood Rd.), 3-, 5-, 10-km trails; restrooms and shelters on trail; rentals, instruction and maps available; nominal trail usage fee; year-round campground. Information: 636 W. Greenwood Rd., Alger, MI 48610. 517-345-2778.

MINNESOTA

All state parks require a vehicle permit. Fee is $1.50 per day or regular users may buy a season pass for $5.00. For additional information, contact the individual area or Minnesota Tourism Division, Dept. of Economic Development, 480 Cedar St., St. Paul, MN 55101.

AITKIN: Brown Lake (12 m N on County Rd. 24), 6 m of marked and groomed trails for intermediate skiers; trail map at courthouse in Aitkin; shelter open weekends, refreshments. **No. Achen Ski Trail** (at Rippleside Elementary School in town), 10 m of marked and groomed trails for beginner to advanced skiers; instruction at city park. Information: Aitkin County Parks, Courthouse, Aitkin, MN 56431. 218-927-2102. **Long Lake Conservation Center** (NE at Palisade), 6 m of marked and groomed novice to intermediate trails; trail map; rentals available; lodging. Information: Long Lake Conservation Center, Palisade, MN 56469. 218-768-4653. **Savanna State Forest, Remote Lake Solitude Area** (NE via US 169 and SR 210 to McGregor, then 15 m N on SR 65 and County Rd. 36), 13 m of marked trails; intermediate to advanced terrain; trail map available; lean-to shelters, outdoor toilets, tent camping; rest areas with picnic tables. Information: State Division of Forestry, McGregor, MN 55760. 218-426-3407. **Savanna Portage State Park** (same location as above), 16 m of marked and groomed intermediate trails; trail map available; campground, toilet, parking area. Information: Supervisor, Savanna Portage State Park, Rt. 3, McGregor, MN 55760. 218-426-3580. **Land O'Lakes State Forest** (W on SR 210, then N on SR 6; 1 m N of Outing), 11.2 m of marked and groomed trails in the Washburn Lake Solitude Area; intermediate to advanced terrain; shelters, toilets, parking area. Information: 218-828-2565 or 792-5383.

ALEXANDRIA: Arrowwood Resort (in town), 2.5 m of marked and groomed trails for intermediate skiers; trail map; instruction and rentals; 170-room lodge, restaurant, cocktail lounge, indoor pool, and sauna. Information: Arrowwood Resort, Alexandria, MN 56308. 612-762-1124. **Kensington Runestone County Park** (on SR 27, 15 m SW), 6 m of marked trails, 3 m of which are groomed; intermediate terrain with shelters en route; trail map available; heated lodge, vending machines, restrooms; camping area. Information: Superintendent, Kensington Runestone County Park, Alexandria, MN 56308. 612-965-2365. **Lake Carlos State Park** (N off SR 29), 2.75 m of marked and groomed trails for intermediate skiers; shelter bldg., pit toilets, picnic grounds. Information: Lake Carlos State Park, Rt. 2, Carlos, MN 56319. 612-852-7200. **Spruce Wetlands** (15 m NW on County Rd. 66), unmarked trails on intermediate to advanced terrain.

AUSTIN: Hormel Nature Center (in town), 4.8-km marked and groomed trail for beginners; trail map; instruction and rentals; free camping at city campground, toilets, interpretive bldg.; snow-shoeing. Information: Hormel Nature Center, Rt. 5, Box 285A, Austin, MN 55912. 507-437-7519. **Lake Louise State Park** (SE via SR 56), 3-m marked trail for novice skiers; trail map; campground, outdoor sanitation. Information: Supervisor, Lake Louise State Park, Rt. 1, Box 136A, LeRoy, MN 55951. 507-324-5249.

BAUDETTE: Red Lake Wildlife Management Area (NW on SR 11 at Roosevelt), 6 m of marked and groomed trails for beginner to intermediate skiers; trail map available; parking area, toilets. Information: Supervisor, Red Lake Wildlife Management Area, Roosevelt, MN 56673. 218-783-5861. **Zippel Bay State Park** (20 m NW Off SR 172), 1-m marked and groomed novice trail on S shore of Lake of the Woods; map available; primitive camping, pit toilets. Information: Supervisor, Zippel Bay State Park, Williams, MN 56686. 218-783-5253.

BEMIDJI: Bemidji City Trail (begins at city arena on 23rd St.), 4-km marked beginner trail; parking area at arena. **Bemidji State University** has 6-km marked and groomed trail for beginner to intermediate skiers; trail map available at university or chamber of commerce; restrooms at parking area. Information: 218-755-3367. **Buena Vista Ski Area** (in town), 15 m of marked and groomed trails for beginner to advanced skiers; rentals and instruction; trail fee, map available; downhill ski facilities, day lodge, food service. Information: Buena Vista Ski Area, Bemidji, MN 56601. 218-243-2231 or 751-5530. **Isle O'Pines** (near town), 25 km of marked and groomed novice to advanced trails; trail fee (guests free), map available; rentals by reservation; housekeeping cabins, some with fireplaces; lodge, game room, snacks. Information: Isle O'Pines, Rt. 3, Box 232, Bemidji, MN 56601. 218-751-2783. **Kohl's Last Resort** (near town), 27 m of marked trails for novice to inter-mediate skiers, 5 m of trails are groomed; trails connect to Buena Vista State Forest; trail map available; snowshoe rental; house-keeping cottages, most with fireplaces; lodge and restaurant. In-formation: Kohl's Last Resort, Rt. 5, Box 247, Bemidji, MN 56601. 218-586-2251. **Lake Bemidji State Park** (NE), 3-m marked and groomed novice trail; map available; camping, toilets. Information:

Supervisor, Lake Bemidji State Park, RR 5, Box 44, Bemidji, MN 56601. 218-751-1472. **Old Tyme Retreat** (near town), 20 km of marked and groomed trails for novice to advanced skiers; 50 km of marked trails within 10-m radius; trail fee (except guests), map available; instruction and guided tours; rentals; housekeeping log cabins, lodge, snacks; meals served with weekend package plan. Information: Old Tyme Retreat, Rt. 4, Box 234, Bemidji, MN 56601. 218-335-6604. **Wolf Lake Resort** (near town), 14 m of marked and groomed novice to advanced trails; trail fee (except guests), trail map; instruction; rentals; housekeeping cottages, lodge, lunch, and beverages available. Information: Wolf Lake Resort, Rt. 3, Box 231, Bemidji, MN 56601.

Bald Eagle Center (E via US 2 near Cass Lake), 20 m of marked trails, some connect to Chippewa National Forest trails; winter camping instruction, lodging for groups only. Information: Bald Eagle Center, Cass Lake, MN 56633. 218-665-2241. **The Home Place Lodge and Ski Tur Centre** (on Squaw Point Rd., S of Cass Lake), 25 km of marked and groomed novice to advanced trails; connecting trails to Chippewa National Forest; trail fee (except for guests), map available; instruction and rentals; housekeeping cabins; lodge with fireplace, waxing room; sauna. Information: The Home Place Lodge and Ski Tur Centre, Squaw Pt. Rd., Cass Lake, MN 56633. 218-335-8802.

Chippewa National Forest (E on US 2; hq at Cass Lake), 640,000-acre forest laced with hundreds of lakes; headwaters of the Mississippi River; 2 large reservoirs; streams and rivers; many m of marked trails and forest roads. Cross-country ski trails managed by the Forest Service include: **Norway Beach Nature Trail** (4 m E of Cass Lake off US 2 at Norway Beach Recreation Area), self-guiding nature trail through 200-year-old pine grove and on section of old railroad logging grade suitable for novice skiers. **Carter Lake Trail** (NE of Bemidji via US 71 to Tenstrike, then E on Forest Rd. 2420, then S on Forest Rd. 2419; trailhead just N of Carter Lake), 4.6 km of marked interconnecting novice to intermediate trails; trail map available. **Meadlow Lake Trail** (NE of Bemidji via Country Rd. 20 to Forest Rd. 2393, then N .5 m), 8.2-km marked and groomed novice to intermediate trail with old homestead site and foot bridge en route, side trail leads to Turtle River; trail map available. Information on preceding 2 trails: District Ranger, Blackduck Ranger District, U.S. Forest Service, Blackduck, MN 56630. 218-835-4291.

BRAINERD: Camp Ripley Ski Area (W on SR 210 to Pillager, then 6 m S on County Rd. 6), 20 m of marked and groomed trails for beginner to advanced skiers; trail map at parking area; open weekends 9 am–5 pm (subject to military operations). Information: Dept. of Natural Resources, 315 Charles St. NW, Brainerd, MN 56401. 218-828-2610. **Crow Wing State Park** (SW off SR 371), 3.6 m of marked and groomed trails for novice to advanced skiers; trail map available; shelters, toilets. Supervisor, Crow Wing State Park, Brainerd, MN 56401. 218-829-8022. **North Country Ski Touring** (just off Pine Beach Rd. on SR 371), 15 km of marked and groomed, beginner to intermediate trails; certified instruction; trail fee, map available; rentals; lounge area with fireplace in ski barn, beverages and homemade pastries; outdoor toilets. Information: North Country Ski Touring, Rt. 10, Box 415, Brainerd, MN 56401. 218-829-0900. **Pillsbury State Forest** (E on SR 210 to Pillager, then 6.5 m N on County Rd. 1), 12.8 m of marked and groomed trails; novice to intermediate terrain; shelters, toilets, parking area. Information: 218-828-2565 or 746-3322. **Ruttger's Bay Lake Lodge** (NE), 15 m of marked and groomed trails for novice to advanced skiers; trail fee (except guests), map available; instruction and rentals; lodge and cabin accommodations, dining room. Ruttger's Bay Lake Lodge, Rt. 1, Box 5, Deerwood, MN 56444. 218-678-2885.

BUFFALO: Carl A. Johnson Park (W; 7 m N of Cokato, 1.5 m E of County Rd. 3), 2 km of marked and groomed intermediate trails; picnic area, toilets. **Harry Larson Memorial Park** (N via SR 25, 8 m NW of Monticello off County Rd. 111), 3 km of marked and groomed intermediate trails; toilets. **Montisippi Park** (N; W end of Monticello), 3 km of marked and groomed novice to intermediate trails; map available; picnic area, toilets. Information and maps for above areas: Public Works Bldg., Buffalo, MN 55313. 612-295-3179. **Lake Maria State Park** (8 m W of Monticello), 5.5 m of marked and groomed intermediate to advanced trails; trail map available; winter camping. Information: Superintendent, Lake Maria State Park, Monticello, MN 55360. 612-878-2325. **Manitou Lakes** (3.5 m SW of Monticello), 20 m of marked and groomed beginner to advanced trails; parking fee, trail map available; ski lodge for group or family rental; wind shelters, picnic area, primitive toilets. Information: Northwest Branch YMCA, Monticello, MN 55360. 612-536-5700. **Sherburne National Wildlife Refuge** (N via SR 25),

13 m of marked trails; novice to intermediate terrain; trail map available. Information: Supervisor, Sherburne National Wildlife Refuge, Rt. 2, Zimmerman, MN 55398. 612-389-3323.

CALEDONIA: Beaver Creek Valley State Park (W), 615-acre park with 2 m marked beginner trail; trail map available; shelter bldg.; winter camping, outdoor toilets. Information: Beaver Creek Valley State Park, Rt. 2, Caledonia, MN 55921. 507-724-2107.

CARLTON: Jay Cooke State Park (SE of town), 3 m of marked trails for intermediate to advanced skiers; shelter, toilets; camping. Information: Supervisor, Jay Cooke State Park, Carlton, MN 55718. 218-384-4610. **Moose Lake State Park** (S off I-35), 965-acre park with 3 m of marked trails for intermediate skiers; trail map available; shelter; outdoor toilets. Information: Supervisor, Moose Lake State Park, Moose Lake, MN 55767. 218-485-4059. **Pine Valley Ski Area** (N via SR 33, on Armory Rd. in Cloquet), 7.5 m of marked and groomed intermediate to advanced trails; competition trails; trail fee, map available; chalet, food service, restrooms. Information: Pine Valley Ski Area, Armory Rd., Cloquet, MN 55720.

DETROIT LAKES: Maplelag (N vis US 59 near Callaway), 20 km of marked and groomed beginner and intermediate trails; trail fee (except guests), trail map available; beginning instruction; moonlight tours; waxing room; housekeeping accommodations; guided tours of maple sugar operation; sauna. Information: Maplelag, Rt. 1, Callaway, MN 56521. 218-375-2986. **Mt. View Ski Trail** (in town), from Industrial Park in town to **Detroit Mountain** downhill ski area; 20 km of marked trail with 4 loops; beginner to advanced terrain; parking area at both ends; day lodge, cafeteria, and restrooms at downhill ski area. Information and trail map: Detroit Lakes Chamber of Commerce, 700 Washington, Detroit Lakes, MN 56501. 218-847-9202. **Pine Lake Trail** (E off SR 34 in Tamarac National Wildlife Refuge), 5 m of marked trails for beginners; trail map available; picnic tables, pit toilets, parking area. Information: Supervisor, Tamarac National Wildlife Refuge, Rochert, MN 56578. 218-847-4355.

DULUTH: City ski trails (within city limits): **Magney-Snively,** 7.5 km of marked and groomed intermediate trails; **Chester Park,** 2.4 km of marked intermediate trails; **Hartley Field,** 2.4-km marked beginner trail; **Amity-Lester,** 9.7-km marked advanced trail; **Lester Park Golf Course,** 2.6-km marked trail for beginners. Information and trail maps: Duluth Dept. of Parks and Recreation, City Hall, Rm. 208, Duluth, MN 55802. 218-723-3614. **Spirit Mountain Ski Area** (9500 Spirit Mountain Place), 7.5 m of marked and groomed trails for novice to advanced skiers; trail fee, map available; instruction and rentals; downhill ski facilities, day lodge, cafeteria, restaurant, cocktail lounge; rental housekeeping villas, campground. Information: Spirit Mountain Ski Area, 9500 Spirit Mountain Place, Duluth, MN 55810. 218-628-2891. (See also Carlton).

EFFIE: Deer Acres Resort and Campground (near town), 8 m of marked and groomed trails for intermediate skiers; instruction and guided tours by reservation; trail map; rentals; lodge accommodations and housekeeping cabins; restaurant; campground. Information: Deer Acres Resort, Effie, MN 56639. 218-653-2281. **George Washington State Forest, Thistledew Area** (E on SR 1), 12 m of marked trails for intermediate to advanced skiers; campgrounds, toilets; trail map at Thistledew Ranger Station or Deer River (SW) Area Hq. Information: Supervisor, George Washington State Forest, DNR Forestry, Deer River, MN 56636. 218-246-8343.

ELY: Hidden Valley Ski Area (NE off SR 169), 10 m of marked and groomed trails for intermediate to advanced skiers; trail map available; downhill ski facilities, day lodge, food service; sleeping bag accommodations and meals for groups. Information: Hidden Valley Ski Area, Box 267, Ely, MN 55731. 218-365-3231 or 365-3097.

FARIBAULT: Cannon River Wilderness Area (4 m N), 6 m of marked beginner to advanced trails; trail map available; picnic shelter, restrooms. Information: Supervisor, Rice County Parks and Recreation, 610 20th St. NW, Faribault, MN 55021. 507-334-6337. **Nerstrand Woods State Park** (NE in Nerstrand), 6 m of marked and groomed trails for beginner to intermediate skiers; trail map available at ranger station; shelter bldg., winter camping, outdoor toilets. Information: Supervisor, Nerstrand Woods State Park, Nerstrand, MN 55053. 507-334-8848.

FERGUS FALLS: Old Smoky Hill (in town), 4 m of marked and groomed trails; downhill ski facilities, warming house. Information: 218-739-2251. **Maplewood State Park** (N via US 59 and SR 108),

4.5 m of marked and groomed trails for novice and intermediate skiers; trail map available; camping, picnic area, toilets. Information: Supervisor, Maplewood State Park, Erhard, MN 56534. 218-863-8383. **Spidahl Ski Gard** (N via US 59 near Erhard), 20 m of marked and groomed trails; beginner to advanced terrain; trail fee, map available; instruction and rentals; warming shelter, food service, restrooms. Information: Spidahl Ski Gard, Rt. 1, Erhard, MN 56534. 218-736-5097.

GRAND MARAIS: Grand Portage National Monument (36 m NE via US 61), 8.5-m marked and maintained portage trail suitable for intermediate to advanced skiers; trail leads over hilly terrain from stockade to Ft. Charlotte; last part of trail is relatively flat; map available; plowed parking area; winter camping permitted; no snowmobiles. Information: Superintendent, Grand Portage National Monument, National Park Service, Box 666, Grand Marais, MN 55604. 218-387-2788. Surrounding the Monument is **Grand Portage Indian Reservation** with an extensive ski trail system. **Grand Portage State Forest** (NE via US 61) has **Border Route Trail** (off US 61, 10 m N of Hoveland on Arrowhead Trail in Pigeon River Section), 22.5 m of marked trails for intermediate to advanced skiers; trails connect to Grand Portage Radisson trail system on the reservation; trail map available. Information: Supervisor, Grand Portage State Forest, Grand Marais, MN 55604. 218-475-2210 or 612-822-0569. **Radisson Inn Grand Portage** (NE via US 61; near Grand Portage), 60 m of marked trails for beginner to advanced skiers; one 15-m section of wide trail, in multi-use area, shared with snowmobiles; instruction and rentals; trail fee (except guests), trail map; accommodations at area. Information: Radisson Inn Grand Portage, Grand Portage, MN 55605. 218-475-2401. **Gateway-Hungry Jack Lodge** (near town), 18 km of marked trails and 9 km of marked and groomed trails for beginner to advanced skiers; instruction; rentals by reservation; trail maps available; lodge, lounge, sauna; housekeeping cabins, some with fireplaces. Information: Gateway-Hungry Jack Lodge, Grand Marais, MN 55604. 218-388-2265. **Gunflint Lodge** (near town), 50 m of marked and groomed novice to advanced trails; shelters en route; instruction and rentals; trail map available; guided tours, cookouts, evening programs; housekeeping cabins; American plan units, meals. Information: Gunflint Lodge, Grand Marais, MN 55604. 218-388-2294.

  Cascade River State Park (10 m SW), 2815-acre park with 15 m of marked and groomed trails on Lake Superior shores; beginner to advanced terrain; trail map; camping, shelter, toilets. Information: Supervisor, Cascade River State Park, Lutsen, MN 55612. 218-387-1543. **Cascade Lodge** (SW via US 61), 30 m of marked and groomed trails with track set; beginner to advanced terrain; one arterial trail shared with snowmobiles; trail connects with Cascade River State Park; trail map available; instruction, group tours; ski and snowshoe rentals; lodge, dorm, motel accommodations; restaurant. Information: Cascade Lodge, Grand Marais, MN 55604. 218-387-9980. **Lutsen Ski Area** (S off US 61, 1.5 m S of Lutsen), 20 m of marked and groomed trails for beginner to advanced skiers; instruction and guided tours; rentals; trail map; trail use fee for chalet and chairlift; downhill ski facilities, day lodge, cafeteria, restaurant, cocktail lounge; year-round resort with varied accommodations; RV hookups for campers. Information: Lutsen Ski Area, Lutsen, MN 55612. 218-663-7212. **Temperance River State Park** (23 m SW), 10 m of marked and groomed trails for intermediate skiers; trail map; camping permitted. Information: Supervisor, Temperance River State Park, Schroeder, MN 55613. 218-663-7476. **George H. Crosby Manitou State Park** (43 m SW, then 10 m NW on SR 1), 6 m of marked and groomed trails for advanced skiers; trail map; camping permitted. Information: Supervisor, George H. Crosby Manitou State Park, Finland, MN 55603. **Environmental Learning Center** (43 m SW on US 61, then NW on SR 1 to Isabella), 30 m of trails; winter recreation courses offered; trails connect with National Forest Lodge trails. Information: Environmental Learning Center, Isabella, MN 55607. 218-293-4345. **National Forest Lodge** (43 m SW on US 61, then NW on SR 1 to Isabella), 60 km of marked beginner to advanced trails; instruction by appointment; rentals; trail map available; snowshoe rentals and trails; rental cabins, lodge with fireplace, family-style meals served. Information: National Forest Lodge, Isabella, MN 55607. 218-293-4411.

GRAND RAPIDS: Sugar Hills Ski Area (S off US 169), 15 m of marked and groomed trails for novice to advanced skiers; trail map available; instruction; rental and retail ski shop; downhill ski facilities, day lodge, cafeteria; nursery; lodge, dorm, and motel accommodations; restaurant, cocktail lounge; package plans available. Information: Sugar Hills Ski Area, Box 369, Grand Rapids, MN 55744. 218-326-3473. **Back O' The Moon Ski Area** (near town), 7 m of marked intermediate trails, groomed with track set;

trail fee (except guests), map available; instruction and rentals; housekeeping cabins with fireplaces, campground, limited food service. Information: Back O' The Moon Resort, Rt. 4, Grand Rapids, MN 55744. 218-326-8648. **Camp Mishawaka** (near town), 14 km of marked and groomed trails for beginner to intermediate skiers; trail fee (except guests), map available; instruction by reservation; lodge and housekeeping cabins; meals by arrangement. Information: Camp Mishawaka, P.O. Box 368, Grand Rapids, MN 55744. 218-326-5667. **Wabana Trails** (16 m N on SR 38 and County Rds. 49 & 59), 5.5 m of intermediate trails in Wabana Wildlife Sanctuary; trail map available at county land dept. in Grand Rapids courthouse. Information: 218-326-2019. **Suomi Hills Recreation Area** (20 m N on SR 38), 8 km of marked, interconnecting trails around numerous small lakes; several campsites en route; beginner to intermediate terrain on Chippewa National Forest; parking area at trailhead. Information and map: Ranger, Marcell Ranger District, U.S. Forest Service, Marcell, MN 56657. 218-832-3161.

Simpson Creek Recreation Area (NW via US 2 to Deer River, then about 17 m NW on SR 46 to County Rd. 33), 12.5 m of marked interconnecting trails for novice to intermediate skiers; color-coded marking system; trail map available; 2 parking areas; Visitor Information Center at jct of SR 46 & County Rd. 35. Information: Ranger, Deer River Ranger District, U.S. Forest Service, Deer River, MN 56636. 218-246-2131. **Bowstring Northwoods Resort** (near Deer River), 9 m of marked and groomed trails for beginners; trail fee, map available; lodge, housekeeping cabins, restaurant, cocktail lounge. Information: Bowstring Northwoods Resort, 101 Inger Rd., Deer River, MN 56636. 218-556-4321.

Remote Lake Cross-Country Ski Area (SW in Savanna State Forest), 13 m of marked and groomed trails; intermediate to advanced terrain; shelter, toilet, parking area. Map and information: DNR Office, Hill City, MN 55748. 218-697-2476. **Quadna Mountain Ski Area** (S of Hill City on US 169), 7 m of marked and groomed intermediate trails; trail map available; instruction and rentals; downhill ski facilities; day lodge, restaurant, bar; indoor tennis; lodge, motel, and condominium accommodations; campground. Information: Quadna Mountain Ski Area, Hill City, MN 55748. 218-697-2324.

HINCKLEY: St. Croix State Park (E via SR 48), 20.8 m of marked trails for novice to intermediate skiers; 75 m of trails shared with snowmobiles; chalet with fireplace and restrooms at trail center; primitive camping, outdoor toilets. Information and map: Supervisor, St. Croix State Park, Rt. 3, Box 174, Hinckley, MN 55037. 612-384-6591. **Banning State Park** (N off I-35), 4 m of marked and groomed trails; intermediate terrain; trail map available; winter camping, outdoor toilets. Information: Supervisor, Banning State Park, Sandstone, MN 55072. 612-245-2668.

INTERNATIONAL FALLS: Voyageurs National Park (E); part of a proposed 100-m ski and hiking trail system is completed; marked and maintained trails include: **Black Bay Narrows Trail** (at end of SR 11 E), 3-m and 6-m loops begin just across the Black Bay Narrows on W end of Kabetogama Peninsula; trails suitable for intermediate skiers. **Lost Bay Trail** (accessible from Ash River Rd., SE off US 53), 12-m trail winds from Eks Bay E past Ek and Agnes lakes, then N past several tiny lakes and W to Jorgens Lake, then loops back to Eks Bay; trail, suited for experienced skiers, is reached by skiing 3.5 m from Ash River Rd. to Kabetogama Lake, then another 3 m across the lake to Lost Bay; trail maps available. Information: Superintendent, Voyageurs National Park, P.O. Box 50, International Falls, MN 56649. 218-283-4492.

JACKSON: Kilen Woods State Park (7 m NW), 2.5-m marked and groomed intermediate trail; parking area, toilets. Information: Supervisor, Kilen Woods State Park, Lakefield, MN 56150. 507-662-6258.

MARSHALL: Camden State Park (7 m SW off SR 23), 4 m of marked and groomed trails for beginner to intermediate skiers; toilets in park. Information: 507-865-4530. **Upper Sioux Agency State Park** (NE via SR 23), 3-m marked beginner to intermediate trail; toilets in park. Information: Supervisor, Upper Sioux Agency State Park, Rt. 2, Box 92, Granite Falls, MN 56241. 612-564-4777.

MINNEAPOLIS-ST. PAUL: Battle Creek (E off US 61; off Winthrop St., 1 block S of Upper Afton Rd., St. Paul), 2 m of marked and groomed trails for advanced skiers; trail map; instruction; downhill ski facilities with chalet, snack bar, restrooms. Information: Battle Creek Ski Area, 2010 White Bear Ave., St. Paul, 55109. 612-770-1361. **Afton State Park** (E in Afton, along St. Croix River), 7 m of marked trails for advanced skiers; trail map available; shelter, toilet, and parking area. Information: Supervisor,

Afton State Park, 5500 Quadrant Ave., Afton, MN 55001. 612-436-5391. **South Washington County Park** (SE via US 61; on Pt. Douglas Dr. in Cottage Grove), 3.2 m of marked trails; beginner to advanced terrain; trail map; picnic tables, toilets. Information: Washington County Parks and Recreation, 11660 Myeron Rd. N., Stillwater, MN 55082. 612-439-6058. **Highland Golf Course** (Edgecumbe Rd. and Montreal Ave. in St. Paul), 6 m of marked and groomed trails for beginner to intermediate skiers; rentals and instruction; trail map available; food service and restrooms. Information: 612-699-6082. **Friendly Hills Park** (in Mendota Hts.), 2.5 m of marked beginner to advanced trails; trail map; warming house, restrooms; ice skating. Also in Mendota Hts. is **Valley Park** with 2.5 m of marked trails for beginner to advanced skiers; open-air pavilion. Information for preceding 2 areas: Mendota Hts. City Hall, 750 S. Plaza Dr., Mendota Hts., MN 55120. 612-454-4059. **Ft. Snelling State Park** (SW at jct of SR 5, 55), 3.5-m marked and groomed beginner trail; trail map available; nature center, restrooms. Information: 612-727-1961. **Hiawatha Ski Touring Area** (46th St. and Longfellow Ave. S., Minneapolis), 3 marked and groomed 3-km trails lighted for night skiing; instruction and rentals; trail map; chalet, food service. Information: Hiawatha Golf Course, 4553 Longfellow Ave., Minneapolis, MN 55406. 612-348-2121. **Wood Lake Nature Center** (on Lake Shore Dr. in Richfield), 3 m of marked and groomed trails suitable for beginners; rentals by reservation for naturalist tour; trail map; museum, interpretive center, restrooms. Information: Wood Lake Nature Center, 735 Lake Shore Dr., Richfield, MN 55423. 612-861-4507. **Central Park—Nine Mile Creek Ski Touring Trail** (104th St. & Morgan Ave. S. in Bloomington), 5-m marked trail for intermediate to advanced skiers; trail map; shelter; parking at Moir Picnic Grounds. Also in Bloomington is **Girard Lake Park Trail** (84th St., 1 block E of France Ave.), 1-m marked beginner trail. Information for preceding 2 trails: Bloomington Park and Recreation Division, 2215 W. Old Shakopee Rd., Bloomington, MN 55420. 612-881-5811. **Hyland Lake Park Reserve** (E. Bush Lake Rd. near 96th St. in Bloomington), 6.4 m of marked and groomed trails; beginner to advanced terrain; rentals and instruction by reservation; trail map; Richardson Nature Center, restrooms, picnic area; parking fee. Information: 612-941-7993. **Minnreg Ski Touring Center** (S off I-35W at Minnreg exit; at Honeywell Country Club), 18 m of marked and groomed trails for beginner to advanced skiers; 10 km of lighted trails for night skiing; trail fee, map available; rentals and instruction; parking area, clubhouse, ski shop; trails connect with nearby Ritter Park. Information: 612-435-6166. **Ritter Park** (S off I-35W; 195th St., W of I-35W), 15 km of marked and groomed beginner to advanced trails; trail map; shelter, restrooms. Information: Parks and Recreation Division, City Hall, Lakeville, MN 55044. 612-469-5354. **Cedar Hills Ski Park** (I-494 W to Eden Prairie; at 9735 Eden Prairie Rd.), 2 m of marked trails suitable for intermediate skiers; rentals and instruction by reservation; trail map; downhill ski facilities, chalet, food service, restrooms. Information: Cedar Hills Ski Park, 9735 Eden Prairie Rd., Eden Prairie, MN 55343. 612-445-4066 or 445-9908. **Edenvale Golf Club** (14500 Valley View Rd. in Eden Prairie), 6 m of marked trails suitable for beginner to advanced skiers; rentals and instruction; guided evening tours; trail map; clubhouse, food service, ski shop. Information: Edenvale Golf Club, 14500 Valley View Rd., Eden Prairie, MN 55343. 612-941-7799. **Jonathan-Chaska Ski Trails** (SW in Chaska), 9 m of marked trails for beginner to advanced skiers; association-sponsored lessons; trail map available; shelter, snacks, toilets. Information: Jonathan Association, Lake Village Center, Chaska, MN 55318. 612-448-4700. **Minnesota Valley Trail** (SW on the Minnesota River Bank), 12 m of trail in 2 segments open for ski touring: **Carver Rapids,** 6 m of marked and groomed trail suitable for intermediate skiers; trail map; shelter, toilets, parking area. **Lawrence Wayside,** 5.8 m of marked and groomed trail for beginners; trail map; shelter, toilet, parking fee. Information: Minnesota Valley Trail, Rt. 1, Jordan, MN 55352. 612-492-6400.

West of Minneapolis is **Carver Park Reserve** (19 m W on SR 7), 13 m of marked and groomed trails; beginner to advanced terrain; rentals and instruction by reservation; ski patrol on trails; trail map; Lowry Nature Center, restrooms, barn with stove, picnic areas; tent camping; parking fee. Information: Hennepin County Park Reserve District, Rt. 1, Box 32, Maple Plain, MN 55359. 612-427-4911 or 473-4693. **Meadowbrook Ski Touring Area** (W on SR 7 to Hopkins; Mead Rd. & Goodrich Ave.), beginner and intermediate trails on golf course; rentals and instruction. Information: 612-348-2121. Next 5 areas, located near Minnetonka (W on SR 7) have about 2 m each of marked and groomed trails on beginner to intermediate terrain: **Big Willow Park** (E of I-494 and W of County Rd. 73 along Minnetonka Blvd.); **Evergreen Park** (S of Minnetonka Blvd. and W of Williston Rd. on Victoria St.); **Lone Lake Park** (on Shady Oak Rd., S of Excelsior Blvd.); **Meadow Park** (on Oakland Rd., E of I-494 and W of County Rd.

61); **Purgatory Creek Park** (on W 55th St., E of SR 101). Information: City Hall, 14600 Minnetonka Blvd., Minnetonka, MN 55343. 612-933-2511. **Luce Line Trail** (W via SR 55 to Plymouth), 2 segments suitable for novice skiers: Plymouth to Orono, 6 m, and Orono to Watertown, 12 m; both segments marked and groomed. Maps and information: DNR, 1200 Warner Rd., St. Paul, MN 55106. 612-296-2553.

    Morris T. Baker Park Reserve (18 m W on US 12; N of County Rd. 24 in Medina), 9.6 m of marked and groomed trails for beginner to advanced skiers; trail map; rentals and instruction by reservation; chalet with fireplace, snack bar, barn with picnic tables, woodburning stove; parking fee. Information: 612-473-7418. **Lake Rebecca Park Reserve** (23 m W on US 12; on County Rd. 55 near Rockford), 12.3 m of marked and groomed trails; beginner to advanced terrain; rentals and instruction by reservation; trail map; picnic areas, fireplaces, toilets; parking fee. Information: 612-473-4693. **Elm Creek Park Reserve** (14 m NW off SR 152 near Osseo), 14.5 m of marked and groomed beginner to advanced trails; rentals; instruction by reservation; trail map available; Eastman Nature Center, picnic area, toilets; parking fee. Information: 612-425-2324. Additional information on above 3 Reserves: Hennepin County Park Reserve District, Rt. 1, Box 32, Maple Plain, MN 55359. 612-473-4693. **Bunker Hills Ski Trails** (N near Anoka; at SR 242 and Foley Blvd.), 19 km of marked and groomed trails; beginner to advanced terrain; rentals and instruction; trail map; restaurant, shelter. Information: Bunker Hills Ski Trails, Coon Rapids Golf Course, Anoka, MN 55303. 612-757-3920.

MOORHEAD: Buffalo River State Park (E off US 10), 2 m of marked trails for novice and intermediate skiers; trail map available; pit toilets. Information: Supervisor, Buffalo River State Park, Rt. 2, Box 118, Glyndon, MN 56547. 218-498-2124.

NEW ULM: Flandrau State Park (S side of town), 1.5-m marked beginner trail; parking area, toilets. Information: 507-354-3519. **Fort Ridgely State Park** (NW of SR 4), 3 m of marked trails; beginner to intermediate terrain; parking area, toilets. Information: 507-426-7840.

PARK RAPIDS: City Trail (in town), 7 m of beginner to intermediate marked trails; parking area. Information: 218-732-3342.

Val Chatel (about 15 m N via County Rd. 4), 8 km of marked and groomed trails; trails connect with **Paul Bunyan State Forest** trails; trail use fee (except guests), map available; instruction and rentals; downhill ski facilities, day lodge, cafeteria, dining room; lodge rooms, housekeeping units. Information: Val Chatel, Park Rapids, MN 56470. 218-266-3306. **Wilderness Bay Resort** (N via US 71), 20 km of marked and groomed trails for intermediate skiers; trail use fee (except guests), trail map; instruction; housekeeping cabins; meals in lodge by prearrangement, snacks. Information: Wilderness Bay Resort, Itasca Star Route, Park Rapids, MN 56470. 218-732-4865. **Itasca State Park** (NW off US 71), 25 m of marked and groomed trails for beginner to advanced skiers; trail map available; outdoor toilets. Information: Supervisor, Itasca State Park, Lake Itasca, MN 56460. **Stave's Resort** (N via US 71 at Lake Itasca), 8 m of marked and groomed trails; beginner to intermediate terrain with trails connecting to Itasca State Park; trail map available; housekeeping cabins (open weekends by reservation only), grocery store, coffee shop. Information: Stave's Resort, Lake Itasca, MN 56460. 218-266-3395 or 233-4995. **Gloege's Outfitting** (S on US 71, then E on SR 227 to Nimrod), 5 m of marked trails; rentals and instruction; accommodations at area; occasional snowmobile use. Information: Gloege's Outfitting, Nimrod, MN 56478. 218-472-3250.

ROCHESTER: Douglas Trail (NW from Rochester to Pine Island), 12-m marked, multi-use trail suitable for novice skiers; snowmobiles on separate trail; map at Regional DNR headquarters in Rochester. Information: 507-288-3129. **Mantorville to Oxbow Ski Trail** (W at Mantorville), 12-km marked trail; beginner to intermediate terrain; trail map. Information: Sierra Club Coordinator, Box 222, Mantorville, MN 55955. 507-635-5157. **Forestville State Park** (SE via US 52 to Preston, then W on US 16), 6-m marked trail for beginners; trail map; campground, outdoor sanitation. Information: Supervisor, Forestville State Park, Rt. 3, Box 28, Preston, MN 55965. 507-352-5111. **Carley State Park** (E on US 14, then N off SR 42 on County Rd. 4), 3.5-m marked trails for beginner to intermediate skiers; trail map; campground, outdoor sanitation. Information: Supervisor, Carley State Park, Plainview, MN 55964. 507-534-3400. **Whitewater State Park** (E on US 14 then N on SR 74), 6 m of marked trails; beginner to advanced terrain; trail map; campground, shelter, pit toilets. Information: Supervisor, Whitewater State Park, Altura, MN 55910. 507-932-3007. **Rice Lake State Park** (W via US 14), 4 m of marked and groomed trails for beginner skiers; trail map; campground, outdoor toilets. Information: Supervisor, Rice Lake State Park, Rt. 3, Owatonna, MN 55060. 507-451-7406.

ST. CLOUD: St. John's University (W via I-94 at Collegeville), 10 m of marked trails; intermediate terrain; trail map available at college Information Center. Information: St. John's University, Collegeville, MN 56321. 612-363-2509. **Tokle Trail** (W via I-94 to Avon, then 3 m S), 4-m marked and groomed trail for beginner to intermediate skiers; instruction and map available. Information: 612-845-4314 or 253-1877. **Eagle Mountain Ski Area** (NW via I-94, then NE on SR 28 to Grey Eagle), 10 km of marked beginner to advanced trails groomed with track set; trail use fee, map available; instruction and rentals; downhill ski facilities with lodge, restaurant; bunkhouse, campground with plug-ins, shelters on trail. Information: Eagle Mountain Ski Area, Box 98, Grey Eagle, MN 56336. 612-285-4567. **Camp Ko-Ac** (SW via SR 23 at Paynesville), 9 m of marked and groomed trails; intermediate terrain; rentals for groups; instruction on request; trail map available; dormitory accommodations, dining hall, recreation hall. Information: Camp Ko-Ac, Box 91, Paynesville, MN 56362. 612-243-4894. **Sibley State Park** (SW via SR 23, then 5 m W on SR 9), 2.6 m of marked and groomed trails; beginner to advanced terrain; trail map; warming house, restrooms; primitive camping. Information: Supervisor, Sibley State Park, New London, MN 56273. 612-354-2443.

SUPERIOR NATIONAL FOREST (in NE part of state), 3 million acres of dense evergreen forest, streams, and over 2000 lakes; includes beautiful wilderness **Boundary Waters Canoe Area** (continues into Canada); unlimited ski touring possibilities in the forest on over 200 m of designated ski trails, plus many m of unplowed forest roads; many marked trails begin near towns of Ely, Grand Marais, and Virginia (see entries); permits required for entering Boundary Waters Canoe Area (no snowmobiles). Information: see towns listed above, or Forest Supervisor, Superior National Forest, P.O. Box 338, Duluth, MN 55801. 218-727-6692.

TAYLORS FALLS: St. Croix Wild River State Park (12 m NW), 4 m of marked trails for beginner to advanced skiers; parking area, toilets; park under development. Information: Supervisor, St. Croix Wild River State Park, Taylors Falls, MN 55084. 612-465-5711. **William**

O'Brien State Park (S on SR 95 near Copas), 9.8 m of marked and groomed trails; beginner to advanced terrain; trail map; limited pack-in camping, pit toilets, water. Information: Supervisor, William O'Brien State Park, Marine on St. Croix, MN 55047. 612-433-2421.

TWO HARBORS: Two Harbors City Trail (in town), 15-km marked and groomed trail for beginner to intermediate skiers; toilet on trail; trail map available at City Hall. Information: 218-834-4386. **Woodland Caribou Cross Country Trail** (38 m N on County Rd. 2), 16 m of marked and groomed trails; intermediate to advanced terrain in the **Finland State Forest;** trail map; shelter and outdoor toilets; parking area. Information: 218-723-4669.

VIRGINIA: Lookout Mountain Ski Trail (3 m N), 9 m of marked and groomed trails for intermediate to advanced skiers; toilets at trailhead. **Olcott Park** (in town), 1-m marked and groomed beginner trail. Instruction by request from Laurentian Nordic Ski Club (Box 222, Virginia, MN 55792). Trail maps and information: Chamber of Commerce, Virginia, MN 55792. 218-741-2717. **McCarthy Beach State Park** (W on US 169 to Hibbing, then N on County Rd. 5), 8 m of marked and groomed, intermediate trails; trail map available; campground, toilets, parking area. Information: Supervisor, McCarthy Beach State Park, Star Route, Hibbing, MN 55746. 218-254-2411.

WABASHA: Kruger Trail (5 m W on SR 60), 2 m of marked trails for intermediate to advanced skiers; trail map, toilets. Information: 612-345-3216. **Snake Creek Trail** (3 m S of Kellogg on US 61), 3.5 m of marked trails; intermediate to advanced terrain; map and information: DNR, Box 69, Lake City, MN 55041. 612-345-3216. **Frontenac State Park** (NW off US 61), 2 m of marked and groomed trails for beginner to intermediate skiers; trail map available; warming house, campground, pit toilets. Information: Supervisor, Frontenac State Park, Rt. 2, Box 295, Lake City, MN 55041. 612-345-3401. **Mt. Frontenac** (NW on US 61; 9 m S of Red Wing), 5 m of marked trails for beginner to intermediate skiers; trail use fee, trail map; limited rentals; instruction; downhill ski facilities, chalet, and cafeteria; motel and dormitory accommodations within 1 m. Information: Mt. Frontenac Ski Area, Rt. 1, Red Wing, MN 55066. 612-388-5826.

WALKER: Shingobee Recreation Area Trail System (6 m SW on SR 34), 12 km of marked and groomed interconnecting trails; beginner to advanced terrain; warming house with restrooms; trail map; separate snowmobile trail; parking area. Information: District Ranger, Walker Ranger District, Chippewa National Forest, Walker, MN 56484. **Howard Lake Ski Trail** (same as above) 10-km marked and groomed trail connects with Shingobee Trail. **Earthome Resort** (SW off SR 34 on Howard Lake Rd.), 3.5 km of marked and groomed trails for novice to intermediate skiers; trail map; rentals; housekeeping cabins, small store, snacks. Information: Earthome Resort, Howard Lake Rd., Akeley, MN 56435. 218-652-2135. **Cut Lake Cross-Country Skiing Area** (S via SR 371 to Pine River, then 10.25 m W on County Rd. 2), 7 km of marked and groomed trails; beginner to advanced terrain; shelter and toilet at parking area. Information and trail map: Land Dept., Cass County Courthouse, Walker, MN 56484. 218-547-3300, ext. 226.

WARREN: Old Mill State Park (NE via County Roads), 1-m marked and groomed trail for novice and intermediate skiers; trail map available, picnic shelter, toilets. Information: Supervisor, Old Mill State Park, Argyle, MN 56731. 218-437-8174.

WINONA: O. L. Kipp State Park (SE via US 14 and US 61), 4.5-m marked and groomed trails; beginner to intermediate terrain; trail map; campground, pit toilets. Information: Supervisor, O. L. Kipp State Park, Rt. 4, Winona, MN 55987. 507-643-6849.

MONTANA

For additional information, contact the individual area or Montana Travel Promotion Unit, Dept. of Highways, Helena, MT 59601.

BOZEMAN: Lone Mountain Ranch (40 m S on US 191, turn W toward Big Sky 4 m, then right 1 m), 35 m of marked and groomed trails at ranch, access to 300 m of marked trails in Spanish Peaks Primitive Area and Yellowstone National Park; beginner to expert terrain varies from semi-open rolling hillsides to very steep alpine meadows, with lots of dry powder snow; trail fee ($2, except guests), trail map; rentals, Nordic ski shop; certified instruction; all-day wilderness tours to backcountry cabin, moonlight tours; mule-drawn sleigh rides; no snowmobiles; accommodations at ranch in log cabins with fireplaces, modern baths and electric heat; meals served family style in dining room; après-ski in Horsefly Saloon; package ski touring vacations available with combinations of lodging, food, and guided tours (package tours entitle guests to a 20% reduction in airfare on major airlines); public transportation from Bozeman to ranch on Yellowstone Park Co. Bus. Operating out of Lone Mountain Ranch, **Yellowstone Nordic** offers an exciting variety of guided tours at the Ranch and to Old Faithful in Yellowstone National Park (snow-coach transportation to park included), where during a full moon, geyser watching by moonlight is an incredible experience. Information for both the above: Bob and Viv Schaap, Lone Mountain Ranch, Box 145, Big Sky, MT 59716. 406-995-4644. **Big Sky of Montana** (43 m S off US 191), about 35-m cross-country trail system on resort property; trailhead, rental and retail shop at golf clubhouse; instruction; major full-service resort area (developed by the late newscaster Chet Huntley) has extensive downhill ski facilities; lodge, condominium, and hostel accommodations; cafeteria, restaurants, bars, entertainment; heated pool, sauna; shops, deli, convention center. Bus service from Bozeman. Information: Big Sky of Montana Resort, P.O. Box 1, Big Sky, MT 59716. 406-995-4211. Toll free: 800-548-4486. **Bridger Bowl** (16 m NE on SR 293), cross-country and racing trails; rental and retail shop; certified instruction; downhill ski facilities, day lodges, cafeterias, restaurant, cocktail lounge, bierstube; accommodations at Bridger Mountain Lodge; numerous accommodations, restaurants and services in Bozeman; bus service between Bozeman and Bridger Bowl. Information: Bridger Bowl Ski Area, Box 846, Bozeman, MT 59715. 406-587-2111.

Gallatin National Forest (N & S of town), 1.7-million-acre forest is laced with hundreds of m of trails and forest roads suitable for cross-country skiing; many of the trails begin at the areas mentioned above. The U.S. Forest Service has prepared a detailed list of recommended ski tours in the Bozeman area. For maps and information: Forest Supervisor, Gallatin National Forest, P.O. Box 130, Bozeman, MT 59715.

BUTTE: Georgetown Lake Area (41 m NW via US 10A), trails maintained by U.S. Forest Service include: 3-m loop for intermediate skiers and .75-m easy loop on campground road; both trails begin at parking area off US 10 across from Georgetown Lake dam. Nearby Echo Lake Trail is easy 1.8-m tour; Discovery Basin Loop Trail is 2.25-m trail suitable for intermediate skiers; both trails begin at **Discovery Basin Ski Area** with downhill ski facilities, cafeteria, restaurant, bierstube; instruction and rentals. Accommodations available at nearby Fairmont Hot Springs resort hotel in Gregson, where facilities include dining room, cabaret, hot springs, pools, and saunas. Information: Discovery Basin Ski Area, Anaconda, MT 59711. Maps and information on above 4 trails: Ranger, U.S. Forest Service, Box H, Philipsburg, MT 59858. 406-859-3211. **Wraith Hill** (12 m W of Anaconda on US 10A), access to cross-country ski trails; downhill ski facilities with day lodge, cafeteria; food and lodging in Anaconda. Information: Wraith Hill Ski Area, Anaconda, MT 59711.

DILLON: Maverick Mountain Ski Area (38 m NW via SR 278 at Polaris), cross-country ski trails; instruction and rentals; downhill ski facilities, day lodge, cafeteria; nearby accommodations with restaurant, lounge, and pool. Information: Maverick Mountain Ski Area, Polaris, MT 59746. 406-834-2412.

GLACIER NATIONAL PARK (hq entry at West Glacier, 32 m NE of Kalispell on US 2), spectacular wilderness with precipitous mountain peaks, 50 glaciers, many lakes, abundant wildlife. Ski tours from **West Glacier** include: 2-m trail beginning at Lake McDonald Lodge (plowed road N from West Glacier) follows a stream to iced-over McDonald Falls; generally level terrain with a few short uphill and downhill spots; recommended for novice skiers. Also starting at Lake McDonald Lodge is easy 6-m tour to Avalanche Campground (permit required for overnight camping), 2 m beyond is Avalanche Lake. 14 m round trip to Apgar Lookout (W at park hq) is a long uphill climb rewarded by great views and a challenging downhill run; suitable, with good snow conditions, for advanced skiers. From Polebridge Ranger Station (N via park road from West Glacier) is 6-m unplowed road N to River Campground and Big Prairie, an easy day trip. Trails from **Walton Ranger Station** (in Essex on US 2) follow Ole Creek and Park Creek; another trail climbs Scalplock Mtn. Tours from **East Glacier Park** include: 9-m round trip to Firebrand Pass on Continental Divide (start at Lubec Guard Station on US 2, 6.5 m W of East Glacier Park), generally uphill and not well marked; elk are usually seen along Calf Robe Mtn. Road N of town is unplowed and leads into Two Medicine Valley; 9.5-m trip to Trick Falls and another 3.5 m to Two Medicine Lake; moderate 400-ft gain in elevation; trails radiating out of Two Medicine are usually difficult to follow and snow depths can be great; beautiful panoramic views of the mountains. **St. Mary** (N of East Glacier Park via SR 89) is information center and starting point for tours on the NE side of the park. Red Eagle Valley (left off SR 89 at St. Mary winter entrance sign, then 300 yds to ranger dwellings) has 3 short loops, plus 14-m round-trip trail to Red Eagle Lake; strong winds may be encountered. 5.8-m unplowed road W off SR 89 (S of St. Mary) leads to Cut Bank Campground; for overnighters, short trips farther up the valley are possible. It is advisable to check your tour plan and current weather conditions at a Ranger Station; overnight campers need permits. Lodging and restaurants are available along the perimeter of the park. For additional tour suggestions and information: Park Superintendent, Glacier National Park, West Glacier, MT 59936.

GREAT FALLS: Kings Hill Pass Area (70 m SW on US 89), unlimited touring possibilities on forest roads; minimum marking, map available; rentals and instruction available at nearby **Showdown Ski Area** (S of pass) with downhill ski facilities, day lodge, cafeteria, saloon, and nursery; food, lodging, and services in Great Falls or White Sulphur Springs (40 m S). Information: District Ranger, U.S. Forest Service, Neihart, MT 59465. 406-236-5321. **Teton Pass** (NW vis US 89 to Choteau, then 32 m NW off US 89), access to unlimited cross-country skiing; rentals and instruction available; downhill ski facilities, day lodge, cafeteria; accommodations, restaurants and services in Choteau. Information: Teton Pass Ski Area, Choteau, MT 59422. 406-466-5749.

HAMILTON: Lost Trail Pass (51 m S on US 93), unlimited cross-country skiing for novice to advanced skiers; timbered high elevation; trail map available; downhill ski facilities with cafeteria, rentals; accommodations at Lost Trail Lodge (6 m N of pass) and in Darby (34 m N). Information: District Ranger, Sula Ranger District, Sula MT 59871. 406-821-3201.

KALISPELL: Flathead National Forest (surrounding town), 2.3-million acre forest with glaciers, glacial lakes, jagged mountains and dense forest; entire forest is available for cross-country skiing with many unplowed roads and marked trails; **Swan Lake Ranger District** (SE off SR 35 & SR 209) has mostly intermediate to advanced terrain with steep sidehills, beautiful views of the Mission Mountains; some avalanche danger; food and lodging in Bigfork. **Hungry Horse District** (E of Kalispell; accessible S off US 2), many trails and roads depart from Izaak Walton Inn (in Essex; see below); other nearby accommodations in Hungry Horse and West Glacier. **Glacier View District** (N off US 2), has 2 easy tours with beautiful views into Glacier National Park, and an intermediate tour near Columbia Falls. **Tally Lake District** (N & W of Kalispell) has many good trails just N of Whitefish and around Tally Lake Campground; motels, restaurants, rentals, and guides available in Whitefish. Forest Service publishes a small booklet with detailed descriptions of recommended tours. Information: Forest Supervisor, Flathead National Forest, P.O. Box 147, Kalispell, MT 59901. 406-755-5401.

   Northern Nordic Ski Touring & Racing Center (16.5 m N via US 93; near turnoff for Big Mtn. Ski Area), 5 km of marked and groomed trails with unlimited touring in surrounding mountain ranges; beginner to intermediate rolling terrain with short downhill; trail fee ($1), trail map; certified instructors offer group and private lessons; guided tours on request; clinics (by special request) include instruction in winter survival, first aid, waxing, conditioning, and technique; rental and retail shop; warming lodge, snacks; food and lodging in Whitefish. Information: Northern Nordic Ski Touring & Racing Center, Box 895, Whitefish, MT 59937. 406-862-3888. **Whitefish Nordic Ski Center** (14 m N in Whitefish), unlimited touring in surrounding area; group and private certified instruction; waxing clinics, snow survival seminar, guided half-day tour, full-day tour with lunch, overnight tours into Glacier National Park; rental and retail shop. Information: Whitefish Nordic Ski Center, 139 2nd St., Whitefish, MT 59937. 406-862-5294. Snow Report: 406-862-3511. **Big Mountain Ski Area** (8 m N of Whitefish), access to unlimited touring; instruction and rentals; downhill ski facilities with day lodges, cafeterias, bierstube, nursery; variety of lodge accommodations (package plans), restaurants, lounges, heated outdoor pool, sauna. Information: Big Mountain Ski Area, P.O. Box 1215, Whitefish, MT 59937. 406-862-3511. **Izaak Walton Inn** (60 m E on US 2 at Essex), located in Flathead National Forest and across the road from Glacier National Park, touring possibilities are unlimited; many trails and unplowed roads depart from the inn;

map of area trails available; instruction and guided tours by reservation; retail and rentals shop; inn has 29 rooms, good food, and comfortable lounge decorated with railroad memorabilia. Information: Sid and Millie Goodrich, Izaak Walton Inn, Box 675, Essex, MT 59916. Telephone: ask Operator for Essex No. 1.

LIBBY: Turner Mountain (22 m NW on SR 506), 3 marked trails begin off SR 506 near downhill ski area with day lodge, snack bar. Information: Turner Mountain Ski Area, Libby, MT 59923. **Libby Ranger District** of Kootenai National Forest maintains about 18 m of marked trails starting from various roads radiating from Libby; beginner to advanced terrain; some trails shared with snowmobiles; trail map available (small fee); rentals, food and lodging in Libby. Information: District Ranger, Libby Ranger Station, Rt. 2, Box 275, Libby, MT 59923.

MISSOULA: Montana Sports Ranch (85 m NE on SR 209 at 40 m marker), marked and maintained trails on 240-acre ranch with access to unlimited skiing in nearby wilderness area; varying terrain for beginner to advanced skiers; average winter snowfall over 130 inches; rentals, instruction, and guided tours available; snowmobiles on separate trails; lodging at ranch with 12 modern rooms, family-style meals served, western bar and lounge; special weekend and group rates; ranch provides transportation to and from Missoula and Kalispell. Information: Montana Sports Ranch, Box 501, Hwy. 209, Condon, MT 59826. 406-754-2351. **Lolo Pass Winter Sports Area** (37 m W on US 12), 18,000-acre area with 30 m of designated ski trails; beginner to advanced terrain on forest roads and trails on timbered slopes; information and warming area at Lolo Pass Visitor Center (open weekends Dec. 1-Mar. 1); accommodations at Lolo Hot Springs (8 m E). Additional information: District Ranger, Powell Ranger District, U.S. Forest Service, Lolo, MT 59847. 208-942-3113. **Marshall Mountain** (4 m E of Missoula), access to unlimited ski touring; instruction; downhill ski facilities with day lodge, snack bar; food, lodging, and services in Missoula. Information: Marshall Mountain Ski Area, Missoula, MT 59801. 406-258-6619. **Montana Snow Bowl** (13 m NW), cross-country ski trails; downhill ski facilities, day lodge, restaurant, lounge; accommodations in Missoula. Information: Montana Snow Bowl, Missoula, MT 59801. 406-549-9777.

RED LODGE: Red Lodge Mountain (6 m W; 65 m SW of Billings), access to unlimited cross-country skiing; downhill ski facilities, day lodge, restaurant, bierstube; food, lodging, and services in Red Lodge. Information: Red Lodge Mountain, Red Lodge, MT 59068. 406-466-2288.

NEBRASKA

For additional information, contact the individual park or Nebraska Game and Parks Commission, 2200 North 33rd St., P.O. Box 30370, Lincoln, NE 68503. For weekly snow reports call 402-464-0641 (in Lincoln), and ask for the Snowline.

BROWNVILLE: Indian Cave State Park (S off SR 67), 3000 acres with densely wooded bluffs along the Missouri River; park rich in history, has riverfront settlement from the 1850s and a cave with early Indian petroglyphs; interconnecting loops and trails total about 38 m, marked for cross-country skiers; trails from camping area near St. Deroin townsite rated beginner to intermediate, spur from campsite to historic Half-Breed Cemetery is a short easy tour; central section of the park, generally more difficult, has a steep climb to the top of Rock Bluff Trail where overnighters will find 6 Adirondac shelters (roof and 3 sides) on the ridge overlooking the river; trails to Bridge and Lemon Hollows recommended for intermediate to advanced skiers; south trails, particularly the road, are easy, and the tour to the cave is scenic and relatively simple. Maps and information at the park office: 402-883-2575.

CHADRON: Chadron State Park (9 m S on US 385), 840 rugged pine-covered acres remarkably well suited for cross-country skiing; 1.3-km, 8-km, and 2.3-km loops around the Chadron Creek, cabins, and base area, recommended for beginners; 2.4-km and 3.4-km marked trails wind through wooded areas rated intermediate terrain; northwest day-use area, with separate parking lot, has marked trailhead for exploratory tours into Dead Horse Canyon, for advanced skiers only; family area with good sledding hill near the pool,

ice skating and fishing on the park lagoon; winter primitive camping restricted to the area behind park headquarters; Multi-Use
Facility consists of 6 units in 3 duplexes, each unit accommodates
4–10 persons, kitchen facilities available by arrangement (reservations through park office: 308-432-2036). **Fort Robinson State Park**
(27 m W on US 20), 40,000 acres including adjacent **Soldiers
Creek Management Unit** (Wood Reserve); beautiful woodlands
along Soldiers Creek thin out into grasslands below dominating
Ponderosa Pine buttes; **Red Cloud Agency Area,** gentle terrain for
beginners, ski route passes winter pasture of the park's buffalo and
long-horned cattle herds; in the opposite direction is an unmarked
road through the woodlands along Soldiers Creek from lower campground to Carter Johnson Lake, also for novices; **Red Cloud Bluffs**
can be reached by several marked trails and a fire road, recommended for advanced skiers; another advanced tour beginning at
Carter Johnson Lake climbs to Smiley Canyon Rd. for a 4- to 6-m
downhill run back to the lower campground, or by cutting through
the woods, back to the lake; just to the N of **James Ranch** (from
homesteading days) are evergreen-covered hills with some horse
trails and fire roads, ideal exploratory touring possibilities for
intermediate and advanced skiers; **Wood Reserve** offers old Hat
Creek to Fort Robinson military road, an easy tour, or Troop Trail,
a challenge for advanced skiers, winds into an area of bluffs. Primitive camping permitted in designated areas; skiers asked to check in
and out with park personnel. Maps and information at park office:
308-665-2660. Accommodations, restaurants, and services in Craw-
ford and Chadron.

PONCA: Ponca State Park (N off SR 12), 836 acres with picturesque
bluffs overlooking the Missouri River; 17 m of horse and foot
trails adaptable to cross-country skiing; **Lewis and Clark Trail,**
trailhead just N of the pool, parallels the river atop the wooded
bluffs for over a mile; for the advanced skier, the northern section
of the park has several challenging trails along steep hillsides and
onto a bluff with probably the best view in the park; unplowed
roads interlace the park, offering good tours for skiers of all skill
levels; ski-backpackers permitted to camp in the day-use area N of
the cabins; bald and golden eagles known to winter-roost in the park.
For trail map and information: 402-755-2284.

NEVADA

For additional information, contact the individual area or Nevada Dept. of Economic Development, Capitol Complex, Carson City, NV 89710.

CARSON CITY: Hope Valley Area of the **Toiyabe National Forest** (37 m SW via SR 88), popular area with meadow and mountain terrain suitable for cross-country skiers; no marked trails; snowmobiles permitted. Lodging, restaurants, and services in Markleeville, CA (15 m). Information: District Forest Ranger, U.S. Forest Service, 1536 S. Carson St., Carson City, NV 89701. 702-882-2766. Snow report: 702-882-9211.

ELKO: Wildhorse Ranch & Resort (65 m N via SR 51), 30 m of trails on 6700-acre cattle ranch adjacent to Humboldt National Forest; marked and groomed trails on varied terrain from flat to mountainous; trail fee ($12); trail map ($1.50); rentals; instruction and guided tours; accommodations at area, family-style Italian food; plowed parking area ($2 per day); snowmobiles on racetrack only. Information: Archie F. Corbari, Jr., Wildhorse Ranch & Resort, Via: Elko, NV 89801. Telephone: Northfork 6471 or 6472 through Elko.

INCLINE VILLAGE: Spooner Lake Ski Touring Trails (13 m S via SR 28; 10 m E of Carson City via US 50 and SR 28), 2.2-m Spooner Meadow Trail for novice skiers is marked with blue survey tape; 1.6-m Spooner Lake Trail, an intermediate trail marked with red survey tape, circles the lake; expert skiers can continue on to Markette Lake via North Creek Canyon Trail from Meadow Trail; map available; parking at trailhead. Information: Park Ranger, Lake Tahoe-Nevada State Park, P.O., Box 3283, Incline Village, NV 89450. 702-831-0494. **Ski Incline** (in Incline Village) offers instruction and rentals; downhill ski facilities with day lodge, warming hut, cafeteria, restaurant; a year-round family resort with condominium lodging available. Information: Ski Incline, P.O. Box AL, Incline Village, NV 89450. 702-831-1821. Snow Report: 702-

831-3211. Unlimited accommodations, restaurants, and services in North Lake Tahoe area. Information: North Lake Tahoe Chamber of Commerce, Box 884, Tahoe City, CA 95730.

RENO: Mt. Rose Ski Area (on SR 27, 22 m SW; 12 m NE of Lake Tahoe), cross-country ski trails into Toiyabe National Forest; primarily a downhill ski area with day lodge, cafeteria, dining room, and bar. Information: Mt. Rose Ski Area, Box 2406, Reno, NV 89505. 702-849-0704. **Slide Mountain Ski Area** (on SR 27, 21 m SW of Reno), another jumping-off place for cross-country skiers; downhill ski facilities with day lodge, cafeteria, and bar. Information: Slide Mountain Ski Area, P.O. Box 2748, Reno NV 89505. 702-849-0852. Unlimited accommodations, restaurants, services, and entertainment in Reno and North Lake Tahoe area.

NEW HAMPSHIRE

For additional information, contact the individual area or New Hampshire Division of Economic Development, Box 856, State House Annex, Concord, NH 03301.

BRETTON WOODS: Bretton Woods Touring Center (I-93 N to US 3 to Twin Mtn., off US 302 just SE of Twin Mtn.), 84 km of marked and partly groomed trails; beginner to advanced terrain with wide open trails in the Presidential Mtn. Range, beautiful views of Mt. Washington; trail fee ($2.50), map available; rentals, instruction, and guided tours; overnight shelter in Pemigewasset Wilderness; downhill ski facilities, day lodge, cafeteria; lounge serves beer and wine; babysitting service; accommodations at Bretton Woods Motor Inn and Rosebrook Townhouses, additional lodging, restaurants and services in Twin Mtn; super ticket (trail fee, rentals and lesson) and package plans available. Information: Bretton Woods Touring Center, Bretton Woods, NH 03575. 603-278-5000.

CLAREMONT: Norsk Ski Touring Center (about 26 m E on SR 11 at New London; from Concord, exit 11 off I-89, then 1.7 m E on

SR 11), 18 m of marked and fully groomed trails at Lake Sunapee Country Club; novice to intermediate terrain with both open and wooded areas, views of Mt. Kearsarge; abundant wildlife; trail fee ($3), trail map available; rentals, sales, group and private instruction; guided nature, moonlight, and luncheon tours; downhill technique clinics, waxing clinics, races, ski movies; no snowmobiles; lodging, restaurant, and tavern at touring center; additional accommodations in New London. Information: Norsk Ski Touring, John and Nancy Schlosser, Rt. 11, New London, NH 03257. 603-526-4685. **Eastman Touring Center** (22 m NE via SR 11 and SR 10 at Grantham; from Concord, exit 13 off I-89), 25 km of marked and groomed trails for all levels of ability; open and wooded terrain; small trail fee, trail map available; rental and retail shop; waxing room, free waxing clinics; certified instructors offer group and private lessons; no snowmobiles; guided tours; restaurant and lounge, showers and restroom facilities; food and lodging in New London. Information: Eastman Community Association, Box 53, Grantham, NH 03753. 603-863-4240. **Gray Ledges Lodge** (22 m NE via SR 11 and SR 10 at Grantham; from Concord exit 13 off I-89, then .8 m S on SR 10, right at Mobil station, .8 m to gate), 50 m of marked and maintained trails; beginner to expert terrain on rolling farmlands with panoramic views and wooded mountainsides with streams; rentals, instruction, and guided tours; variety of accommodations in lodge, motel, family rooms, bunkhouse; lodging for groups; restaurant, recreation room with fireplace; package plans. Information: Gray Ledges Lodge, Grantham, NH 03753. 603-863-1002. **Dexter's Inn Nordic Center** (13 m E on SR 103 at Sunapee; from Concord exit 12 off I-89 to SR 11 to SR 103B), 200 acres with 12 m of marked and groomed beginner to expert trails on meadows and rolling wooded hills with beaver ponds; adjacent to 400 acres of village-owned property with trails; trail fee, map available; rentals; waxing room; group and private instruction, guided tours; no snowmobiles; food and lodging at inn. Information: Dexter's Inn Nordic Center, Frank or Shirley Simpson, 50 Stagecoach Rd., Sunapee, NH 03782. 603-763-5571. **Mount Sunapee State Park** (16 m E off SR 103 at Mt. Sunapee), 10 m of marked novice and intermediate trails; rental and retail shop; trail map; downhill ski facilities with day lodge, cafeteria; variety of inns, motels, and restaurants nearby. Information: Mt. Sunapee Ski Area, Mt. Sunapee, NH 03772. 603-763-2356.

COLEBROOK: Wilderness Ski Area (10 m E on SR 26), 25 m of marked and groomed trails; novice to advanced terrain with wooded and open mountainous areas; trail fee ($2, except hotel guests), trail map available; rentals and instruction, guided tours by appointment; downhill ski facilities, day lodge, cafeteria; accommodations at Balsams Hotel (group rates and package plans); additional lodging, restaurants in Colebrook. Information: The Balsams Hotel, Dixville Notch, NH 03576. 603-255-3400.

FRANCONIA: Cannon Mtn./Franconia Notch State Park (3 m S off SR 3), 5 interconnecting, color-coded trails totaling 5.25 m; beginner to intermediate terrain on abandoned US 3 and on old logging roads; trailhead at Echo Lake parking lot; trail map available; rentals, instruction, and guided tours at touring center in Peabody Slopes day lodge (just W of parking lot on SR 18); downhill ski facilities, 2 day lodges, 2 cafeterias, nursery; no snowmobiles. One motel, restaurant and lounge located directly on trails; additional food, lodging, and services in Franconia. Information: Cannon Mtn. Ski Area, Franconia, NH 03580. 603-823-5563. Snow report: 603-823-7771. Franconia lodging reservation service: 603-823-5661. **Franconia Inn Cross Country Center** (exit 38 off I-93), 60 m of marked interconnecting trails, 40 m of which are continuously groomed; beginner to expert terrain; trail fee ($2), trail map available; trail system linked with other area trails making it possible to ski to another inn for lunch; rentals, group and private instruction, guided tours; no snowmobiles; food and lodging at inn (special ski week rates). Information: Franconia Inn, Rt. 116, Easton Rd., Franconia, NH 03580. 603-823-5542. **Sunset Hill Touring Center** (exit 38 off I-93, SR 117 to Sugar Hill, then left on Sunset Rd. .25 m), 25 m of marked and color-coded trails, groomed with track set; beginner to expert terrain on wooded mountain trails with superb views; trail map available; warming hut with potbellied stove and free hot soup; rentals, group and private instruction, guided tours, moonlight tours; no snowmobiles; lodging at inn (35 rooms), dining room. Information: Sunset Hill House, Sugar Hill, NH 03585. 603-823-5522.

HENNIKER: Pole and Pedal (E of Concord on US 202 in Henniker), about 25 km of marked and groomed trails including a 7.5-km loop; beginner to advanced terrain with additional touring possibilities on old area logging roads; rentals and instruction, warming and waxing room; guided tours (group rates). Information: Pole and Pedal Shop, Box 327, Henniker, NH 03242. 603-428-3242.

JACKSON: Jackson Ski Touring Foundation (in Jackson), a nonprofit foundation, maintains 125 km of marked trails, 50 km of which are groomed and tracked, in Mt. Washington Valley and through adjacent private lands; variety of trails include: 7.8-km novice trail along river, wilderness trails, and 15.1-km trail from Jackson village to Wildcat Mt.; trail donation ($2 adults, $1 children), detailed trail map ($1), village map free; group and private certified instruction, guided tours; accommodations and food at 12 lodges and inns on trail system (variety of vacation plans); no snowmobiles. Information: Jackson Ski Touring Foundation, Box 90, Jackson, NH 03846. 603-383-9355. **Appalachian Mountain Club** (8 m N on SR 16), 25 m of marked trails in Pinkham Notch area; novice to expert mountainous terrain with sharp ascents and descents; trails connect to Jackson Ski Touring Foundation trail system; trail map available; instruction and ski workshops; lodge with bunk accommodations for 107; 2 sitting rooms with fireplaces; family-style breakfast and dinner served, trail lunches available; no snowmobiles. Information: Appalachian Mountain Club, Pinkham Notch Camp, Gorham, NH 03581. 603-466-2727. **Eastern Mountain Sports** (on SR 16A in Jackson) supports Jackson Ski Touring Foundation trail system (see above); rental and retail shop with snack bar; group and private certified instruction; lodge accommodations (50% discount for rentals by lodge guests). Information: Eastern Mountain Sports, Inc., Rt. 16A, Jackson, NH 03846. 603-383-9641. Daily Trailways bus service from Boston. Mt. Washington Valley package plans available. Information: Mt. Washington Valley Chamber of Commerce, Box 385, North Conway, NH 03860. 603-356-3171.

LACONIA: Gunstock Ski Touring Trails (exit 20 off I-93, E of Laconia on SR 11A), 10–12 km of marked and groomed trails for novice to expert skiers; wooded and open terrain with spectacular views of Lake Winnipesaukee; no trail fee; touring center building has rental and retail shop, information and trail maps; instruction available; downhill ski facilities with day lodge, restaurant, lounge; nursery; no snowmobiles; 28 inns and motels, restaurants and services in Laconia area. Information: Gunstock Ski Area, P.O. Box 336, Laconia, NH 03246. 603-293-4341. **Brickyard Mountain**

Resort (6 m N on US 3), 5 m of marked and groomed trails; beginner to expert terrain near and overlooking Lake Winnipesaukee; trail fee ($3, except guests), map available; rentals and instruction; guided tours for hotel guests only; downhill ski facilities, day lodge, cafeteria, nursery; resort hotel with 105 rooms, 2 dining rooms, 2 lounges, entertainment; heated indoor pool, sauna, health club. Information: Brickyard Mountain Resort, Rt. 3, Laconia, NH 03246. 603-366-4316. Snow report: 800-258-0343.

LEBANON: Moose Mountain Lodge (N in Etna), many m of marked trails begin at lodge; beginner to advanced terrain with breathtaking views of the Green and White Mountains; rentals available; accommodations and hearty food (for up to 30 guests) at rustic log lodge. Information: Moose Mountain Lodge, Etna, NH 03750. 603-643-3529. **La Salette Ski Touring Center** (E on SR 4A in Enfield Center), 25 m of marked trails for novice to expert skiers; rentals and instruction; skating rink, toboggan run, snowshoe trails; food and lodging at area; weekend and season rates. Information: La Salette Ski Touring Center, Rt. 4A, Enfield Center, NH 03748. 603-632-4257.

LINCOLN: Loon Mountain Ski Touring Center (exit 32 off I-93, then 2 m E on SR 112), 10.5 m of marked and groomed, novice to intermediate trails; access to numerous trails in adjacent White Mtn. National Forest; no trail fee, map available; rentals, instruction and guided tours; downhill ski facilities, base lodge, cafeteria, restaurant, cocktail lounge; nursery; lodging at The Inn at Loon Mtn.; additional lodging, restaurants, and services in Lincoln. Information: Loon Mountain Ski Touring Center, Lincoln, NH 03251. 603-745-8111. Lodging reservation service: 603-745-8146.

MANCHESTER: Charmingfare Ski Touring Center (9 m E off SR 101 in Candia), 700 acres with 20 m of marked and groomed trails; beginner to intermediate gently rolling, open and wooded terrain; trail fee ($2), trail map available; rentals; EPSTI-certified instructors offer group and private lessons; no snowmobiles; clubhouse with snack bar and lounge; lodging, restaurants, and services in Manchester. Information: Charmingfare Ski Touring Center, Box 146, Candia, NH 03034. 603-483-2307. **Plausawa Valley Ski Touring Center** (10 m N on US 3; Hooksett exit off I-93), 12 m of marked and groomed trails for novice to intermediate skiers; open and wooded terrain with river view; trail fee ($1), trail map available; rental and retail shop, instruction; citizens' races; center open weekends and holidays plus full-moon nights, weather permitting; restaurant and lounge at clubhouse; lodging, restaurants, and services in area. Information: Plausawa Valley Ski Touring Center, Rt. 3, Pembroke, NH 03275. 603-228-1441.

NASHUA: Hollis-Hof Ski Touring Center (7 m W in Hollis on Richardson Rd.), 50 m of marked trails, 10 m of which are groomed; mostly rolling farmlands with open fields, some intermediate woods trails; trail fee ($2), map available; rentals, group and private instruction, guided tours; warming shelter with hot and cold drinks, snacks; no snowmobiles; food and lodging in Nashua. Information: Hollis-Hof Ski Touring Center, 53 Richardson Rd., Hollis, NH 03049. 603-465-2633.

PETERBOROUGH: Windblown (on SR 124, 8 m SE via SR 123; from Boston, SR 2 to I-495, then SR 119 to W. Townsend, MA, then right on SR 124), 18 m of marked interconnecting and maintained trails, 10 m of which are groomed with track set; beginner to expert rolling open and wooded terrain with brooks and nice distant views; trail fee ($2.50 adults, $1.50 ages 10–20, under 10 and over 65 free), trail map; warming hut located deep in woods has emergency phone and is available to overnighters with reservations, food, and sleeping bags; retail shop, ski and snowshoe rentals; instruction; no snowmobiles; restaurant open weekends; food, lodging, and services in Peterborough. Information: Al Jenks, Windblown, Turnpike Rd., New Ipswich, NH 03071. 603-878-2869. **Temple Mt. Ski Area** (4 m E on SR 101; 23 m W of Nashua), 35 m of marked and maintained trails, 8 m of which are groomed; beginner to expert terrain on open fields and open and wooded mountain ridges with elevations from 1486 ft to 2200 ft; trail fee ($2), all skiers must check in and out; trail fee includes free use of Alpine area T-bar lift to reach ridge-top trails; instruction, guided tours plus special Monadnock Region tours and moonlight tours, free ski clinics, citizens' races; downhill ski facilities with 2 day lodges and snack bars, nursery. Numerous accommodations, restaurants, and services nearby (lodging: Monadnock Region Assoc., 603-924-3611). Information: Temple Mt. Ski Area, Rt. 101, Peterborough, NH 03458. 603-924-6949. **Woodbound Inn Touring Center** (S in Jaffrey; 1.5 m off SR 119 and US 202 on Contoocook

Lake Rd.), 18 m of marked and groomed trails for novice to intermediate skiers on open and wooded terrain; trail fee ($2), map
available; rentals, instruction and guided tours; no snowmobiles;
food and lodging at inn. Information: Woodbound Inn, Jaffrey,
NH 03452. 603-532-8341. **The Inn at East Hill Farm** (W of Peterborough; E of Troy off SR 12), 8 m of marked trails for beginner
to intermediate skiers; trail fee ($2, except inn guests), gratis coffee;
some instruction for beginners; rentals; rope tow, tobogganing,
sleigh rides, snowmobiling; food and lodging for up to 90 at inn;
indoor skating rink, indoor pool, sauna. Information: The Inn at
East Hill Farm, Troy, NH 03465. 603-242-6495. **Summers Ski and
Mountain Touring Center** (W of Peterborough; ½ m W of jct of
SR 137 and SR 101), 20 m of marked and maintained trails, groomed
as necessary; beginner to advanced trails along streams, past an
active beaver pond, and through beautiful stands of hardwood
forest with occasional excellent views of Mt. Monadnock; trails
connect to **Mt. Monadnock Recreation Area** (603-532-8880) and
Mt. Monadnock State Park (603-532-8862) trail systems; trail fee
($1), trail map available; ski shop, rentals, instruction, free lessons
on Wed. nights (with reservation); guided tours with advance reservation; warming/waxing hut (heated on weekends only) with coffee,
tea, and hot chocolate available; winter camping by permit; snowshoeing off trails; no snowmobiles. Information: Summers Ski and
Mountain Touring Center, Box F, Rt. 101, Dublin, NH 03444.
603-563-8556. **Sargent Camp Ski Touring Center** (6 m N of Peterborough on Windy Row), operated by Boston University; 15 m of
marked and groomed trails on flat to hilly forested terrain for
novice to advanced skiers; trail fee ($1.50), trail map available;
skiers must sign in and out at the Ski Adventure Lodge of the
Outpost; group and private lessons, guided environmental tours
(for groups of 4–12), snowshoe orientation; ski and snowshoe
rentals; designated snowshoe trails; no snowmobiles, no pets; trailhead lodge, winterized cabins and dormitories, meals served family
style (food and lodging by reservation only, up to 150); open weekends and NH school vacations. Information: The Human Environ-
ment Institute, Sargent Camp, RFD 2, Peterborough, NH 03458.
603-525-3311. In Boston: 617-353-3202. Snow report: 603-525-9338.
Crotched Mountain Touring Center (N on US 202, then E on SR
47), 45 m of novice to expert marked trails on open and wooded
terrain and on old logging roads; rental and retail shop, instruction,
guided tours; trail map; warming hut; downhill ski facilities with

base lodge, cafeteria, cocktail lounge; nursery; food and lodging in Francestown and Peterborough. Information: Crotched Mountain Ski Area, Rt. 47, Francestown, NH 03043. 603-588-6384.

WATERVILLE VALLEY: Waterville Valley Ski Touring Center (exit 28 off I-93, then 11 m E on SR 49), over 35 m of marked beginner to expert trails on open and wooded terrain, along streams and over old logging roads; trails groomed daily and patrolled regularly; trail fee ($2, adult; $1, 12 and under), rental and retail shop, waxing service, group and private instruction; special "Starter Kit" includes trail fee, lesson and rentals; ski workshops, citizens' races, scheduled nature tours; snack bar and restaurant next to touring center. A full-service resort area with downhill ski facilities, variety of lodging, restaurants, bars, and plenty of après-ski; choice of ski-touring vacation plans. Information and reservations: Waterville Valley Ski Touring Center, Waterville Valley, NH 03223. 603-236-8311. Snow report, toll free: 800-258-8983 (from MA, CT, RI, NY, NJ, PA, DE, DC, MD, VA, VT, ME; 800-552-0388 from NH).

WOLFEBORO: The Nordic Skier (19 N. Main St.; 100 m N of Boston; 65 m W of Portland, ME), 20 m of groomed trails with track set by enthusiastic area skiers; no trail fee; unlimited touring possibilities on open and forested rolling terrain with hidden meadows and old logging roads around picturesque Wolfeboro on the east shores of Lake Winnipesaukee; The Nordic Skier (shop) is area nucleus for rentals, sales, instruction, moonlight tours, waxing clincs, trail maps; warming hut and lunch at Abenaki Ski Area, a town-operated facility (3.5 m N on SR 109A); snowmobiles on separate trails; winter camping at Wolfeboro Campground; numerous inns, motels, restaurants and services in Wolfeboro. Information: The Nordic Skier, P.O. Box 297, Wolfeboro, NH 03894. 603-569-3151. **Moose Mountain Ski Area** (E off SR 109 near Brookfield, on Mountain Rd.), 12 m of marked and groomed beginner trails on flat and hilly wooded terrain; rentals; downhill ski facilities with day lodge, cafeteria; winter camping. Information: Moose Mountain Ski Area, Brookfield, NH 03872. 603-522-3639.

NEW JERSEY

For additional information, contact the individual area or New Jersey Office of Tourism & Promotion, Division of Economic Development, Dept. of Labor & Industry, P.O. Box 400, Trenton, NJ 08625.

ALLAIRE STATE PARK (off SR 549, 6 m N of Lakewood), 2630-acre park with restored ironmaking village dating to early 1800s; trails suitable for cross-country skiing. Information: Superintendent, Allaire State Park, Box 220, Farmingdale, NJ 07727.

ALPINE: Palisades Interstate Park (9 m N of George Washington Bridge, on Palisades Interstate Pkwy.), about 7 m of trails at **State Line Lookout Area;** trails follow old fire roads and bridle paths on mostly flat terrain, some hills; skiers may use the closed section of old Rt. 9W or any of the fire trails that begin at the NW corner of the parking lot; Trail A, easy 1 m; Trail B, more difficult; Trail C, most difficult, 2½ m long with a steep hill; no snowmobiles. Fort Lee is nearest town with restaurants and services. Information: Superintendent, Palisades Interstate Park Commission, P.O. Box 155, Alpine, NJ 07620. 201-768-1360.

MORRISTOWN: Morristown National Historical Park (Bernardsville exit off I-287, N on US 202, then W on Tempe Wick Rd.): **Jockey Hollow** area has 19 m of marked trails on 1500 acres; beginner to advanced terrain with hills and streams, hardwood forest, wildlife, historic site with reconstructed soldiers' huts; trail maps posted; parking area at Jockey Hollow Visitor Center; no snowmobiles. Information: Superintendent, Morristown National Historical Park, P.O. Box 1136R, Morristown, NJ 07960. 201-539-2016.

NEWFOUNDLAND: Craigmeur Ski Area (from I-80 exit 37, then 8 m W on SR 513; from SR 23, Green Pond exit, then 2 m S on SR 513), marked and maintained trails on 5 wooded acres for novice skiers; trail fee ($4), free trail map; group and private instruction; rentals for adults and juniors; downhill ski facilities with day lodge, restaurant, snack shop, cocktail lounge, vending machines. Accommodations at nearby motel (Howard Johnson) on Green Pond Rd.; public transportation from N.Y.C. on Northeast Coach Lines. Information: Craigmeur Ski Area, Green Pond Rd., Newfoundland, NJ 07435. 201-697-4501.

NEWTON: Fairview Ski Touring Center (W via SR 94, County Rts. 610, 617, & 624), 25 m of marked and maintained trails on 600 acres; easy to difficult skiing on open fields and wooded mountainous terrain; trail fee ($3), map available; certified instructors offer group and private lessons; guided tours; rentals for adults and juniors; lodging in heated cabins with bath; fireplace and dining room in main lodge, meals served family style; special weekend package rates include 2 nights' lodging, 5 meals, 2-day trail pass; no snowmobiles. Information: Mr. Dan McCain, Fairview Lake YMCA Camps, RD 5, Box 210, Newton, NJ 07860. 201-383-9282.

RINGWOOD STATE PARK (on Sloatsburg Rd. in Ringwood), cross-country skiing permitted at Ringwood Manor, site of restored ironmaster's home, and in Shepard Lake and Skyland sections of park; terrain suitable, but not designated for skiing. Information: Superintendent, Ringwood State Park, RD, Box 1304, Ringwood, NJ 07456.

STOKES STATE FOREST (besected by US 206, N of Branchville), 14,887-acre forest along the Kittatinny Mountains in the NW part of the state; many m of roads and trails, including the Appalachian Trail, open to cross-country skiing and showshoeing; scenic overlooks along the ridge; Tillman Ravine, a natural area in the southern part of the forest, has an interesting gorge with tall hemlocks and steep banks; snowmobiles restricted to specific trails on NE side of US 206; parking area at Visitor Center (on US 206). Information: Ranger, Stokes State Forest, RR2, Box 260, Branchville, NJ 07826.

SUSSEX: Sleepy Hollow Park Kamp Grounds (on SR 565; 3 m from Playboy Club), 300-acre area; trail fee ($3 adults, $2 children under 12); certified instructors offer private and group lessons, group tours; Nordic racing programs; adult and junior rentals (hourly rates); centrally located day lodge with fireplace, separate game room for children. Information: R. Von Oesen, Manager,

Sleepy Hollow Park Kamp Grounds, SR 565, Sussex, NJ 07461. 201-875-6211. **Great Gorge/Vernon Valley Ski Areas** (E; off SR 23 at Hamburg, then 3 m N on SR 94), marked and maintained trails for cross-country skiers; 2 adjacent downhill ski facilities, day lodges, restaurants, cafeterias, cocktail lounges; nursery; accommodations at nearby Playboy Hotel; additional lodging, restaurants, and services nearby. Information: Manager, Great Gorge/Vernon Valley Ski Areas, McAfee, NJ 07428. 201-827-2000.

WASHINGTON CROSSING STATE PARK (on SR 29 & SR 546, N of Trenton on the Delaware River), site of Washington's landing in 1776, has trails suitable for cross-country skiing. Information: Superintendent, Washington Crossing State Park, RR 1, Box 337, Titusville, NJ 08560.

STATE PARKS and **STATE FORESTS** with suitable terrain, but no formally designated cross-country trails and areas include: Abram S. Hewitt Forest (Hewitt); Allamuchy Mt. Park and Stephen's Section (Hackettstown); Cheesequake Park (Matawan); Delaware & Raritan Canal Park and Bull's Island Section (Belle Mead); Hacklebarney Park (Long Valley); Jenny Jump Forest (Hope); Norvin Green Forest (Butler); Round Valley Park (Lebanon); Spruce Run Park (Clinton); Voorhees Park (Glen Gardner); Wawayanda Park (Highland Lakes); Worthington Forest (Colombia). Information: Bureau of Parks, P.O. Box 1420, Trenton, NJ 08625.

NEW MEXICO

For additional information, contact the individual area or New Mexico Dept. of Development, Tourist Divison, 113 Washington Ave., Santa Fe, NM 87503.

ALAMOGORDO: Lincoln National Forest has good cross-country ski possibilities on forest roads and trails in **Cloudcroft Area** (20 m E on US 82); beginner to expert mountainous terrain at 8000- to 9000-ft elevations with some open, relatively flat meadow areas; forest map available (50¢). Information: District Ranger, Cloudcroft Ranger District, Box 288, Cloudcroft, NM 88317. 505-682-2551. **Ski Cloud Country** (off US 82, 3 m E of Cloudcroft) offers ski touring; downhill ski facilities with day lodge, restaurant, snack bar; accommodations and dining at luxurious Cloudcroft Lodge. Information: Ski Cloud Country, Cloudcroft, NM 88317. 505-682-2511. Additional lodging, restaurants, and services in Cloudcroft.

ALBUQUERQUE: Sandia Peak Area of **Cibola National Forest** (E on US 66 to SR 14, then 13 m N via SR 14 and SR 44), 5 m of marked trails through spruce forest with open alpine meadows, suitable for beginner and intermediate skiers; average elevation of 10,450 ft; trails annually maintained by U.S. Forest Service and New Mexico Ski Touring Club; no trail fee, free trail map; rentals and instruction available in Albuquerque; 31,000 acres of Sandia Mountain have been designated as wilderness; inquire at Ranger Station for use permit; trails located near top terminal restaurant of Sandia Peak Tramway; unlimited lodging, restaurants, and services in Albuquerque. Information: District Ranger, Sandia Ranger District, Star Route Box 174, Tijeras, NM 87059. 505-281-3304.

CHAMA: Chama Pass Area (14 m N on SR 17 in Colorado; E of Antonito, CO) unlimited touring possibilites on many m of Forest Service trails and on open meadow areas; terrain varies from very east to most difficult with rolling foothills, mesalike mountains, great open meadow areas surrounded by aspen and pine forest, long downhills for telemark buffs; beautiful views of Chama Valley from the ridge; popular easy tours include: 3.5-m trail to Trujillo Meadows Reservoir and old area narrow-gauge railroad grade, parts of which are used for annual ski race; snowmobiles permitted, but tend to use separate areas; 10,000-ft elevation generally assures excellent snow conditions; access to area from plowed parking area at top of pass. Information: District Ranger, La Jara Ranger District, Rio Grande National Forest, Monte Vista, CO 81144. **Edward Sargent Fish & Wildlife Area** (at northern town limits), 20,208 acres of rolling foothills with Forest Service roads and large open meadows suitable for novice to intermediate skiers; wilderness area with scenic backdrop of Chama Peak and surrounding mtns.; unused county road runs through area affording an open trail from which to launch an endless variety of tours; no snowmobiles permitted. Information: New Mexico Dept. of Fish & Game, Villagra Bldg., Santa Fe, NM 87107. Instruction, rental, and retail ski shops, variety of lodging, restaurants, and services in Chama; annual ski race held within town limits. For additional information on above areas: Iron Horse Trading Co., Chama, NM 87520. 505-756-2476.

SANTA FE: Santa Fe National Forest (E & W) has numerous areas with excellent cross-country skiing possibilities: **San Pedro Parks Wilderness Area** (10 m E of Cuba on SR 126), trail for intermediate to advanced skiers on unplowed forest road to wilderness boundary, then trails to large meadows on plateau, about 10 m one way; elevations range from 8500 to 10,000 ft. Information: District Ranger, Cuba Ranger District, Cuba, NM 87013. 505-289-3264. **Fenton Hill Area** (N of Jemez Springs), 7-m tour one way on unplowed roads along SR 4 between Jemez and Los Alamos for beginners to expert skiers; touring possibilities also in Redondo Campground and Jemez Falls areas. Information: District Ranger, Jemez Ranger District, Jemez Springs, NM 87025. 505-829-3535. **Pecos Wilderness Area** (E) has **Winsor Trail,** 5 m one way, on forested and open mountain slopes for expert skiers; elevations range from 10,300 to 11,040 ft; trailhead at Santa Fe Ski Area (on SR 475, 16 m NE), also good touring in nearby Peralta Canyon and Tesuque Peak areas. Information: District Ranger, Tesuque Ranger District, 1155 Siler R., Santa Fe, NM 87501. 505-988-6322. Permit needed to enter wilderness areas.

TAOS: Carson National Forest (hq on Cruz Alta Rd., S of town) a million acres of beautiful country with unlimited ski touring possibilities. Expert 4.5-m trail, one way, to Williams Lake in **Wheeler Peak Wilderness Area;** trail follows Forest Rd. 62 into high mountain area surrounded by 13,000-ft peaks; trail elevations range from 9460 to 11,140 ft; potential avalanche area; permit needed to enter Wilderness Area; trailhead at **Taos Ski Valley** (4 m N on US 64, then 15 m NE on SR 150), full-service resort area with downhill ski facilities, numerous accommodations, choice of restaurants and après-ski. (Information: Taos Ski Valley, Inc., Taos Ski Valley, NM 87571. 505-776-2266). **Columbine-Hondo Area** has tour for expert skiers on Forest Rd. 71 along Columbine Creek to either Forest Trail 69 or 72 to Gold Hill (12,711 ft) and Goose Lake area; trailhead and parking at Columbine Campground (E of Questa on SR 38). **Sawmill Park Area** has several intermediate trails: Forest Rd. 58 and Forest Trails 91 and 140 follow Middle Fork Red River to Middle Fork Lake; Forest Trails 56 and 55 follow

East Fork Red River to **Sawmill Park** featuring en route a beautiful m-long meadow along meandering trout stream; Forest Trail 56 continues to Lost Lake in Wheeler Peak Wilderness Area; trailhead and parking S of town of Red River at jct of Forest Rds. 58 and 58A. Good touring in **Latir Peaks Area** (E of Questa, N of SR 38), with high, rounded summits, broad meadows, and tiny lakes. Information and maps for above areas: District Ranger, Questa Ranger District, P.O. Box 110, Questa, NM 87556. 505-586-0520. Ski touring guides and instructors operate out of **Red River** (E of Questa on SR 38), a lively old gold mining town with **Red River Ski Area** (Box 303, Red River, NM 87558. 505-754-2223) and **Powder Puff Mountain Ski Area** (Box 786, Red River, NM 87558. 505-754-2941); wide choice of accommodations, restaurants, and night spots. Canjilon Ranger District (W of Taos; off US 84), recommends good cross-country skiing from SR 110 N to **Canjilon Lakes.** For maps and additional information: Forest Supervisor, Carson National Forest, P.O. Box 558, Taos, NM 87571.

NEW YORK

For additional information, contact the individual area or New York State Dept. of Commerce, Division of Tourism, 99 Washington Ave., Albany, NY 12245. Additional information on trails in Adirondacks and Catskill Forest Preserve and in State Forest and Wildlife Management Areas: New York State Dept. of Environmental Conservation (DEC abbreviation used in text), 50 Wolf Rd., Albany, NY 12233. Additional information on trails in state parks: New York State Dept. of Parks & Recreation, Albany, NY 12238.

ADIRONDACK PARK: Over 2-million-acre preserve with beautiful mountains and lakes, and spectacular scenery; offers numerous ski touring possibilities:

    Schroon Lake: Hoffman Notch Trail (via I-87 to Schroon Lake; W from village on Hoffman Rd. to Young's Rd. to Potash Hill Rd.), 7-m trail for intermediate skiers; terminates on northern end on road connecting North Hudson and Newcomb; stream crossings are not bridged. **Pharoah Lakes Wilderness Area Ski Trails** (northern perimeter entrance points approached via SR 74, NE of Schroon Lake; southern entrance via Pottersville to village of Adirondack), area has a network of trails that connect 22 small and large ponds; novice and intermediate scenic terrain with cliffs and ledges, plus many open areas due to effects of past forest fires. Information: DEC. **Wills Run Ski Touring & Hiking Trails** (off US 9 at south end of village on Hoffman Rd.), 20 m of marked and maintained, interconnecting trails for beginner to expert skiers; trails connect to Hoffman Notch Trail (see above); trail donation appreciated; free trail map; rentals, group and private instruction; scheduled events include 3–4-m pond tour, 4–5-m mountain tour, moonlight tours, and touring seminars; no snowmobiles; warming hut and waxing area, hot drinks and snacks; food and lodging in Schroon Lake (3 m). Information: Wills Run Ski Touring & Hiking, RD 1, Hoffman Rd., Schroon Lake, NY 12870. 518-532-7936.

Lake Placid: Mt. Van Hoevenberg Recreation Area (7 m E on SR 73), site of the 1980 Olympic cross-country and biathlon Nordic skiing events; about 20 m of trails laid out to international cross-country ski trail standards, designed for both formal races and recreational skiing, make this one of the best Nordic ski trail systems in the East; trails are laid out in interlocking loops so a tour of any length can be selected; all trails begin and terminate at the central stadium; an additional 32-m (50-km) trail constructed for the 1980 Olympic ski event; warming hut and waxing room; extensive parking facilities. Information: DEC. Nearby **Adirondak Loj** (8 m S off SR 73 at end of Adirondak Loj Rd.) has beginner and intermediate, marked and maintained trail system; trails connect to state trails, for experienced skiers, in **Adirondack High Peaks Wilderness Area;** flat to mountainous terrain with breathtaking views; no trail fee, free trail map; instruction and guided tours ($50 per day); no rentals; food and lodging at rustic Adirondak Loj (reservations recommended); plowed parking area ($1 per day, non-members); winter camping facilities include heated Campers and Hikers Bldg. with small trading post, 11 lean-tos and 45 tent sites; no snowmobiles; additional lodging, restaurants in Lake Placid. Information: The Adirondack Mountain Club, P.O. Box 867, Lake Placid, NY 12946. 518-523-3441. Or: 172 Ridge St., Glens Falls, NY 12801. 518-793-7737. **Upper Saranac Lake-Lake Clear Area** (19 m W via SR 86 to Lake Clear Junction, then 3 m

W on SR 30 to DEC's Saranac Inn hq; trails start just W of hq), area has several short novice loops on both sides of SR 30; a 5-m bridle path to Fish Pond, rated intermediate, has one steep spot. Information: DEC. **Lake Placid Club Resort** (I-87 to exit 30, then SR 9 and SR 73 to Lake Placid), 12 m of marked and groomed trails on over 800 acres; beginner to expert terrain includes golf course and wooded trails; trail fee ($1.50, except club guests); rentals, group and private instruction; guided tours can be arranged; ice skating (rentals), paddle tennis, squash; package plans offer food, lodging, and use of resort facilities including Mt. Whitney downhill ski area; a luxury resort with accommodations, gourmet dining, lounge, après-ski; conference rooms, shops. Information: Lake Placid Club Resort, Lake Placid, NY 12946. 518-523-3361. **Bark Eater Lodge** (16 m E via SR 73 at Keene), extensive trail system plus access to miles of untracked wilderness; rentals, sales and instruction; lodge accommodations and home-cooked food served family style; families and small groups welcome. Information: Bark Eater Lodge, Keene, NY 12942. 518-576-2221. **Whiteface Chalet** (10 m N on SR 86 in Wilmington), marked and maintained trails for novice to intermediate skiers; small trail fee; rentals and instruction; food and lodging. Information: Whiteface Chalet, Wilmington, NY 12997. 518-946-2207. **Paleface Lodge & Ski Center** (14 m NE on SR 86; 1 m W of Jay), 25 m of marked and maintained trails; many slight slopes and gentle forest trails for beginners to expert skiers; no trail fee, trail map available; no rentals; instruction and guided tours; cafeteria, bar, and lounge; motel accommodations; snowmobiles permitted; additional food and lodging in Wilmington (2 m). Information: Paleface Lodge & Ski Center, P.O. Box 163, Jay, NY 12941. 518-946-2272. **Mount Pisgah** (W on SR 86, on Trudeau Rd. at Saranac Lake), trails for cross-country skiers; downhill ski facilities; food and lodging in Saranac Lake. Information: Mount Pisgah Ski Area, Trudeau Rd., Saranac Lake, NY 12983. 518-891-1990. Other winter activities in Lake Placid include: indoor and outdoor ice skating, tobogganing, sleigh rides, downhill skiing, ski jumping, bobsledding/luge, snowmobiling, and scenic airplane flights. Cross-country ski rentals at Eastern Mountain Sports (on Main St. next to Hotel Marcy) and Equipe Sports (on Saranac Ave.). Variety of accommodations, restaurants, and services in Lake Placid, site of 1980 Winter Olympic Games. Additional information: Lake Placid Chamber of Commerce, Olympic Arena, Lake Placid, NY 12946. 518-523-2445.

North Creek: Siamese Ponds Wilderness Area (5 m NW on SR 28 to North River, then 1 m beyond is road to left marked for Thirteenth Lake and Garnet Hill Lodge), trail runs N to S along Thirteenth Lake, then follows Sacandaga River to SR 8, 10 m W of Wevertown; 2.5-m side trail to Siamese Ponds; S end of trail goes over shoulder of Eleventh Mtn., descent down N slope of mountain is steep and can be hazardous; rest of route, generally easy grades. Information: DEC. **Garnet Hill Lodge & Ski Touring Center** (same directions as above), 30 km of marked and groomed trails for novice to intermediate skiers; direct access to Adirondack Park trails; trail fee ($2, adults; $1, children), trail map available; rental and retail shop, snack bar in Ski Barn; group and private certified EPSTI instruction by appointment; guided tours; lodge accommodations, home-cooked meals, comfortable living room with massive garnet-stone fireplace. Information: Garnet Hill Lodge, North River, NY 12856. 518-251-2821. **Gore Mountain Ski Center** (off SR 28, 2 m S of North Creek), ½-m loop for novices, 4-m trail for intermediates, and 3-m, more challenging wilderness trail; trail maps available at main lodge; major downhill ski area with 2 day lodges, cafeteria, cocktail lounge; nursery; ice skating, toboggan and sled slope. Information: Gore Mountain Ski Center, North Creek, NY 12853. 518-251-2411. Area operated by NY State Dept. of Environmental Conservation. **Gore Mountain Ski Touring Center** (in North Creek), 25 km of beginner to expert, marked and maintained trails; trail fee ($2, adult; $1, junior 14 & under), trail map available; rental and retail shop; group and private instruction; brown-bag lunchroom, coffee available. Information: Gore Mountain Ski Touring Center, Cunningham's Ski Shop, Inc., Main St., North Creek, NY 12853. 518-251-2466. **Santanoni Preserve** (SR 28N to Newcomb), 5-m trail begins at barrier on N side of Lake Harris Inlet and leads to Camp Santanoni; another trail branches off and leads to Moose Pond; trails are woods roads suitable for intermediate skiers. Information: DEC. Food, lodging, and services in North Creek.

Northville: Northville-Lake Placid Trail, 132-m wilderness foot trail runs N from Northville and emerges from the forest a few m from Lake Placid; numerous sections are suitable for skiing; beginning at S end of trail, interesting tours for mostly intermediate skiers include: **Benson to Silver Lake Lean-to** (3.2 m N of Northville on SR 30 to Benson Rd., follow road 6 m to iron bridge, bear right on dirt road at a triangle where paved road turns sharply left, continue 1 m or as far as plowed road); round trip to Silver Lake is 12.6 m; a gentle continuous climb with just a few steep spots is rewarded with long downhill return tour. **South from Piseco** (N on SR 30 to Speculator, then W on SR 8; trail crosses SR 8 at Piseco just E of Piseco Central School), 8-m trail generally downhill to suspension bridge over Sacandaga River; elevation loss is about 600 ft, return trip is uphill. **North from Piseco,** trail is almost level for first 2.5 m, then trail ascends a wet-weather streambed which can be rocky; beyond this point, trail is generally level to Fall Stream crossing; next, trail climbs a series of upgrades, then descends to Jessup River, 7 m from Piseco; travel beyond Jessup River not recommended. **Stephens Pond, Cascade Pond, and Tirrell Pond** (trail crosses SR 30, 3 m E of Blue Mtn. Lake village): S of SR 30, trail leads to Cascade Pond and Rock Pond; N of SR 30, trail connects north end of Tirrell Pond and the Blue Mtn. Lake-Long Lake Hwy. Information: DEC.

   Old Forge: Big Otter Lake Truck Trail (2 m S on SR 28 at Thendara; turn W on dirt road just before the railroad bridge, park at the gate at end of road), interesting 8-m intermediate trail to Big Otter Lake; 4 possible short side tours. **McKeever Truck Trail** (S on SR 28 at McKeever; turn E on dirt road on S side of Moose River bridge), 6-m intermediate trail follows along South Branch of Moose River. **Third Lake to Limekiln Trail** (6 m NE on South Shore Rd.; trail begins ½ m SW of Petrie Rd.), 7-m tour on old logging roads and area trails from northern end of Third Lake to road system in Limekiln Lake Public Campsite; intermediate terrain. **Loop Trail Around Black Bear Mtn.** (N on SR 28 to Eagle Bay; from jct of Big Moose Rd. and SR 28, 1.25 m to marked trailhead), 2-m intermediate loop around eastern end of Black Bear Mtn.; trail returns to SR 28 about ½ m farther E from start. **Cascade Lake Trail** (1 m from Eagle Bay on Big Moose Rd.), 1-m tour to Cascade Lake; continuing around lake and back to start is 5-m round trip, recommended for intermediate skiers. Information: DEC. **McCauley Mountain Hiking and Touring Trails** (in Old Forge), 5.2-m trail around McCauley Mtn. and 4-m trail around Gray Lake; trails marked by red triangles nailed to trees; trail map available; downhill ski facilities with day lodge and cafeteria. Information: McCauley Mountain Ski Area, Old Forge, NY 13420. 315-369-3225. Nearby **Thendara Golf Course,** open to the public, is excellent beginner terrain. **Inlet Ski Touring Center** (just N of Old Forge on South Shore Rd.), over 50 m of marked and partly groomed wilderness trails adjacent to touring center; interconnecting trail system marked with color-coded markers; beginner to expert terrain; no trail fees; detailed map available; rental and retail shop; group and private instruction, guided tours; citizens' races; snowshoeing permitted; no snowmobiles; warm-up room; restaurant (½ m). Information: Inlet Ski Touring Center, Walter C. Schmid, South Shore Rd., Inlet, NY 13360. 315-357-3453. For additional information, snow conditions, or accommodations: Tourist Information Center, Old Forge, NY 13420. 315-369-6983.

Tupper Lake: Cold River Horse Trail (6 m E on SR 3 to Wawbeek Corners, pass Panther Pond, and turn S on Ampersand Rd.), 30-m horse trail system with grades and widths suitable for skiing; many parts of trail system require endurance, skill, and favorable snow conditions, although numerous in and out tours possible; 10-m tour to Racquette Falls popular intermediate route. **Five Ponds Wilderness Area** (W via SR 3; 8 m W of Cranberry Lake, then 2 m S to village of Wanakena), remote area with about 40 m of trails for experienced skiers with winter survival training; a 9-m loop is possible in combination with High Fall truck trail, a mostly level route, and blue-marked Leary Trail with a number of ups and downs, tour rated expert. Information: DEC. **Big Tupper Ski Area** (off SR 30, 2 m S of Tupper Lake), 3.7-m and 3-m trails for cross-country skiers; rentals; downhill ski facilities with day lodge, cafeteria, and cocktail lounge. Information: Big Tupper Ski Area, P.O. Box 820, Tupper Lake, NY 12986. 518-359-3651. Lodging: Chamber of Commerce, Tupper Lake, NY 12986.

Warrensburg: Warren County Cross-Country Ski Trail (exit 23 off I-87; N via US 9 and County Rd. 40 in Warrensburg), 10 m of marked interconnecting trails for novice to expert skiers; parking lot, picnic area, restrooms. Information: Warren County Tourism Dept., Municipal Building, Lake George, NY 12845. 518-792-9951, ext. 245. Snow report: 518-793-1300.

ALBANY: Five Rivers Environmental Education Center (SW on SR 443 in Delmar; entrance sign 1 m past Bethlehem Central School), North Loop Trail suitable for novice skiers; trail map and brochure describing animal tracks available at trailhead; trails open daily (8:30 am–4:45 pm), center's buildings with interpretive displays and lectures open weekdays. **Rensselaerville State Forest** (SW via SR 85 and SR 359 near Rensselaerville), extensive, open pine forest glades offer about 4 m of skiing for beginners; glades parallel a forest road. **Partridge Run Wildlife Management Area** (SR 85 to

Rensselaerville, then 3 m N on SR 6 to SR 13), 8 m of marked trails and roads suitable for novice skiers; separate snowmobile trails; skiers should not use area during big-game hunting season. **Featherstonhaugh State Forest** (9 m W of Schenectady off Lake Rd. near Mariaville) has 2-m loop on flat terrain and a second loop on slightly hilly terrain. Information for above areas: DEC. **John Boyd Thacher State Park** (15 m SW via SR 85 & SR 157), novice to intermediate trails on wooded, rolling, and lakeside terrain; ice skating, sled and toboggan slopes; snowmobiles in designated areas. **Thompson's Lake State Park** (SW; 3 m W of Thacher on SR 157), flat beginner terrain; ice skating, sledding, ice fishing; snowmobiles in designated areas; camping area. **Grafton Lakes State Park** (12 m E of Troy on SR 2), wooded rolling and lakeside terrain; ice skating, ice fishing; snowmobiles in designated areas. Information on above 3 parks: NY State Dept. of Parks & Recreation. **Beresford Farms Ski Touring Center** (20 m W; NY Thruway exit 24, US 20 W to Duanesburg, then 2.5 m S off SR 7 on Chadwick Rd.), 800 acres of beginner to advanced marked trails on rolling farmland with stands of mixed hardwoods; trails groomed with track set, 5 m of trails have 2 sets of parallel tracks; 2 m of trails lighted; trail fee ($2), trail map available; rental and retail shop, instruction, waxing and racing clinics, citizens' races, dogsled races, ice skating, tobogganing; The Horse Barn offers homemade soups, charcoal-grilled hot food, and big fireplace. Food and lodging in Duanesburg. Information: Beresford Farms, RD 1, Delanson, NY 12053. 518-895-2345. **Trail North's Apple Barn** (N on I-87 to SR 146, then N on Barns Rd. to Focastle Farms), marked and groomed trails with track set on 180 acres of rolling orchard; trail fee ($1.50); rentals and instruction (group rates); waxing clinics; restaurant (specialty is homemade apple pie), country store, fudge shop, and boutique. Information: Trail North, 895, New Loudon Rd., Latham, NY 12110. 518-785-0340. Touring center: 518-399-6111.

BUFFALO: Alpine Recreation Area Ski Touring Center (SE on SR 240 at West Falls), 10 m of marked and groomed, interconnecting trails on beginner to advanced terrain; 60-acre area for open field skiing; trail fee ($2, adult; $1, junior), trail map available; rental and retail shop; group and private instruction; moonlight tours, sleigh rides, ice-skating rink, winter picnic facilities; warming lodge with fireplace. Information: Alpine Recreation Area, 298 Ellicott Rd., West Falls, NY 14170. 716-662-1400. **The Nordic Way at Colden Langlauf Trails** (35 m SE via I-90 to SR 400 to Maple St.

to Center Rd.), 7 m of marked and groomed trails with track set; beginner to advanced terrain of open and forested rolling hills with streams and bridges; trail fee ($2, adult; $1, children under 11), trail map available; rental and retail shop; instruction; guided tours include moonlight tour with basic instruction and tour to Holland Village with return transportation; restaurant, bar, brown-bag lunchroom; snowmobiles on multiple-use trail; motels and restaurants nearby. Information: The Nordic Way, 8536 Center Rd., Holland, NY 14080. 716-941-6675 or 6676.

CAMDEN: Erie Bridge Inn (I-90 exit 34, N on SR 13 to Camden, then N on Main St. to Oswego St., then 1 m to Florence Hill Rd.), marked and maintained, beginner to expert trails on 160 acres with access to adjoining **Mad River State Park** trails; heavily wooded rolling terrain with beautiful views and lots of snow; trail fee ($2), trail map available; rental and retail shop, instruction; lodge accommodations with breakfast and dinner, homemade breads a specialty; snack bar; no snowmobiles. Information: Erie Bridge Inn, Florence Hill Rd., Camden, NY 13316. 315-245-1555.

CATSKILL: North Lake Ski Trails (W on 23A to Haines Falls, then N on road to North Lake Public Campsite; at 2.2 m a sign will mark road to Kaaterskill Falls, then 1 m to parking lot), 19th-century carriage roads plus trails at campsite suitable for novice skiers; escarpment trail should be used with caution particularly on south-facing exposures where the edges may be icy. **Overlook Mountain Ski Route** (SW via County Rd. 16 to Platte Clove, then S on Prediger Rd., trail starts at end of road; or SR 212 to Woodstock, then 2.5 m N on County Rd. 33 and Meads Mountain Rd.), old 7.6-m road over Overlook Mountain connected Tannersville with Meads and Woodstock; northern end suitable for intermediate skiers, southern end continuously steep and rated expert. Information on above trails: DEC. **Cortina Valley Ski Area** (W off SR 23A), 10 m of marked and groomed, novice to expert trails; trail fee ($2), trail map available; rentals and instruction; downhill ski facilities, day lodge serves hot and cold food; no snowmobiles; motel accommodations at area, restaurants nearby. Information: Cortina Valley Ski Area, P.O. Box 287, Haines Falls, NY 12436. 518-589-6500. **White Birches Ski Touring Center** (W on SR 23 at Windham), 15 m of marked and groomed trails with track set; ski patrol; rental and retail shop; instruction; citizens' races; warm-up lodge with fireplaces. Information: White Birches Ski Touring Center, Windham, NY 12496. 518-734-3266.

COBLESKILL: Petersburg State Forest (5 m S via County Rd. 4 from Warnerville), about 3 m of unmarked roads and lanes wind through forest; intermediate terrain. **Leonard Hill State Forest** (S via SR 145, SR 30 and County Rd. 17 to Broome Center, then Sarbrucher Rd. 1.5 m E to Gilboa town line sign; directly opposite is woods road to forest), 3-m intermediate tour to fire tower; many overlooks en route and outstanding view from fire tower. Information: DEC.

CORTLAND: James B. Kennedy Memorial Forest (8 m S; access via SR 90, SR 131, and SR 132), about 10 m of trails and unplowed town roads; hilly terrain, rated intermediate to expert, with a few steep spots. Information: DEC. Directly N of state forest is **Greek Peak Ski Area** (off SR 90 near Virgil), 27 m of marked and maintained beginner to expert trails; open and wooded terrain; no trail fee, map available; rentals, instruction and guided tours; downhill ski facilities, 2 day lodges, cafeteria, restaurant, dining room, country store; townhouse and condominium accommodations; snowmobiles in designated areas. Information: Greek Peak Ski Area, RD 2, Courtland, NY 13045. 607-835-6111. Snow report: 607-835-3615. **Fillmore Glen State Park** (NW on SR 38; 1 m S of Moravia), suitable terrain for cross-country skiing, although no marked trails. Information: N.Y. State Dept. of Parks & Recreation.

DANSVILLE: High Tor Wildlife Management Area (NE off SR 21, just E of Naples), about 8 m of trails on hilly intermediate terrain with outlooks of Canandaigua Lake; separate designated snowmobile trails. **Rattlesnake Hill Wildlife Management Area** (6 m W on SR 436, then ¾ m SW on Shute Rd., then S on Wallsworth Rd. 1 m to parking lot), about 6 m of interconnecting loops on woods roads and trails; gently rolling intermediate terrain on top of a plateau with nice overlooks. Skiers should not use above areas during big-game hunting season. Information: DEC. **Stony Brook State Park** (3 m S on SR 36), suitable terrain for cross-country skiing, although there are no marked trails. Information: N.Y. State Dept. of Parks & Recreation. **Swain Ski Area** (SW via SR 36 & SR 70 at Swain), trails for cross-country skiers; downhill ski facilities, day lodge, cafeteria, restaurant, nursery. Information: Swain Ski Area, Swain, NY 14884. 607-545-6511.

GLENS FALLS: Glen Falls International Cross-Country Ski Trail (exit 19 off I-87; in Crandall Park on Upper Glen St. in Glens

Falls), designated as a National Recreation Trail by the Dept. of the Interior; 6 m of marked and groomed trails with track set daily; novice to intermediate terrain on heavily forested area; some trails lighted for night skiing (daily 7 am–11 pm); no trail fee, trail map available; free instruction offered in weekly recreational classes; fun races every Wed. night; site of the Glens Falls International Ski Race; children's rentals and lessons; guided tours; plowed parking area. Information: City of Glens Falls Recreation Dept., City Hall, 42 Ridge St., Glens Falls, NY 12801. 518-792-3141, ext. 45. **Moreau Lake State Park** (exit 17S off I-87 in South Glens Falls), trails on flat open terrain suitable for novice skiers; rentals and instruction available on weekends and holidays; winter camping. Information: N.Y. State Dept. of Parks & Recreation. **Queensbury Country Club** (N on SR 9L at jct of SR 149), marked and groomed trails for novice to advanced skiers; rentals; warm-up area by Franklin fireplace; home-cooked food and cocktails in clubhouse; game room. Information: Queensbury Country Club, Inc., RD 1, Lake George, NY 12845. 518-793-3711. Variety of accommodations, restaurants, and services in Glens Falls/Lake George area; information: Warren County Publicity, Municipal Center, Lake George, NY 12845. 518-792-9951, ext. 245.

HUDSON: Olana State Historic Site (5 m S on SR 9G), 19th-century home of landscape painter Frederick Edwin Church has 7 m of marked carriage trails that wind through woods and over fields of 400-acre site; hilly terrain overlooking the Hudson River is suitable for beginner to intermediate skiers; area of lake cleared for ice skating; open daily 9 am–4 pm. **Clermont State Historic Park** (S on SR 9G; N of Tivoli), trails for novice to intermediate skiers. **Taconic State Park** (E via SR 23 and SR 22; SE off SR 22 at Copake Falls), marked trails and old logging roads wind through park; trails connect to other area trails including Appalachian Trail; hilly to mountainous terrain along state line, suitable for intermediate to expert skiers; snowmobiling in designated areas. Information: N.Y. State Dept. of Parks & Recreation. **Beebe Hill State Forest** (NE via SR 23 & SR 22 to Austerlitz, just beyond village, turn left on Osmer Rd., continue 1.6 m to Barrett Pond; woods road W to forest is just beyond pond), about 3 m of marked trails in forest; because of some steep pitches, area is rated expert. Information: DEC.

ITHACA: Connecticut Hill Wildlife Management Area (13 m W on SR 13, then N on Carter Creek Rd.), area on top of a steep-sided plateau with numerous interconnecting, unplowed woods roads; most roads are unmarked and skill in map reading is necessary; area generally rated expert with just 1 novice route; valley approach roads, usually unplowed, allow the chance for a long downhill run back to the car from the top of the plateau area; skiers should not use area during big-game hunting season. Information: DEC. **Buttermilk Falls State Park** (2 m S on SR 13) and **Robert H. Treman State Park** (5 m SW on SR 13) offer rolling wooded terrain for novice skiers; sled and toboggan slopes; snowmobiles permitted. **Taughannock Falls State Park** (8 m N on SR 89) has a 4.2-m multi-use trail; large sledding hill. Information for above 3 parks: N.Y. State Dept. of Parks & Recreation. **Podunk Cross-Country Ski Center** (NW via SR 96; on Podunk Rd. in Trumansburg), 10–12 m of marked trails with access to nearby state and federal lands; trail maps available; rental and retail shop has Finnish equipment; EPSTI-certified instruction; ski films, citizens' races; lodge with wood-burning stove, snacks and hot drinks, brown-bag lunch area. Information: Osmo O. Heila, Podunk Cross-Country Ski Shop, RD 1, Podunk Rd., Trumansburg, NY 14886. 607-387-6716.

JAMESTOWN: The Chautauqua West Trail is a 15-m-long marked footpath extending from North Harmony State Forest on the south (W via SR 474; 1 m W of Panama), to Mt. Pleasant State Forest on the north (2.5 m SW of Mayville on SR 430); generally flat terrain suitable for novice skiers; trail is marked where it intersects major highways. Information: DEC. **Peek'n Peak Ski Center** (E via SR 474, then N off SR 426, S of Finley Lake), 15 m of marked and groomed interconnecting trails for novice to advanced skiers; trail fee ($1.50, adults; $1, children 12 & under), trail map available; rental and retail shop; group and private instruction (learn-to-ski package; lessons and tours include daily trail fee); half-day, full-day and overnight tours for intermediate to advanced skiers; year-round luxury resort with elegant Old English atmosphere; downhill ski facilities, 2 day lodges, cafeterias; lodging, dining room, pub, entertainment, coffee shop; indoor pool, sauna, indoor tennis; no snowmobiles. Information: Peek'n Peak Ski Center, Box 100, Clymer, NY 14724. 716-355-4141.

KINGSTON: Slide Mountain Trail (best reached from the South via US 209 to Ellenville, then SR 55 to Curry; at Curry, turn N on County Rd. 19 and go about 5 m to intersection of Claryville Rd. and West Branch Rd., take left fork and follow West Branch Rd. about 13 m to Winisook Lake; trail departs to right and is marked with DEC sign), follow yellow trail markers about .9 m, then take left fork and follow red markers up Slide Mtn.; 2.9-m trail to summit (4180-ft elevation) is an old jeep road part of the way; ascent to top is recommended for skiers experienced in ski mountaineering. At .9-m fork (see above) continue to follow yellow markers to right for **Claryville Trail;** 4-m trail climbs from 2000 ft at Winisook Lake through a pass SW of Slide Mtn. at 3100 ft and follows East Branch River down to end of Denning Rd. N of Claryville at 2100 ft; route recommended for intermediate skiers (to reach S end of trail, at intersection of Claryville Rd. and West Branch Rd., turn right on Claryville Rd. and continue about 7 m to end; road name changes to Denning Rd.). **Stissing Mountain State Forest** (on E side of Hudson River; SR 199 E off Taconic State Pky., ½ m to County Rd. 53 S, continue 3 m to Hicks Hill Rd., then ½ m on Hicks Hill Rd. to parking area), multiple-use area has skiable woods roads; hilly terrain suitable for novices. Information: DEC. **Belleayre Mt. Ski Center** (exit 19 off I-87 at Kingston, 38 m W on SR 28 to Highmount, then follow signs ½ m to ski area), about 3 m of marked trails at ski area on semiflat to mountainous terrain for novice to expert skiers; access to many m of marked hiking trails in surrounding Catskill Park; no trail fee, map available; rentals; certified EPSTI group and private instruction, 2-hour lesson combining intensive instruction with guided tour recommended for beginners (lesson reservations advised); guided tours offered; major downhill ski facilities operated by DEC; 3 day lodges, cafeterias, nursery, ski shop; no snowmobiles. Information: Belleayre Mtn. Ski School, Pine Hill, NY 12465. 914-254-5601. Snow report: 914-254-5600. Public transportation via Adirondack-Pine Hill Trailways to Highmount. Accommodations: Central Catskill Association, Fleischmanns, NY 12430.

    Frost Valley YMCA (W via SR 28 to Big Indian, then 15 m S on County Rd. 47; from S, SR 17 to Liberty, N on SR 55 to Curry, then N via County Rds. 19 & 47), 35 m of interconnecting, marked, and maintained trails on 2200 acres in the center of the Catskill Park Preserve; several m of trails regularly groomed with track set; varied terrain for beginner to expert skiers from flat open fields to heavily wooded mountain trails with overlooks and waterfalls; many m of streamside trails along legendary Neversink River; access to many m of adjacent state trails; snow cover averages 4 months per year because of 2000-ft elevation; trail fee ($2.50), trail map available; rentals; free instruction for beginners and intermediates; guided tours by reservation; ice skating, snowshoeing, tobogganing, ice hockey, astronomy (available to guests); no snowmobiles; wide range of accommodations includes cabins and 10 lodges with rooms, dormitories, and lounges; family-style meals in dining hall; package plans available. Public transportation via Shortline bus to Liberty or Trailways bus to Big Indian. Information: Frost Valley YMCA, Oliverea, NY 12462. 914-985-7400; nights: 914-985-7205. **Bobcat at Catskill Ski Center** (W on SR 28 to Andes, then follow signs 2.5 m to ski area), marked trails for cross-country skiers on beginner to expert terrain; rental and retail shop; group and private instruction, guided tours; trail fee ($2.50), trail map available; downhill ski facilities, day lodge, cafeteria, cocktail lounge; no snowmobiles; accommodations, restaurants in Andes (2.5 m). Information: Bobcat at Catskill Ski Center, Bovina Center, NY 13740. 914-676-3143. **Williams Lake Hotel** (S of Kingston; exit 18 off I-87, SR 32 N to SR 213, then W to Binnewater Rd., then N), 10 m of marked and maintained trails on varied rolling terrain for beginner to advanced skiers; rentals and instruction; trail fee ($3, except hotel guests), trail map available; downhill ski slope, ski jumps, ice skating, tobogganing; no snowmobiles; year-round resort hotel, American plan, entertainment. Public transportation via Adirondack Trailways to Rosendale. Information: Williams Lake Hotel, Rosendale, NY 12472. 914-658-3101. **Hidden Valley Lake Ski Touring Trails** (S of Kingston; exit 18 of I-87, 8 m N on SR 32 to Rosendale Shopping Center, then at top of hill past center, turn left to County Rd. 26, turn left again and keep right on Whiteport Rd. 1.5 m), many m of marked and groomed trails with track set; Nordic ski patrol; night skiing; rentals and instruction; workshops and safety clinics; guided tours and moonlight tours; citizens' races; group dormitory accommodations with food on weekends; campgrounds, heated restrooms. Information: Outdoor Inns, Inc. C.P.O. Box 190, Kingston, NY 12401. 914-338-4616.

LE ROY: Frost Ridge (exit 47 off I-90, ½ m S on SR 19, ½ m E on North Rd. to Conlon Rd.; 19 m W of Rochester), about 5 km of marked trails on 350 acres of gently rolling, open and wooded farmland; rentals, instruction, guided tours; downhill ski facilities, day lodge with cafeteria and pub; limited snowmobiles; winter camping (50 sites). Information: Frost Ridge Recreation Area, Conlon Rd., LeRoy, NY 14482. 716-768-9730.

LONG ISLAND: Bethpage State Park (37 m E of NYC via Southern State & Bethpage Pkys.), golf course with flat and rolling terrain suitable for novice to intermediate skiers; downhill ski slope with tow; sledding. Information: 516-249-0701. **Caumsett State Park** (42 m E of NYC; on West Neck Rd., 7 m N of Huntington), rolling, wooded novice to intermediate terrain overlooking Long Island Sound; naturalist programs by reservation. **Connetquot River State Park** (on SR 27, 50 m E of NYC), many m of touring possibilities on flat wooded terrain; naturalist programs by reservation. **Heckscher State Park** (50 m E of NYC via Southern State & Heckscher Pkys.), wooded flat scenic novice terrain on Great South Bay. Information: 516-581-2100. **Nissequogue River State Park** (50 m E of NYC on SR 25 in Smithtown), wooded novice terrain with hiking and fire trails suitable for cross-country skiers; naturalists lead tours. **Sunken Meadow State Park** (46 m E of NYC via Northern State & Sunken Meadow State Pkys. in Kings Park), scenic terrain on the Sound. **Wildwood State Park** (73 m E of NYC on SR 25-A in Wading River), rolling wooded terrain for novice to intermediate skiers; overlooks of the Sound. For more information and schedule of programs: Long Island State Park and Recreation Commission, Belmont Lake State Park, Babylon, NY 11702. 516-669-1000.

Nassau County Parks open to cross-country skiers include: Christopher Morley Park (in Roslyn), North Woodmere Park (in Woodmere), Grant Park (in Hewlett), Bay Park (in East Rockaway), Cow Meadow Park (in Freeport), Wantagh Park (in Wantagh), Eisenhower Park (in East Meadow), Cantiague Park (in Hicksville). For additional information and events: 516-292-4288. **Suffolk County Parks** do not permit skiing on bridle trails because trails are used throughout winter for horseback riding. Several public golf courses are open to cross-country skiers. Information: Suffolk County Dept. of Parks & Recreation, 516-567-1700.

MASSENA: Robert Moses State Park (NE of town; 2 m N on SR 37 on an island on the St. Lawrence Seaway), 14 m of marked and maintained trails; gentle open and wooded novice terrain;

special events and weekend treasure hunts; sledding area, snow-mobiles in designated areas; picnic area, warming station, restrooms. Information: Massena Chamber of Commerce, Inc., P.O. Box 387, Massena, NY 13662. 315-769-3525 or 315-769-8663 (weekends).

MONTICELLO: The Concord Hotel Ski Touring Center (on SR 42; 2 m N off SR 17 at Monticello), 1-m and ¼-m beginner trails, ¾-m intermediate trail, and 3-m advanced trail; marked and groomed trails laid out on golf course; trail fee ($5; hotel guests, $2.50), trail map available; rentals, group and private instruction, guided tours; snowshoeing (rentals, instruction, and marked trails); snowmobiling on set course; indoor and outdoor ice skating (rentals and lessons), 820-ft tobogganing run; downhill ski facilities; chalet, cafeteria, lounge; 1425-room year-round resort hotel, American plan; children's program, teen activities; health clubs; night clubs; meeting and banquet rooms; package plans. Public transportation via Shortline bus. Information: The Concord Hotel, Kiamesha Lake, NY 12751. 914-794-4000.

NEWBURGH: Orange County Ski Area (W; off SR 416, 2.5 m S of Montgomery), 2 m of groomed trails for beginner to intermediate skiers on Stony Ford Golf Course; no trail fee, map available; rentals and instruction (student and group rates); ice skating on 1-acre rink and lighted 6-acre pond, snowshoeing, tobogganing; downhill ski facilities; snowmobiles on separate trail; snack bar in Golf/Ski Center bldg. Information: Orange County Ski Area, RD 3, Rt. 416, Montgomery, NY 12549. 914-457-3000.

NEW PALTZ: Mohonk Mountain House (exit 18 off I-87, W on SR 299 at Lake Mohonk), over 100 m of trails, 54 m marked and maintained; beginner to expert terrain in Shawangunk Mtn. Range with panoramic views; trail fee ($3), trail map available; rentals and instruction; guided tours for hotel guests; no snowmobiles; trailhead lodge and limited lunch for day guests; old Victorian mansion has capacity for 350 guests, American plan. Public transportation via Trailways bus to New Paltz, hotel limousine pickup. Information: Mohonk Mountain House, Lake Mohonk, New Paltz, NY 12561. 914-255-1000; NYC: 212-233-2244. **Lake Minnewaska Ski Touring Center** (exit 18 off I-87, SR 299 W to US 44 & SR 55), access to 150 m of trails in Shawangunk Mtns.; 15 m of marked and groomed trails for beginner to expert skiers; trail fee ($5, Sat., Sun.;

$3.50, Mon.–Fri.), trail map available; rentals, group and private instruction; special midweek Learn-to-Ski Program; scheduled touring workshops; annual citizens' race; accommodations in charming old-fashioned hotel with wood-burning fireplace in most guest rooms, dining room, Wine Cellar. Public transportation to New Paltz, hotel limousine pickup. Information: Lake Minnewaska Resort, Lake Minnewaska, NY 12561. 914-255-6000. **Hudson Valley Winery** (exit 18 off I-87, SR 299 E to US 9W S, then follow signs), about 15 m of marked trails wind through the winery's vineyards and woods; beginner to expert terrain with Hudson River views; admission fee ($4, adults; $3, children), includes tours of wine cellars and tasting; rentals and lessons; open weekends. Information: Hudson Valley Winery, Highland, NY 12528. 914-691-7296. **Nevele Country Club** (exit 17 off I-87, W on SR 52 to Ellenville), 1000 acres of rolling terrain with lake, waterfalls, and wooded areas; no marked trails; rentals and instruction, guided tours; chalet, restaurant, coffee shop; accommodations at area. Information: Nevele Country Club, Ellenville, NY 12428. 914-647-6000.

OLEAN: Phillips Creek State Forest (E via SR 17 & SR 244; 9 m E of Belmont), 7 m of marked trails and woods roads for novice skiers; sign with trail layout located at entrance. Information: DEC. **Allegany State Park** (W via SR 17; 7 m of Salamanca), marked and maintained trails on gently rolling, wooded terrain; many m of hiking trails in park suitable for intermediate to advanced skiers; parking and trailhead at Bova Ski Slope Area; ice skating; snowmobiles in designated areas; winter camping. Information: N.Y. State Dept. of Parks & Recreation.

PALISADES INTERSTATE PARK is in several sections on W side of Hudson River N of NYC. **Harriman State Park** (35 m N of NYC via Palisades Interstate Pky.), marked trails on wooded rolling terrain suitable for novice to intermediate skiers; snowmobiles in designated areas. **Bear Mountain State Park** (45 m N of NYC via Palisades Interstate Pky.), many m of marked trails suitable for novice to intermediate skiers; **Appalachian Trail** crosses Bear Mtn. Bridge and passes through park; downhill ski facilities at **Silver Mine Ski Area** with day lodge and food service; ski jump, ice skating, sledding available in park. **Rockland Lake State Park** (18 m N of NYC via US 9W), trails on wooded terrain with overlooks of Hudson River; ice skating and sledding. Information: Palisades

Interstate Park Commission, Bear Mtn. State Park, Bear Mtn., NY 10911. 914-786-2701.

POTSDAM: High Flats State Forest (S on SR 56 to Colton, then cross Raquette River and continue about 3.5 m on Colton-Parish-ville Rd., turn SE on Rodwell Mill Rd., then left on Crowley Rd., parking area and lodge at end of road), marked intermediate ski trail leads into state forest; return loop possible via unplowed French Hill Rd.; trail maintained by Clarkson College and open to the public. Information: DEC.

SARATOGA SPRINGS: Saratoga Mt. Ski Touring Center (exit 13N off I-87; at **Saratoga Spa State Park**), 2000 acres with about 20 m of marked and groomed trails; beginner to intermediate terrain on rolling open and wooded areas with brook, geysers, and springs; all park facilities are open to the public free; the touring center, owned and operated by the Farra family, is located in golf club-house; retail and rental shop; group and private lessons by EPSTI instructors; special ski activities include movies, lectures, demon-strations, moonlight tours, NASTAR races, Bill Koch League weekly races for ages 8–16, annual Saratoga Skinny Skis Ski Race on Washington's Birthday weekend; ice-skating rink, warming room, restrooms, picnic area; food and lodging in park at beautiful Gideon Putman Hotel (Winter Ski Package; 518-584-3000); wide variety of accommodations and restaurants in Saratoga Springs. Public transportation via Amtrak and Trailways bus. Information: Ron Farra Family, Saratoga Mtn. Ski Touring Center, Saratoga Spa State Park, Saratoga Springs, NY 12866. 518-584-2008 or 584-2256.

SHERBURNE: The Brookfield Horse Trails is an extensive trail system of about 130 m; 2 recommended sections for skiers include: **Vidler Road Loop** (NE via SR 80 & SR 8 to Brookfield; .8 m E of Brookfield on Skaneateles Turnpike, than 1.6 m N on Vidler Rd.), 5-m intermediate trail with some steep spots which can be taken in a climbing direction by touring in a clockwise direction. **Fairground Road Loop** (3 m N from Brookfield on Fairground Rd.), another 5-m intermediate loop; clockwise direction recommended to avoid steep downhill run on NE part of trail. **Albert J. Woodford Memorial Forest** (N on SR 12 to Sangerfield, then 2.5 m E on US 20 to Janus Rd. and DEC sign), many unplowed town roads, truck trails, and skiable lanes through forested area; gently rolling terrain suitable for novice skiers. Information: DEC. **The Rogers Environmental Education Center** (1 m W of Sherburne on SR 80), many walking paths and trails open to novice skiers; information, programs, interpretive brochures, trail maps at center buildings (open Mon–Fri. and noon–5 pm Sat. & Sun.). Information: Rogers Environmental Education Center, Box Q, Sherburne, NY 13460.

SYRACUSE: Green Lakes State Park (10 m E via SR 290 or SR 5), rolling wooded terrain suitable for intermediate skiers; ice skating, sled and toboggan slope; snowmobiles in designated area; campground with outdoor toilets. Information: N.Y. State Dept. of Parks & Recreation. **90 Acres Ski Center** (8 m E; 1 m E of Fayetteville on SR 5), 7 m of marked and groomed trails for novice to advanced skiers on 80 acres of open and wooded rolling terrain; access to 300-acre state park; trail fee ($1.50), trail map available; rentals; EPSTI-certified instruction (3-lesson package); guided tours; downhill ski facilities, day lodge; indoor tennis, platform tennis; bar and lounge; no snowmobiles. Information: 90 Acres Ski Center, 8012 E. Genesee St., Fayetteville, NY 13066. 315-637-9023. **Toggenburg** (SE via SR 91 to Fabius, then E off SR 80), trails for cross-country skiers; downhill ski facilities, day lodge, cafeteria, nursery. Information: Toggenburg Ski Area, Fabius, NY 13063. 315-683-5842. **Country Hills Farm** (S via I-81; on North Rd. near jct of I-81 & I-90), 18 m of marked and groomed trails with track set; some lighted trails for night skiing; open and wooded rolling hills with maple and pine forest; trail fee ($2; special family rates available), trail map; rental and retail shop; EPSTI-certified instructors; ski clinics, citizens' races, Christmas camp (4 days of skiing, winter camping, and winter ecology study), snowshoe class (how to make your own); lodge accommodations, cafeteria, dining room; no snowmobiles. Information: Country Hills Farm, Tully, NY 13159. 315-696-8774.

TURIN: Lesser Wilderness State Forest (N on SR 26 to Houseville, then W on Carpenter Rd.; trail entrance is at top of steep rise after hairpin turn; park on shoulder of road), marked trails and woods roads have gentle grades suitable for novice skiers; located on E edge of Tug Hill Plateau, forest receives heavy snowfall and season begins early and lasts until last spring. Information: DEC. **Whetstone Gulf State Park** (N off SR 26), hilly wooded terrain for novice to expert skiers; no trails; heated shelter. Information: N.Y. State Dept. of Parks and Recreation. **Snow Ridge Ski Area** (off SR 26 N of Turin), 6 m of marked and groomed trails along top of ridge with spectacular views of the Black River Valley; access to unlimited skiing on surrounding state land; beginner to expert terrain; no trail fee, map available; rentals and instruction; downhill ski facilities, day lodge, cafeteria, restaurant, bar, entertainment; nursery; no snowmobiles; lodging, restaurants at area and nearby; package plans. Information: Snow Ridge Ski Area, Turin, NY 13473. 315-348-8456; toll free (N.Y. State): 800-962-8419.

WATERTOWN: Tug Hill State Forest (S via I-81; on SR 177, 5.5 m E of Rodman and 2 m W of Barnes Corners), access from small green storage shed on N side of SR 177; 3 trails of 2.2 m, 1 m, and 1.8 m form a figure-8 shape; novice terrain. Information: DEC.

WHITE PLAINS: Ward Pound Ridge Reservation (NE near Connecticut state line; on SR 121 near jct of SR 35 at Cross River), 4500-acre area with 3 interconnecting loops of 2 m, 4 m, and 6 m on varied open and wooded terrain for beginner to advanced skiers; trails marked with color-coded signs; no trail fee, trail map available; parking fee ($1 residents; $2 nonresidents); sledding, tobogganing, snowshoeing; snowmobiles on designated trails; winter camping in specific shelters. Information: Superintendent, Ward Pound Ridge Reservation, Cross River, NY 10518. 914-763-3493.

NORTH CAROLINA

For additional information, contact the individual area or North Carolina Division of Travel and Tourism, Dept. of Commerce, 430 North Salisbury St., Raleigh, NC 27611.

BLUE RIDGE PARKWAY, a mountaintop drive with an average elevation of 3000 ft, extends from Virginia SW through Asheville to Cherokee; numerous overlooks with spectacular views; entire pkwy is a potential ski touring trail; skiers permitted to use sections closed to vehicles. Sections apt to be closed due to snow conditions include: (NE of Asheville) Craggy Gardens and Mt. Mitchell area,

Blowing Rock sections; (SW of Asheville) Mt. Pisgah area, Soco Gap. Information: Park Ranger, Blue Ridge Parkway, 700 North-western Bank Bldg., Asheville, NC 28801.

GREAT SMOKY MOUNTAIN NATIONAL PARK (half in Tennessee) has Forest Service roads, old logging roads, and trails suitable for cross-country skiing, snow permitting. Deep Creek and Nolan Creek Rds. (N off US 19 at Bryson City) offer good tours; Kephart Prong Trail near the Oconaluftee Ranger Station is recommended; the road from Smokemont Campground (off US 441) to Towstring Rd. down along the Oconaluftee River is a good beginner tour; Clingmans Dome road off US 441 on the state line is very popular (see Tennessee). The Park Service requires chains for driving in the park during extreme conditions. Information: Superintendent, Great Smoky Mountain National Park, Gatlinburg, TN 37738. Oconaluftee Ranger Station: 704-497-3081.

MT. MITCHELL STATE PARK (34 m NE of Asheville), with the highest peak in Eastern America, has good cross-country ski terrain with many trails and old logging roads; access is via the Blue Ridge Parkway, which may be closed to vehicles. Information: Superintendent, Mt. Mitchell State Park, Rt. 5, Box 400, Burnsville, NC 28714. 704-675-4611.

WESSER: Nantahala Outdoor Center has rental equipment (money refunded if no snow); instruction and guide service available; groups of 5 or more renting equipment get a guide free. For rental and accommodation information and snow conditions: Nantahala Outdoor Center, Wesser, NC 28713. 704-488-6407.

NORTH DAKOTA

For additional information, contact the individual area or North Dakota Travel Division, State Highway Dept., Bismarck, ND 58505.

BISMARCK: Fort Lincoln State Park (4 m S of Mandan on SR 1806), 2 m marked trail on the site of Custer's last headquarters before the disastrous Battle of Little Big Horn; reconstructed blockhouses and Slant Indian Village with earth lodges, occupied about 1750. Information: Superintendent, Fort Lincoln State Park, Mandan, ND 58554. 701-663-3049. **Lake Sakakawea State Park** (1 m N of Pick City), located on a peninsula on the south shore of the lake; 3-m cross-country ski trail runs through park's interpretive nature area; separate snowmobile area. Information: Superintendent, Lake Sakakawea State Park, Riverdale, ND 58565. 701-748-2313.

CAVALIER: Icelandic State Park (4 m W on SR 5), 3.5-m marked trail through 200-acre Gunlogson Arboretum with early homestead. Information: Superintendent, Icelandic State Park, Cavalier, ND 58211. 701-265-4561. **Tetrault Woods State Forest** (1½ m S of Walhalla on SR 32), 2.5-m marked trail recommended for cross-country skiing. Information: State Forest Service, NDSU & Institute of Forestry, Bottineau, ND 58318. 701-228-2278.

GRAND FORKS: Turtle River State Park (22 m W on US 2), 3-m cross-country ski trail in beautiful wooded valley along the Turtle River; downhill ski area with rope tows, chalet, and snack bar; nearby ice-skating rink; group camping facilities; separate snowmobile area. Information: Superintendent, Turtle River State Park, Arvilla, ND 58214. 701-343-2011.

MEDORA: Theodore Roosevelt National Memorial Park (Medora exit off I-94, then follow signs), 74,000 acres of scenic badlands along the Little Missouri River; skiing is permitted on all hiking trails; North Unit of park offers .5-m Squaw Creek Nature Trail which begins at the campground and passes through woodland along the river; Caprock Coulee Nature Trail is a 5-m loop with an overlook and shelter at midpoint; Buckhorn Trail, a 1-m tour, leads to a prairie dog town; another trail from the campground ends at Achenback Spring; South Unit touring possibilites include 3-m Jones Creek Trail and 12-m Petrified Forest Trail that leads into the rugged backcountry; many partially marked trails and routes are skiable; check with the park ranger; winter backcountry camping allowed, permit (free) required, no fires; separate snowmobile areas. Limited services in Medora; accommodations and restaurants in Belfield (16 m), Dickinson (34 m), and Beach (25 m). For maps and information: Superintendent, Theodore Roosevelt NMP, Medora, ND 58645. 701-623-4466 or 4467.

MINOT: Trestle Valley Ski Area (in Minot), cross-country rentals available; downhill ski facilities with day lodge and food service. Information: Manager, Trestle Valley Ski Area, Minot, ND 58701. 701-838-5426.

RUGBY: Lake Metigoshe State Park (32 m N on US 281, then 12 m W on SR 43), 3 m of marked and groomed trails on rolling glacial moraine and through deciduous forest along the shores of the lake; snowshoeing, ice fishing, and winter camping; snowmobile trails. Information: Superintendent, Lake Metigoshe State Park, Bottineau, ND 58318. 701-263-4651. **Turtle Mountains** (area in north central ND roughly defined by Canada on the N, US 281 on E, US 2 on S, and US 83 on W), many m of marked trails through beautiful wooded hills interspersed with lakes; 5 areas with marked trails include Hahn Recreation, Turtle Mountain, Strawberry Lake, Hartley-Boundary Lake, and Pelican Lake; also about 20 m of unmarked trails. For detailed maps and information: State Forest Service, NDSU & Institute of Forestry, Bottineau, ND 58318. 701-228-2278.

Bottineau Winter Park (N of Bottineau), 3 m of marked trails for cross-country skiers; downhill ski facilities, chalet and snack bar. Information: Manager, Bottineau Winter Park, Bottineau, ND 58318. 701-263-4556.

OHIO

For additional information, contact the individual area or Ohio Dept. of Economic and Community Development, P.O. Box 1001, Columbus, OH 43216.

ANDOVER: Pymatuning State Park (2 m E off SR 85), winter ski workshop for beginners to advanced with hours of skiing through park woods and over meadows; 27 year-round deluxe housekeeping cabins. Information: Ohio Division of Parks and Recreation, Fountain Square, Columbus, OH 43224.

CHESTERLAND: Alpine Valley Ski Area (10620 Mayfield Rd.), marked trails for cross-country skiers; instruction and rentals available; downhill ski facilities, snack bar, lounge, lodging at area. Information: Alpine Valley Ski Area (10620 Mayfield Rd., Chesterland, OH 44026. 216-285-2211.

CLEVELAND: Cuyahoga Valley National Recreation Area (hq 2 m E of Peninsula on SR 303), 30,000-acre park stretches over 20 m along the Cuyahoga River linking urban areas of Cleveland and Akron; preserves rural character of the river valley and the century-old Ohio and Erie Canal system; cross-country skiing available in many parts of the park including: 16-m **Bike and Hike Trail** along an abandoned railroad bed on eastern park boundary; **Virginia Kendall Park** has extensive trail system suitable for ski touring, also sledding, tobogganing, ice skating, and winter ecology hikes. Information: Superintendent, Cuyahoga Valley National Recreation Area, Box 158, Peninsula, OH 44264. 216-653-9036.

STATE PARKS: 41 state parks offer good ski touring possibilities on many m of hiking, bridle, and bicycle trails, and on unplowed park roads; because of the snow belt and terrain, most of the parks recommended are in the eastern part of the state; park personnel will suggest areas and trails suitable for skiers; snowmobiles on designated trails. Information: Ohio Division of Parks and Recreation, Fountain Square, Columbus, OH 43224.

OREGON

Sno-Park permits, required in many winter recreation parking locations throughout the state, are available at Motor Vehicles Division field offices and at many ski resorts, sporting goods stores, and similar facilities near winter recreation areas. A daily permit costs $1, an annual permit $5.

For additional information, contact the individual area or Oregon State Highway Division, Travel Information Section, Salem, OR 97310.

ASHLAND: Bull Gap Rd. 392D (I-5 S to Mt. Ashland exit, then 7 m W on Mt. Ashland access road to parking area), 6-m round trip tour for beginner and intermediate skiers through Shasta Red Fir forest with views of Mt. Shasta and occasional views of Mt. Mc-Loughlin; Rogue River National Forest map available (50¢); winter camping and snowmobiles permitted; plowed parking area (Sno-Park permit needed). Information: Ashland Ranger District, U.S. Forest Service, 2200 Hwy. 66, Ashland, OR 97520. 503-482-3333. **Mt. Ashland Ski Area** (1 m up road), cross-country ski rentals; downhill ski facilities with day lodge, cafeteria. Accommodations, restaurants, and services in Ashland. Information: Mt. Ashland Ski Area, P.O. Box 220, Ashland, OR 97520. 503-482-6406.

BAKER: Elkhorn Mountains/Anthony Lakes Area (22 m NW off I-80N), over 100 m of forest roads suitable for cross-country skiers on mountainous terrain with lots of powder snow; U.S. Forest Service has plans to mark 25–50 m of trails in near future; instruction and rentals available at **Anthony Lakes Ski Area** (off I-80N at North Powder, then 22 m W on access road), downhill ski facilities, day lodge, cafeteria, 4 rental cabins. Accommodations, restaurants, services in North Powder, Baker, and La Grande. Information: Baker Ranger District, Wallowa-Whitman National Forest, Rt. 1, Box 1, Pocahontas Rd., Baker, OR 97814. Ski area information: Anthony Lakes Corp., P.O. Box 89, North Powder, OR 97867. 503-963-6913.

BEND: Mt. Bachelor Nordic Sports Center (22 m W on paved highway), 2-km and 5-km marked and maintained trails with access to many more leading through scenic Deschutes National Forest; instruction and guided tours; map available; rental and retail shop; downhill ski facilities with 3 day lodges (Nordic center in Main Lodge), cafeterias, restaurant, cocktail lounge; day-care center. Daily bus service to Mt. Bachelor from Bend and Sun River (Trailways: 530-382-2151). Numerous accommodations, restaurants, and services in Bend. Information: Mt. Bachelor Ski Area, P.O. Box 828, Bend OR 97701. 503-832-2442. **Swampy Lakes Nordic Ski Trails** (12 m W on SR 46), 19.25 m of marked interconnecting trails; 2-m easy trail on gentle terrain; 3-m and 5.75-m more difficult trails with some narrow steep spots offer rewarding views; 8.5-m most difficult trail, a long tour mostly on forest roads, has 2 shelters en route. Deschutes National Forest trail map available. Information: Pacific Northwest Regional Forest Service Office, P.O. Box 3623, Portland, OR 97208.
   Sunriver Lodge (15 m S off US 97), 1-10 km of marked trails

on golf course, 50 km of marked U.S. Forest Service trails in beautiful surrounding wilderness area; 10 km of trails are groomed; trail
map available; certified PNSIA instructors offer group and private
classes; guided tours by appointment; rentals; ice skating, sleigh
rides; year-round luxurious resort community with accommodations
in condominiums and homes; choice of restaurants, cocktail lounges,
après-ski; Country Mall with variety of shops, professional services,
and post office, supermarket adjacent; bus service to Mt. Bachelor
(39 m). Information: Sunriver Lodge, Sunriver, OR 97701. 503-
593-1221.

CRATER LAKE: Crater Lake National Park (60 m N of Klamath
Falls via US 97 and SR 62), 250-sq-m park surrounding deepest
lake in the U.S.; 40-m **Rim Drive** circling caldera's edge offers
unexcelled vistas; entire rim tour normally takes skiers 3–4 days in
good weather; road is unmarked and under a 15–20-ft snow pack,
and can be difficult to follow; in some areas, steep and icy sidehills
make detours necessary, and avalanche danger is present on all
slopes; also skiers advised to stay off snow cornices on the caldera
rim; route should be undertaken by experienced, well-equipped
winter travelers only; no shelters en route; overnight camping
permits required. 3-m marked trail starts at Rim Village, runs S to
join **Pacific Crest Trail,** which crosses SR 62 just W of Mazama
Campground; another marked trail begins at Vidae Fall on the Rim
Drive (E of Rim Village) and runs S along Sun Creek; farther E
off Rim Drive is 6-m unplowed road to the Pinnacles, unmarked,
but used for touring; park-sponsored interpretive, guided snowshoe walks on weekends, no charge; snowmobiles on designated
route only. South and West Entrance roads to Rim Village open
all year; Park hq in Munson Valley (just S of Rim Village) open
daily 8 am-5 pm for general information; cafeteria in Rim Village
open 9 am-4 pm, weather permitting. Accommodations, restaurants,
and services available immediately adjacent to park and in Klamath
Falls and Medford. Information: Superintendent, Crater Lake
National Park, P.O. Box 7, Crater Lake, OR 97604. 503-594-2211.

EUGENE: Gold Lake Cross Country Ski Trails (43 m E on SR 58
at Willamette Pass), 4 marked trails and forest roads totaling
about 22 m for beginner and intermediate skiers, plus many m of
unmarked side trails for advanced skiers; mostly forested terrain
with beautiful views of jagged peaks of the Cascade Range with

elevations of 4000 ft and over; 2 interconnecting trails to Upper Marilyn Lake and Gold Lake begin at jct of SR 58 and Gold Lake Rd. plowed parking area (Sno-Park permit needed); another 6.9-m trail follows Waldo Lake Rd. from Gold Lake to Shadow Bay on Waldo Lake, unmarked trail shared by snowmobiles; overnight camping permitted, shelter at Gold Lake Campground; short .6-m trail connects to **Willamette Ski Area** with downhill ski facilities, day lodge and cafeteria (open weekends). Map and information: Oakridge Ranger District, Willamette National Forest, 46375 Highway 58, Westfir, OR 97492. 503-782-2291. **Odell Crescent Snow Trails** (on SR 58, just E of Willamette Ski Area), many m of trails include: 12-m Diamond View Trail from W end of Odell Lake through **Diamond Peak Wilderness Area** past Fawn Lake to E end of Odell Lake near parking area (on SR 58 close to Odell Creek Bridge); also from here trails lead S to Crescent Lake; just S of Crescent Lake are 4–5 interconnecting short loops around the base of Little Odell Butte; Davis Lake Trail (N side of SR 58, across from Odell Creek Bridge), 13-m round trip with interconnecting loops to Sunset Cove on Odell Lake. Accommodations and food at Odell Lake Lodge and Crescent Lake Lodge; additional lodging, restaurants, and services in Oakridge. Trail map and information: District Ranger, Crescent Ranger Station, Deschutes National Forest, Box 208, Crescent, OR 97733. 503-433-2234.

HOOD RIVER: Cooper Spur Ski Area (24 m S off SR 35), located on the N slope of Mt. Hood; many m of cross-country trails in Mt. Hood National Forest accessible from area; winter mountaineering program; rentals and repairs available; downhill ski facilities with day lodge, cafeteria. Information: Cooper Spur Ski Area, P.O. Box 23, Parkdale, OR 97047. 503-386-2777.

KLAMATH FALLS: McLoughlin Ski Trails (32 m NW on SR 140), 4 marked trails of 6.25 m, 7.75 m, 13 m, and 14.25 m; interconnecting trails over mostly timbered terrain at the base of Mt. McLoughlin and between Lake of the Woods and Fourmile Lake; Pacific Crest Trail passes through area; Fish Lake Parking Area has food service, telephone, and first aid; 4 other parking areas on SR 140; snowmobiles share area. Information: Klamath Ranger District, 1936 California Ave., Klamath Falls, OR 97601. **Fish Lake** (39 m NW on SR 140), 8 m of beginner to intermediate trails in area, with marked 1.5-m trail connecting to Pacific Crest Trail; restaurant (Fri.–Sun. during winter), cabin rentals, grocery store, and gas station at Fish Lake Resort. Information: Terry & Toni McCardle,

Fish Lake Resort, P.O. Box 40, Medford, OR 97501. Telephone: Dial Operator, ask for Fish Lake Toll Station No. 1, White City, OR. **Oux Kanee Cross-Country Ski Trail** (7 m N of Chiloquin on US 97); trailhead at parking area off highway on Forest Rd. 9732; 3 loops of 4.1 m, 5.7 m, and 8.5 m totaling 10 m; gently sloping terrain suitable for beginners; nearby Oux Kanee Overlook has year-round picnic and toilet facilities. Information: Chiloquin Ranger District, P.O. Box 357, Chiloquin, OR 97624.

PENDLETON: Spout Springs Ski Area (41 m NE off SR 204), over 15 m of marked trails at ski area and in adjacent **Umatilla National Forest;** instruction, rental, and repair service available; downhill ski facilities with 2 day lodges and cafeterias, main lodge with 12 rooms and restaurant. Additional lodging, restaurants, and services in Weston (16 m E). Information: Spout Springs Lodge, Inc., Rt. 1, Weston, OR 97886. 503-566-2015.

PORTLAND: Mt. Hood Area Cross-Country Ski Trails (53 m E on US 26 in Government Camp area), about 75 m of marked trails and forest roads in **Mt. Hood National Forest,** plus a variety of other places to tour, not specifically marked as ski trails; U.S. Forest Service offers a free map, designed to be used with a topographical map and compass, showing 16 area trails, names, length, range of difficulty, and brief descriptions. 8 trails begin at Government Camp ranging from a 1-m beginner loop, with a spectacular view of Mt. Hood, to 12-m intermediate West Leg Trail, an endurance test with a 6-m uphill grade, then a good 6-m downhill run; several m W on SR 35 at Barlow Pass, 4 trails start from the parking area including difficult Twin Lakes Trail, which follows the Pacific Crest National Scenic Trail for part of a 6-m tour to Wapinitia Pass on US 26, S of Government Camp; just beyond Barlow Pass on SR 35 is easy White River Trail, popular novice area with a bowl ½ m up the west side of the river; avalanche danger exists at the end of the trail at timberline; Sahalie Loop novice trail and Bennett Trail for advanced skiers begin near Mt. Hood Meadows Ski Area turnoff; Pocket Creek Trail begins 3 m E of Mt. Hood Meadows on SR 35, popular with novice skiers because first 2 m relatively level with a series of clearouts. Map and additional information: U.S. Forest Service, Winter Recreation Sports Section, P.O. Box 3623, Portland, OR 97208. 503-221-3644. Four nearby downhill ski areas cater to cross-country skiers: **Mt. Hood Meadows** (off SR 35, 10 m NE of Government Camp), 12 m of beginner to expert trails with access to area Forest Service trails; instruction and guided tours available; midweek Ladies Day program for all skill levels with ski technique and winter survival instruction; day lodge has cafeteria and restaurant. Information: Mt. Hood Meadows Ski Area, P.O. Box 47, Mt. Hood, OR 97041. 503-337-2222. Snow report: 503-227-7669 (SNOW). **Multorpor-Ski Bowl** (in Government Camp), access to many m of area Forest Service trails; 2 day lodges, 2 cafeterias, Beer Stube. Information: Mt. Hood Multorpor-Ski Bowl, P.O. Box 85, Government Camp, OR 97028. 503-662-4274. **Summit Ski Area** (in Government Camp), rental services and trail access; near State Hwy. parking area, start of several area U.S. Forest Service trails; day lodge, cafeteria. Information: Summit Ski Area, P.O. Box 85, Government Camp, OR 97028. 503-272-3330. **Timberline Lodge Ski Area** (6 m access road off US 26 at Government Camp), some unmarked cross-country ski trails, plus access to area U.S. Forest Service trails; rentals and instruction available; luxurious accommodations at lodge, a magnificent structure built of native stone and timber, a WPA project during Roosevelt era and now a designated National Historic Site; dining room, cafeteria, 2 cocktail lounges, entertainment; year-round heated outdoor swimming pool. Information: Timberline Lodge, Government Camp, OR 97028. 503-272-3311. Snow report: 503-222-2211. Additional lodging, restaurants, services; ski rentals and repairs in Government Camp. Daily bus service (Continental Trailways) from Portland.

SISTERS: Hoodoo Ski Bowl (22 m W on US 20), at summit of Santiam Pass with panoramic views of Oregon Cascades of **Willamette National Forest;** 20 m of marked trails on and around Hoodoo area plus vast open terrain leading to Big Lake; downhill ski facilities with 2 day lodges, restaurant; Nordic instruction, rentals, and repairs. Lodging, restaurants, services in Sisters. Information: Hoodoo Ski Bowl, Box 20, Hwy. 20, Sisters, OR 97759. Telephone: Portland toll operator (area code 503), ask for Hoodoo 1 or 2.

SWEET HOME: Sweet Home Ranger District of **Willamette National Forest** maintains several cross-country trails: **Heart Lake Road** (32 m E on US 20 at Tombstone Pass), 4-m beginner tour on flat roadbed across hillsides with clearcuts and timber stands; no snowmobiles. **Lava Lake Road** (40 m E on US 20), 15- to 20-m trail on slightly rolling roadbed, suitable for beginners and intermediates; snowmobiles permitted. Maps available for both trails; Oregon Sno-Park permits needed. 4 more trails are under consideration. Information: U.S. Forest Service, 4431 Hwy. 20, Sweet Home, OR 97386. 503-367-5168.

PENNSYLVANIA

For additional information, contact the individual area or Pennsylvania Dept. of Commerce, Bureau of Travel Development, 206 South Office Bldg., Harrisburg, PA 17120.

ALLENTOWN: Apple Valley Cross-Country Ski Area (12 m S on SR 100 & 29), 5 m of marked and maintained trails on 300 acres of wooded valley, open fields, and orchards for novice to expert skiers; trail fee ($2.50), map available; instruction and rentals; trailhead lodge, hot coffee; no snowmobiles. Information: Apple Valley Cross-Country Ski Area, RD 1, Zionsville, PA 18092. 215-966-5525.

COUDERSPORT: Susquehannock Trail System (11 m E on US 6; northern entrance just W of Denton Hill State Park), 85-m marked trail system on old logging roads, railroad grades and foot trails, passes through several state parks with picnic areas en route; access from a number of area roads and state parks; varied mountainous terrain with open fields and wooded valleys for novice to expert skiers. Short trail connects to **Susquehannock Lodge** with accommodations for 38 guests, informal atmosphere, large fireplace, and home-cooked meals served family-style; rentals for guests; trail maps and packed lunches; no snowmobiles. Information: Wil & Betty Ann, Susquehannock Lodge, Rt. 6, RD 1, Ulysses, PA 16948. 814-435-2163. 5 minutes from the lodge is **Denton Hill Ski Area** with access to trail system; downhill ski facilities, day lodge, cafeteria. Information: Denton Hill Ski Area, Coudersport, PA 16915. 814-435-6372.

ERIE: Wilderness Lodge (SR 8 SE to Wattsburg; then 2.8 m E on Jamestown St. to Weeks Valley Rd., 2.5 m to lodge, near state border), 10 m of well-marked trails with access to unlimited acres for bushwhacking; mostly wooded terrain for beginner to expert skiers with trails tunneling through pine and hemlock groves; trails groomed daily with track set; one trail connects to Peek'n Peak Resort (see Jamestown, NY); Nordic Ski Patrol; trail fee ($2), map available; group and private instruction, guided tours; rental and retail shop; accommodations and restaurant in attractive rustic lodge. Expansion underway of both trail system and lodging facilities. Information: James & Nansi Janes, Wilderness Lodge, RD 2, Weeks Valley Rd., Wattsburg, PA 16442. 814-739-2946.

GETTYSBURG: Gettysburg National Military Park (Visitor Center on Taneytown Rd; open daily except Jan. 1, Dec. 25), 3600-acre park surrounding Gettysburg; no marked cross-country ski trails to date, but many ski enthusiasts find excellent touring on numerous foot, bridle, and bicycle trails throughout the park, and 2 large areas are closed to vehicular traffic during snow season; with a park map in hand, a recreational ski tour is also an interpretive tour of one of the greatest battlefields of the Civil War; hilly terrain with both open and heavily wooded areas suitable for all skiers; no winter camping or snowmobiles. Information: Park Superintendent, Gettysburg National Military Park, Gettysburg, PA 17325. 717-334-1124.

HANOVER: Codorus State Park (4 m S on SR 216) surrounds Lake Marburg; 100-acre area and 15 m of maintained hiking trails suitable for novice skiers; rolling terrain with views of the lake from most trails; free park map available; snowmobiles on designated trail. Lodging, restaurants, and services in Hanover. Information: Park Superintendent, Codorus State Park, RD 3, Box 118, Hanover, PA 17331. 717-637-2816.

HARRISBURG: Gifford Pinchot State Park (Lewisberry exit off I-83 S, then SR 177 S to Alpine Rd.; use Conewago parking area), 8 interconnecting, marked hiking and nature trails suitable for cross-country skiers; beginner to intermediate terrain on overgrown fields and through hardwood forest areas; no winter camping or snowmobiles. Information: Park Superintendent, Gifford Pinchot State Park, RD 1, Lewisberry, PA 17339. 717-432-5011.

LIGONIER: Ligonier Mountain Outfitters (E on SR 30 at Laughlin-town), 25 m of intermediate to expert marked and maintained trails through state-owned forested mountain wilderness; private and group instruction, guided tours; rentals. Information: Ligonier Mountain Outfitters, Box 206, Rt. 30, Laughlintown, PA 15655. 412-238-6246. **Laurel Mountain Ski Area** (7 m E off SR 30), marked trail suitable for cross-country skiers; downhill ski facilities, day lodge, cafeteria. Information: Laurel Mountain Ski Area, P.O. Box 527, Ligonier, PA 15658. 412-238-6622. Both areas adjacent to **Laurel Mountain State Park** and **Linn Run State Park.** Accommodations, restaurants, and services in Ligonier.

NEWTOWN: Tyler State Park (1 m E; access from Newtown Rd./ SR 332), 1711-acre park located on both sides of Neshaminy Creek in Bucks County; about 5.5 m of marked bicycle and hiking trails suitable for cross-country skiing; park offers interesting historic homes dating back to 1700s and a covered bridge. Information: Superintendent, Tyler State Park, Newtown, Bucks Co., PA 18940. 215-968-2021.

READING: French Creek State Park (15 m SE via US 422 E to SR 82, S to SR 724 E, then SR 345 S), about 10 m of marked hiking trails for novice to intermediate skiers on wooded rolling hills with plateaus and 2 lakes; abundant wildlife; tent/trailer family camping area; no snowmobiles; adjacent to park is **Hopewell Village National Historic Site** with buildings and remains of a typical early American ironmaking community; 8 m of the Horse Shoe Trail pass through the park. Information: Park Superintendent, French Creek State Park, RD 1, Box 347, Elverson, PA 19520. 215-582-1514. **Horse Shoe Trail** runs 120 m NW through state from Valley Forge State Park (NW of Philadelphia) to meet the Appalachian Trail at Rattling Run Gap near Harrisburg Reservoir (NE of Harrisburg).

SCRANTON: Bruce Lake Natural Area (E on I-84 to exit 26, then S ¼ m on SR 390), 2300-acre forested preserve with 100-acre swamp, 2 lakes, and many species of wildlife; 4 m of woods roads and about 5 m of marked hiking trails on gentle hilly terrain; trail map available; backpack camping on 10 designated sites (permit required, 2 night limit, $3 per night); no snowmobiles; adjacent Promised Land State Park has heavy snowmobile use and is not recommended for skiers. Accommodations, restaurants, services in

Lake Wallenpaupack area. Information: Park Superintendent, Promised Land State Park, Greentown, PA 18426. 717-676-3428.

SOMERSET: Kooser State Park (10 m W off SR 31), 170-acre park with 3 m of marked trails, groomed as necessary; beginner terrain through beautiful wooded area along brook with several ramped bridges and around pretty Kooser Lake; snowmobiles on separate trails; winter camping permitted. Information: Superintendent, Kooser State Park, RD 4, Box 256, Somerset, PA 15501. 814-445-8673. Snow report: 412-238-6622 (24-hour service). **Hidden Valley Ski Touring Center** (12 m W on SR 31; 8 m E of turnpike Donegal exit), 40 m of marked trails through hardwood forest with scattered open fields and pine groves; beginner and intermediate trails groomed; trail fee ($2), map available; group and private instruction, guided tours; scheduled ski clinics and citizens' races including annual Genesee Cup race; downhill ski facilities; day lodge with cafeteria, warming hut with wood stove; year-round resort with accommodations for over 100 at inn; private home rentals available. Bus service to Somerset; with a call, Hidden Valley car will pick you up. Information: Hidden Valley Ski Touring Center, RD 4, Somerset, PA 15501. 814-445-6014. **Seven Springs Ski Area** (10 m W at Seven Springs), marked trails for cross-country skiers; downhill ski facilities with day lodge, cafeteria, restaurant, cocktail lounge; year-round resort with lodge, chalet and cottage accommodations; heated indoor and outdoor pools, sauna. Information: Seven Springs Ski Area, RD 1, Champion, PA 15622. 814-352-7777. Nearby **Laurel Ridge State Park** has 35 m of marked trails. Information: Superintendent, Laurel Ridge State Park, RD 3, Rockwood, PA 15557. 412-455-3744.

STARLIGHT: Inn at Starlight Lake (just over New York border; SR 17, exit at Hancock, NY, then SR 191 S over Delaware River to SR 370, turn right, proceed 3.5 m, turn right again, 1 m to inn), 18 m of marked, maintained and groomed trails on rolling farmland and woods with some steep areas and 3 natural lakes; color-coded marked trails for beginner to advanced skiers; trail fee ($2, for day guests), map available; group instruction, guided day and night tours; no snowmobiles; rentals; accommodations in comfortable lodge rooms or cottages; hearty meals and home-baked bread served in dining room, late-night snacks, wines and spirits served in the Stovepipe Bar. Short Line Bus service to Hancock, NY; prearranged bus pickup for inn guests at no charge. Information: Inn at Starlight Lake, Starlight, PA 18461. 717-798-2519.

STATE COLLEGE: Black Moshannon State Park (9 m NW on US 322, then 7 m NW via county roads), 12 m of beginner to intermediate marked trails on mostly flat wooded terrain around a spring-fed lake; winter camping and snowmobiles in designated areas; trail map available; small downhill ski area with day lodge (9:30 am–5:00 pm, daily), no food service; plowed parking area. Information: Park Superintendent, Black Moshannon State Park, Box 104, RD 1, Philipsburg, PA 16866. 814-342-1101.

STROUDSBURG: Delaware Water Gap National Recreation Area (at Stroudsburg, on both Pennsylvania and New Jersey sides of the Delaware River), about 50 m of unmarked roads and trails on flat terrain along the river and over very hilly areas above the Gap; scenic area with views, pretty waterfalls, and streams; snowmobiles on designated trail only. Information: Superintendent, Delaware Water Gap National Recreation Area, National Park Service, Bushkill, PA 18324. 717-588-6637. **Hickory Run State Park** (W on I-80 to exit 41, then 6 m S on SR 534), 15,000-acre park with 12 m of marked and maintained trails on mostly wooded flat to very hilly terrain; trail map available; plowed parking area; snowmobiles on separate trails. Information: Superintendent, Hickory Run State Park, RD 1, Box 81, White Haven, PA 18661. 717-443-9991. **Fernwood Ski Area** (N on US 209 at Bushkill), trails for cross-country skiers; downhill ski facilities, day lodge, restaurant; accommodations at area. Information: Fernwood Ski Area, Bushkill, PA 18324. 717-588-6661. **Mt. Airy** (NW off SR 611, 3 m S of Mt. Pocono), cross-country ski trails; downhill ski facilities; snowmobile trails; accommodations for 2000 at area. Information: Mt. Airy Lodge Resort Hotel, Mt. Pocono, PA 18344. 717-839-8811. Additional lodging, restaurants, and services in Stroudsburg, Milford, Delaware Water Gap, and White Haven.

UNIONTOWN: Fort Necessity National Battlefield (11 m E on US 40), site of defeat of Lt. Col. George Washington in the opening battle of the French and Indian War on July 3, 1754; 700 acres with hiking/interpretive trails and open meadow areas suitable for cross-country skiers; beginner to intermediate terrain with mixed hardwood and conifer forests on rolling hills with sharp ravines; trail map

ng or snowmobiles; plowed parking area
kends during winter). Lodging, restaurants,
n. Information: Park Ranger, Fort Neces-
The National Pike, Farmington, PA 15437.

n State Park (US 6 S to Clarendon, turn right
at traffic light, then 5 m to park), some marked
of logging roads and abandoned railroad grades
d surrounding state game lands and **Allegheny**
terrain varies from flat open areas to wooded hilly
suitable for beginner to expert skiers; topographical
ffice ($2); winter camping permitted; snowmobiles
trails; warming shelter and plowed parking area at
dging, restaurants, and services in Warren, Tiona, and
information: Superintendent, Chapman State Park, RD
n, PA 16313. 814-723-5030.

HODE ISLAND

ll Rhode Island state parks, forests, and preserves are open to
isitors. The areas mentioned below are recommended as having
suitable terrain for cross-country skiing. For additional information:
Tourist Promotion Division, Rhode Island Dept. of Economic
Development, One Weybosset Hill, Providence, RI 02903.

CHEPACHET: George Washington Management Area and adjacent
Casimir Pulaski Memorial State Park (5 m W on US 44), 7000
acres of lakes, ponds, streams, and woodlands; many m of marked
and maintained trails and forest roads; trail system extends into
Connecticut parks.

HOPE VALLEY: Arcadia Management Area and **Beach Pond
State Park** (N of town; bisected by SR 165), many wooded acres
with lakes, streams and rivers; extensive trail system connects to
Pachaug Trail in Connecticut.

NEWPORT: Norman Bird Sanctuary (3rd Beach Rd. in Mid
450-acre refuge with pond and marked trails; cross-count
welcome.

SOUTH DAKOTA

The Black Hills of western South Dakota, interlaced with
railroad beds, logging and forest service roads, and hiking tr
offer unlimited possibilities for the cross-country skier. The Eas
Prairie region has numerous marked trail systems in state pa
which prohibit any type of motorized vehicles on hiking trails
well as in designated natural areas. The snow season in the easte
region is short, with an unbroken snow cover usually from Ne
Year's to mid-February. Park managers are on duty year round a
most state park and recreation areas and can give up-to-date report
on snow conditions.

For additional information, contact the individual area or South
Dakota Division of Tourism, Joe Foss Bldg., Pierre, SD 57501.

BROOKINGS: Oakwood State Park (25 m NW; 10 m N of Volga
off US 14), 255 wooded acres lying between Oakwood Lakes; ¾-m
marked trail plus Scout Island is set aside for cross-country skiers.
Popular with local skiers is the **Big Sioux River** from Brookings to
Dell Rapids; when frozen, and with good snow cover, the river
provides an excellent opportunity for a long tour. **Oak Lake Girl
Scout Camp** (22 m NE; S of Astoria), a private area which allows
skiing on 500 acres with woods, prairie, and a lake; closed to
hunting and snowmobiles. For permission to ski, contact camp
caretaker: Ms. Nancy Ryger, Sioux Falls, 605-336-2978.

CUSTER: Bear Mountain Area (15 m NW; 3 m N on US 16 and
385 to Forest Service Rd. 297, follow the signs leading to the Boy
Scout Camp, about 8 m; trailhead and parking area are clearly
marked before you reach the camp), interconnecting loops totaling
about 25 m; maintained trails wind through stands of ponderosa
pine, Black Hills spruce, quaking aspen, and paper birch; breathtaking views of the distant Needles and Harney Peak, highest peaks

E of the Rockies; abundant wildlife. **Jewel Cave National Monument** (13 m W on US 16), 1275 acres of beautiful canyons and caverns with jewel-like calcite crystal encrustations; trails newly developed by rangers, stop at the Visitor Center for information (daily 8-5). **Upper Limestone and Deerfield Lake Areas** (25 m NW), uncrowded region with miles of untracked snow on open meadows and abandoned logging roads; all Forest Service roads well marked and most secondary roads unplowed; many of the trails follow General George Armstrong Custer's exploratory route through the Black Hills in 1874; a popular region for winter camping. **Harney Peak Area** (N via SR 89), many m of marked trails through some of the most spectacular scenery in the state including the Needles, Cathedral Spires, 7242-ft Harney Peak, and Mt. Rushmore; interconnecting loops vary in length from 1½ m to 9 m; trailheads at Sylvan Lake, Willow Creek Campground, Horse Thief Lake, and Iron Mt. Picnic Ground; Forest Service trail map available. **Pagent Hill** (within the city limits), limited cross-country skiing, good area for beginners; sledding and tobogganing. Accommodations, restaurants and services available in Custer. Information: Custer Chamber of Commerce, Custer, SD 57730. Maps and additional information for central **Black Hills National Forest:** Supervisor, U.S. Forest Service Headquarters, Custer, SD 57730.

Yellow Hair Outfitters (516 Mt. Rushmore Rd.) has rentals; tours and lessons arranged with advance notice.

LEAD: Deer Mountain Ski Area (3.5 m SW off US 85), 8 loops totaling 15 m of interconnecting marked and groomed trails on varied terrain of rolling hills, with some steep inclines on trails into the wooded isolated areas of the Black Hills National Forest; 5-m trail on an abandoned railroad grade joins Terry Peak Ski Area trails, overlooks along the way provide perfect spots for a picnic lunch; map available for color-coded marked trails; rentals and sales at Deer Mt. lodge; instruction available; downhill ski facilities with day lodge, warming room, cafeteria, fireplace, bar and lounge. Deer Mt. hosts annual Ski for Light cross-country expedition, a program to introduce visually handicapped persons to Nordic skiing through instruction by sighted guides, and races and contests. Information: Sherman Teigan, Area Manager, Deer Mt. Ski Area, Box 622, Deadwood, SD 57732. 605-584-3230. **Terry Peak Ski Area** (5 m W of Lead off US 85), 4.5 m of trails beginning at the lodge on gentle rolling terrain and abandoned railroad bed (joins Deer Mt.

to the S); numerous other tour possibilities in the Terry Peak/
Trojan area of the Black Hills include another old railroad bed
which follows Annie Creek to Elmore, mostly downhill grade;
downhill ski facilities with day lodge, 2 restaurants, lounge, ski
shop, and cross-country rentals. Information: Terry Peak Ski Area,
136 Sherman St., Deadwood, SD 57732. 605-578-1501.

Numerous restaurants and accommodations are in the old mining
towns of Lead and Deadwood. "Ski Bus" service from Rapid City
(50 m) and Sturgis operates weekends; scheduled stops at various
motels; arrives at ski areas about 10 am, departs at 4 pm. Information
and reservations: Stagecoach West, P.O. Box 264, Rapid City,
SD 57709.

MILBANK: Hartford Beach State Park (15 m N off SR 15), 320-
acre park on the shore of Big Stone Lake; 4 marked trails on
heavily wooded terrain; ample parking facilities.

PIERRE: Farm Island Recreation Area (SE), 336-acre area connected
by a causeway to Old Farm Island in the Missouri River, land
leased as a nature study area by the Dept. of Game, Fish, & Parks;
skiing permitted on marked trails on the island; closed to motorized
vehicles. Just up the river is **LaFramboise Island** (connected to
Pierre by a causeway), a recreational reserve under the jurisdiction
of the U.S. Army Corps of Engineers; trails suitable for skiing;
closed to motorized vehicles; (contact local Corps office for information).

REDFIELD: Fisher Grove State Park (7 m E on US 212), 306-acre
park located on a loop of the James River; 1 marked trail and a golf
course open to cross-country skiers; entire park designated game
refuge; motorized vehicles restricted to paved roads.

SIOUX FALLS: Union County State Park (37 m S off I-29), marked
trails with overlooks in 499-acre park. **Newton Hills State Park**
(off Fairview exit about 15 m SE on SR 11), marked trails and
snow-packed roads offer good cross-country skiing on heavily
wooded terrain on the Big Sioux River; 948-acre park. **Beaver
Creek Nature Area** (off US 16, 8 m E), marked trail on 160-acre
area closed to motorized vehicles. **Lake Herman State Park** (28 m
N on I-29, then W on SR 34; 2 m W of Madison), ¾-m trail and
a number of roads throughout the park open to cross-country

skiers; 175-acre park with gently rolling hills and woods. Rentals available in Sioux Falls at Sun and Fun Specialty Sports and Terry Peak Ski and Sports.

SPEARFISH: Spearfish Cross-Country Trails (SW via Tinton Rd./ Forest Service Rd. 134), 3 interconnecting marked loops of 2 m, 4 m, and 5.5 m plus a spur to an overlook near the rim of Spearfish Canyon; trails located in the northern Black Hills National Forest; terrain recommended for beginner through advanced skiers; parking area on W side of road across from trailhead; map available. Information: District Ranger, U.S. Forest Service, Spearfish, SD 57783.

TENNESSEE

For additional information, contact the individual area or Tennessee Tourist Development, 505 Fesslers Lane, Nashville, TN 37210.

CHEROKEE NATIONAL FOREST, 615,000 acres in 2 sections, NE and SW of Great Smoky Mtns.; areas with elevations over 5000 ft are apt to have snow conditions suitable for cross-country skiing. Roan Mountain area (30 m SE of Elizabethton via US 19E) has marked trails and state park facilities; marked and maintained **Appalachian Trail,** with elevations mostly above 5000 ft, winds S through the forest from Damascus (VA), crosses US 19E just E of Roan Mtn. at the state border, then continues S along the main ridge (also the state line) to Great Smoky Mtns.; just N of Erwin, an access road off US 19W & 23 leads to public campgrounds and Appalachian Trail. Information: District Ranger, Cherokee National Forest, P.O. Box 400, Cleveland, TN 37311. 615-476-5528.

GATLINBURG, at the gateway to Great Smoky Mountain National Park, is a year-round family resort for downhill ski enthusiasts; 120-passenger aerial tramway connects the village and ski area; accommodations for 25,000, about 100 restaurants, numerous shops and services. Information: Gatlinburg Chamber of Commerce, Gatlinburg, TN 37738.

GREAT SMOKY MOUNTAINS NATIONAL PARK (half in North Carolina) claims nearly 65 inches of snow each winter; access via US 441 from Gatlinburg. Portions of the **Appalachian Trail** both N and S from Newfound Gap (on US 441) are suitable for cross-country skiing; trail S leads to **Clingmans Dome,** highest point in the park (6642 ft), with superb views en route; also, Fornery Ridge Rd., when closed, is a 7.5-m ski tour from Newfound Gap to Clingmans Dome; N from the Gap, trails lead to Mt. LeConte, with several interconnecting trails in the area from Gatlinburg, Greenbrier Cove, Alum Cave, and Sugarlands; in SW part of the Park, touring possibilities include winter closed roads to Cades Cove; overnight tours in the park require permits. Information: Superintendent, Great Smoky Mountains National Park, Gatlinburg, TN 37738. 615-436-5615.

UTAH

For additional information, contact the individual area or Utah Travel Council, Council Hall, Capitol Hill, Salt Lake City, UT 84114, or Utah Ski Association, 19 East 200 South, Suite 15, Salt Lake City, UT 84111.

ALTA: Alta Ski Area (33 m SE of Salt Lake International Airport on SR 210 in Little Cottonwood Canyon), some 26 ski touring routes have been mapped and numbered by the **Wasatch National Forest** service; 3 easy routes lead from the top of Alta Germania and Albion lifts along ridges to Brighton, with return route from Brighton Millicent lift; numerous other trails lead into the mountains from various points along Little Cottonwood Canyon; most routes are rated difficult and most difficult and will vary with snow conditions and avalanche danger; area is famous for its light, dry powder snow; Alta Cross-Country Ski School offers a complete instruction program from basic diagonal stride to advanced racing technique and downhill skiing with telemark turns; class and private lessons by certified ISIA instructors; guided tours with picnic lunch; trail map available; tours and lessons leave from **Snowpine Lodge,** which has retail shop, rental and repair service, cafeteria with sundeck, lounge with fireplace, accommodations—modified American Plan (information: Snowpine Lodge, Alta, UT 84070. 801-742-3274). Alta, a major resort area, has extensive downhill ski facilities, wide variety of lodge accommodations, excellent restaurants, après-ski, shops, and services. Information: Alta Ski Lifts, Alta, UT 84070. Ski School: 801-742-2600; snow report: 801-742-3333. Alta Reservation Service: 801-742-2040 or 533-8308. Just W of Alta is **Snowbird,** with access to unlimited ski touring possibilities; rentals, instruction, and guided tours; a full-service resort village with downhill ski facilities, lodges, cafeterias, restaurants, ski shops, boutiques, delicatessen, general store, pharmacy, post office; variety of accommodations. Information: Snowbird Resort, Snowbird, UT 84070. 801-742-2222; snow report: 801-521-8102. Snowbird reservations: 801-742-2000. Shuttle service between Alta and Snowbird. Scheduled bus, taxi or car rentals available from Salt Lake City International Airport.

BRIGHTON: Brighton Ski Bowl (on SR 152, 25 m E of Salt Lake City in Big Cottonwood Canyon), access to many m of ski touring possibilities in **Wasatch National Forest;** Forest Service map shows routes to Alta along ridge from top of Brighton's Millicent lift and a route E to Park City; routes vary in difficulty according to snow conditions and avalanche danger; rental and retail shop; instruction and guides available; downhill ski area, cafeteria, restaurants, lodging. Information: Brighton Ski Bowl, Brighton, UT 84121. 801-359-3283. 5 minutes away is **Silver Fork Lodge,** a good starting point for ski touring. Information: Silver Fork Lodge, Star Route, Brighton, UT 84121. 801-649-9551.

CEDAR CITY: Cedar Breaks National Monument (E via SR 14 & SR 143), a huge multicolored amphitheater with beautiful eroded limestone formations; there are no trails within the monument, although skiing is permitted on 6-m length of SR 143 when it is closed; terrain is suitable for beginner to intermediate skiers with large meadows in a spruce/fir area; however, adverse weather conditions often require that skiers be skilled enough to recognize and deal with hazardous conditions; area map available; snowshoeing permitted; winter camping (check-in required); snowmobiles on designated trail only; access to the monument depends on snow conditions, which may force closure of SR 143. Food, lodging, and services at Brian Head, Cedar City, and Parowan. Information: Park Ranger, Cedar Breaks National Monument, P.O. Box 749, Cedar City, UT 84720. 801-586-9451. **Brian Head Ski Area** (off I-15 at Parowan, then 12 m SE on SR 143), access to excellent cross-country ski trails; downhill ski facilities with cafeteria, ski shops, day-care child service; snowmobile trails; condominium lodging, 2 restaurants, dance hall, boutique, general store, liquor store, post office, gas station. Information: Brian Head Ski Area, P.O. Box 38, Cedar City, UT 84720. 801-586-4636.

OGDEN: Powder Mountain Ski Resort (17 m NE off SR 39; 55 m NE of Salt Lake International Airport), marked and maintained cross-country ski trails; rentals and repairs; instruction and guides; downhill ski facilities, day lodges, cafeteria, restaurant, lounge; accommodations at area Coalition Lodge (P.O. Box 152, Eden UT 84310. 801-745-3779); additional food, lodging, and services in Ogden. Information: Powder Mountain Ski Resort, P.O. Box 110, Eden UT 84310. 801-745-3771.

PANGUITCH: Bryce Canyon National Park (24 m SE via US 89 & SR 12), 36,000-acre park with 20-m escarpment exposing beautiful and bizarre rock formations, famous for their vivid colors; 62 m of marked and maintained trails; varied terrain with 900-ft elevation change; park entrance fee ($2), map available; guided snowshoe hikes; no winter facilities in park; winter camping ($2); snowmobiles permitted; food and lodging 4 m outside park. Information: Superintendent, Bryce Canyon National Park, Bryce Canyon, UT 84717. 801-834-5322.

PARK CITY: White Pine Ski Touring Center (at Park City Golf Course), 5 km of trails with track set on golf course; trail fee ($1); rental and retail shop; certified instructors offer lessons in basic and advanced technique, racing, deep-powder skiing and telemark turns; clinics in winter survival; citizens' races; guided half- and full-day tours into the Wasatch Mountains; 3- and 5-day tours into the High Uinta Mountains, where varied terrain offers a challenge or a relaxing tour in any direction, overnight lodging in heated cabins with food and bedding supplied. Touring center's **White Pine Lodge** (2 m N of Park City off SR 224) has 5-km trail with track set and access to 15 m of trails with warming huts en route, in the White Pine Canyon; home-cooked natural foods available in relaxed atmosphere of day lodge; day and overnight tours in upper areas of White Pine Canyon and to Brighton and Alta. Information: White Pine Touring Center, P.O. Box 417, Park City, UT 84060. 801-649-8701.

Park City, an old silver-mining town, is now a full-service year-round resort with extensive downhill ski facilities; rental and retail cross-country ski equipment available at numerous ski shops; variety of lodging in hotels, inns, condominiums, and old Victorian rooming houses; fine restaurants, restored saloons, entertainment; shops and services. Information: Park City Ski Corp., P.O. Box 39, Park City, UT 84060. 801-649-8111. Reservations: Central Reservations of Park City, P.O. Box 1060, Park City, UT 84060. 801-649-8266. Nearby **Park West,** with access to ski touring trails, has rental and retail ski shop for cross-country ski equipment; ski school offers instruction; downhill ski facilities, day lodge, cafeteria, lounge with entertainment; accommodations at Park West Condominiums; free shuttle bus to and from Park City. Information: Park West, P.O. Box 1598, Park City, UT 84060. 801-649-9663. Bus service, limousines, and rental cars available from Salt Lake International Airport to Park City.

PROVO: Uinta National Forest (hq in Provo), 797,000 acres with high mountains rising to 12,000 ft above desert, deep canyons with waterfalls, several thousand m of forest roads and trails. For recommended touring routes in Provo area, contact Pleasant Grove Ranger District, P.O. Box 228, Pleasant Grove, UT 84062. 801-785-3563. For touring routes near Heber City, contact Heber Ranger District, Federal Bldg., Heber City, UT 84032. 801-654-0470.

VERNAL: Dinosaur National Monument (E on US 40 to Jensen, then 7 m N on SR 149 to Quarry Visitor Center), park with spectacular canyons cut by the Green and Yampa Rivers, has fossil remains of dinosaurs and other ancient animals; no formal designated trails, but access to skiable snow areas from Quarry Visitor Center (8:00 am–4:30 pm, daily); area map available; snowmobiles on designated roads only; plowed parking area and winter campground at Quarry; food, lodging, and services in Vernal and Dinosaur, CO. Information: Superintendent, Dinosaur National Monument, Box 210, Dinosaur, CO 81610. 303-374-2216.

VERMONT

For additional information, contact the individual area or Vermont Agency of Development and Community Affairs, Travel Division, Montpelier, VT 05602.

ARLINGTON: Arlington Inn (on US 7), partly marked and snow-mobile-packed novice to expert trails; 150 acres of mountainside terrain with views of Arlington and south; trail fee ($1); rentals; lodging at Inn, breakfast (for Inn guests) and dinner served. Information: Arlington Inn, Arlington, VT 05250. 802-375-6532.
West Mountain Inn (½ m W off US 7, on SR 313), 150 acres on a small mountain with 10 m of marked trails on flat open pasture for beginners, rolling hills for intermediates, and access to challenging trails for more advanced skiers; trail map available; rentals; no snowmobiles; Inn has 10 units, gourmet country dining and full bar. Information: West Mountain Inn, Box 481, Arlington, VT 05250. 802-375-6515.

BOLTON VALLEY: Bolton Valley Resort (midway between Montpelier and Burlington; exit 10 or 11 off I-89, access road off US 2), 27 m of beginner to expert marked trails; terrain varies from gentle easy hills to extremely rugged expert 14-m trail to Trapp Lodge in Stowe, 2 trails on part of **Long Trail** with shelters for winter camping; trail fee ($1 weekdays, $2 weekends), trail map available; group and private instruction; rental and retail shop; downhill ski facilities; year-round resort with accommodations in Bolton Valley Lodge, Black Bear Lodge, and Trailside Condominiums; cafeteria, cafe, pizza parlor, dining room, tavern with entertainment; nursery; grocery. Information: Bolton Valley Resort, Bolton Valley, VT 05477. 802-434-2131.

BRANDON: Churchill House Ski Touring Center (4 m E on SR 73), 22 m of marked trails, part of which are groomed and track set; beginner to advanced trails include Leicester Hollow Trail along glacial canyon and brook leading to Silver Lake, and dramatic Ridge Trail with views of the Adirondacks; trail fee ($2), trail map available; rental and retail shop with ski equipment and accessories; instruction and guide service; guided overnight tours arranged between a succession of inns on the 50-m **Vermont Ski Touring Trail** (Churchill House Inn is at midpoint); also day tours to nearby areas; citizens' races include annual 60-km Hennessey Cognac American Marathon on part of the Vermont Ski Touring Trail, Blueberry-Churchill XC Race, and Brandon Scramble, a 5-km fun race; no snowmobiles; lodging at Churchill House Inn, furnished to retain its 19th-century heritage; hearty country food served family style, fresh French bread a specialty; stockpot soup lunch served to day skiers. Information: Marion & Mike Shonstrom, Churchill House Inn, RFD 3, Brandon, VT 05733. 802-247-3300. **Blueberry Hill Ski Touring Center** (12 m E off SR 73), 40 m of marked and maintained trails over gently rolling to challenging terrain on national forest and Central Vermont Power lands; trail fee ($3) and map; no snowmobiles; group and private instruction; guided tours including tours to inns on Vermont Ski Touring Trail (S to Churchill House Inn, N to Middlebury Snow Bowl); citizens' races; rental and retail shop; lodging and meals at area inn by reservation. Information: Blueberry Hill Ski Touring Center, RFD, Goshen, VT 05733. 802-247-6735.

BRATTLEBORO: Living Memorial Park (1.2 m W on SR 9, then left through covered bridge, drive to top of park), trail starts at picnic shelter; 1-m lighted trail (Mon.–Sat. 7–10 pm) for novice skiers on gentle rolling terrain; ice skating and downhill ski slope; no snowmobiles; warming shelter, snack bar; plowed parking area; operated by Recreation & Parks Dept. Information: Superintendent, Living Memorial Park, P.O. Box 513, Brattleboro, VT 05301. 802-454-5808.

BROOKFIELD: Green Trails Country Inn (by the Floating Bridge in historic Brookfield Village), 20 m of marked and maintained interconnecting trails for novice and intermediate skiers over rolling meadows with highland vistas and through wooded areas; 3-m trail leads to 400-acre **Allis State Park** with marked trails and Adirondack shelters; trail donation appreciated, trail map available; rental and retail shop; instruction; no snowmobiles; the inn, a refurbished 1840 white clapboard farmhouse, offers rooms with bath as well as apartment units; down-home country cooking, cocktails, wine list, and old player piano at the Fork Shop Restaurant, once a pitchfork factory. Reservations and information: Green Trails Country Inn, Box 402, Brookfield, VT 05036. 802-276-2012.

BROWNSVILLE: Mt. Ascutney Ski Area (exit 8 or 9 off I-91; 6 m W of Windsor on SR 44), about 5 m of marked novice to intermediate trails; no trail fee, map available; rentals; group and private instruction, guided tours; downhill ski facilities with day lodge, cafeteria, lounge with entertainment; nursery; a family area with slopeside condominium and private home rentals; additional lodging, restaurants, services in Brownsville, Windsor, and White River Junction. Information: Mt. Ascutney Corp., Rt. 44, Brownsville, VT. 05037. 802-484-7711.

CHESTER: Ski Tours of Vermont (in Chester), variety of special guided tours for weekends or weeks; inter-inn tours, tours for individuals, groups, and families; winter camping and survival instruction. Information: Ski Tours of Vermont, RFD 1, Chester, VT 05143. 802-875-3631.

CRAFTSBURY COMMON: The Inn on the Common/Craftsbury Ski Touring Center (35 m N of Barre via SR 14), 47 m of marked, maintained, and partly groomed trails on widely varied terrain from gentle looping forest trails to difficult mountainous treks; group and private instruction; wilderness tours into areas with abundant wildlife, moonlight tours; trail lunch available; race training and waxing clinics; rental and retail shop; trail fee ($2; guests of the Inn and Center, free), trail map; The Center has 23 dormitory bedrooms, 2 apartments, indoor recreation and game rooms, meals served in a rustic dining hall; The Inn on the Common has luxurious bedrooms furnished with antiques, sumptuous dinners and breakfasts. Information: Penny & Michael Schmitt, The Inn on the Common; Russell Spring, The Craftsbury Center, Box 56; Craftsbury Common, VT 05827. The Inn: 802-586-9619; The Center: 802-586-2514.

GRANVILLE: Puddledock Ski Touring Trails (N on SR 100), 4 m of beginner trails on Granville Gulf State Reservation; trails marked with red metal rectangles and arrows $2'' \times 5''$; good snow cover necessary for rough terrain; maps available from dispenser at trailhead; parking area adjacent to SR 100 in Granville Gulf. Information: Agency of Environmental Conservation, Dept. of Forests, Parks & Recreation, Montpelier, VT 05602.

GREENSBORO: Highland Lodge Ski Touring Center (1.5 m N between SR 14 & SR 16; 35 m from Canada), over 30 m of marked and maintained trails on rolling hills of fields and woods overlooking Caspian Lake; beginner to expert terrain; trail fee ($2; guests free) includes map; group and private instruction; guided tours (special family rates); ski shop with rentals, repairs, and sales; no snowmobiles; pretty country lodge has 12 bedrooms with bath, 3 non-housekeeping cottages; breakfast and dinner served in the lodge dining room, light lunches in the ski shop; discount and package plans available. Information: Dave and Carol Smith, Highland Lodge, Greensboro, VT 05841. 802-533-2647.

JAY: Sunshine Ski Touring Center (E on SR 242; 5 m S of Canadian border; 3 m from Jay Peak Ski Area), over 40 m of color-coded marked trails for beginner to mountaineer expert meander through wooded areas with a few open meadows and spectacular views; 15-plus m of trails are groomed with tracksetter; selection of downhill trails for the telemark enthusiast; trail fee ($1.50), trail map (50¢); trails to neighboring villages enable day tourers to stop for lunch at a country restaurant; certified instruction; rental and retail shop; special tours, clinics and biweekly citizens' races; no snowmobiles; hotel, restaurant and cocktail lounge on premises. Information: Richard Lahr, Sunshine Ski Touring Center, Rt. 242, Jay, VT 05859. 802-988-4459.

JEFFERSONVILLE: Smugglers' Notch (S on SR 108), 32 m of marked, picturesque trails, 16 m of which are groomed; group and private instruction; rentals; day and evening guided tours with wine and cheese get-together after evening tours; extensive downhill ski facilities; full-service resort area with deluxe condominium lodging within walking distance of trails; restaurants, lounges, recreation center, heated indoor pool, saunas, indoor tennis, ice-skating rink; nursery; package plans. Information: Smugglers' Notch Ski Area, Jeffersonville, VT 05464. 802-644-8851. Reservations: 800-451-3222.

KILLINGTON: Mountain Meadows Ski Touring Center (off US 4 in Killington, on Thundering Brook Rd.), 40 m of marked trails, 15 m of which are meticulously groomed; trail system spreads out across Kent Lake and the surrounding hills of the beautiful mountain valley in the heart of Killington; mostly novice to intermediate terrain; trail fee ($3), free trail map: EPSTI-certified group and private instruction, video instruction available; half-day and full-day picnic tours by arrangement; moonlight tours include rentals, use of head-lamps, short lesson, tour around Kent Lake and the Appalachian Trail, and wine party afterward; Ladies' Day program (Wed.) includes lesson, tour and lunch; lodge on S end of Vermont Ski Touring Trail; rental and retail shop; buffet "souper-snack" lunches served to day skiers; accommodations and meals at Mountain Meadows Lodge; additional lodging (upwards of 7000 beds), restaurants, and services in area. Information: John S. Tidd, Mountain Meadows Ski Touring Center, Killington, VT 05751. 802-775-7077. Reservations: 802-775-1010. **Killington Ski Area** (off US 4; 11 m E of Rutland), 5 m of marked trails for novices to experts through wooded areas, along brooks, and into open meadows with panoramic views; extensive downhill ski facilities; ski touring center located in Snowshed Base Lodge along with rental, repair, and retail shop, cafeteria, Angus Tavern Restaurant, nursery. Major resort area with budget to luxury accommodations, variety of restaurants, après-ski, and services. Information: Killington Ski Area, Killington, VT 05751.

LONDONDERRY: Viking Ski Touring Center (on Little Pond Rd.), 17 m of marked beginner to intermediate interconnecting trails on gently rolling woodland and open fields; 10 m of trails expertly groomed; trail fee ($3); detailed map has short descriptions of each trail; Nordic Ski Patrol on duty when available; area near extensive backcountry trail system in the **Green Mountain National Forest;** EPSTI-certified instructors offer group and private lessons; variety of scheduled tours on weekends, most 15 to 20 km long, on public trails in Landgrove/Peru area of the national forest; scheduled backcountry tours for good intermediate and expert skiers; all tours accompanied by Nordic Ski Patrol member equipped with radio communication; some tours include lunch; scheduled cross-country races; rental shop; ski shop; waxing and warming hut; snacks, hot and cold drinks available. Lodging, restaurants, and services in Londonderry, Landgrove, and Weston. Information: Viking Ski Touring Center, Little Pond Rd., Londonderry, VT 05148. 802-824-3933. **Wild Wings Ski Touring Center** (W on SR 11 in Peru) a small family operation offering 7 m of marked and groomed trails, plus access to unlimited touring possibilities in Green Mountain National Forest; instruction, rentals and warming room. Information: Wild Wings Ski Touring Center, Box 132, Peru, VT 05152. 802-824-6793. **Timber Ridge Ski Area** (7 m E on SR 121 in Windham), many m of cross-country trails start at the downhill ski area base lodge; alpine and Nordic ski shop; cafeteria, sundecks. Information: Timber Ridge Ski Area, Windham, VT 05359. 802-824-6806.

LUDLOW: Okemo Mountain Ski Area (1 m N off SR 100 & SR 103), marked and maintained trails vary from 1.5-m novice loop to 6-m trail for advanced skiers; instruction and guided tours; rental, repair and retail shops; special children's rates; downhill ski facilities with day lodge, cafeteria, cocktail lounge; nursery; lodging, restaurants, and services in Ludlow. Information: Okemo Mountain Ski Area, Ludlow, VT 05149. 802-228-4041. **Fox Run Resort** (in Ludlow), 100 acres with marked and maintained trails for novice to advanced skiers; trail fee ($1); instruction and guided tours; rentals; lodging at area. Information: Pat Garvey, Fox Run Resort, P.O. Box O, Ludlow, VT 05149. 802-228-8871.

LYNDONVILLE: Burke Mountain Recreation Touring Center (exit 23 off I-91; 7 m N on SR 114 in E. Burke), 32 m of marked and maintained interconnecting trails for beginner to expert skiers through forests and over open fields with view of Willoughby Gap; trail fee ($2), map available; certified EPSTI group and private instruction; guided tours; rental and retail shop; downhill ski facilities with day lodge, cafeteria, lounge; nursery; condominium lodging at area, reservation service for nearby lodging; Cross-Country Learn-to-Ski plan includes trail fee, lessons, rental equipment for 5 days (Mon.–Fri.). Information: Burke Mountain Recreation, Inc., E. Burke, VT 05832. 802-626-3305. **Lyndon Outing Club** (1 m E), cross-country skiing; downhill ski facilities, day lodge, cafeteria. Information: Lyndon Outing Club, Lyondonville, VT 05851. 802-626-9876. **Darion Inn Ski Touring Center** (in E. Burke), large old Vermont farm with 25 m of groomed trails with machine-set tracks; instruction and guided tours; rental, repair, and retail shop; private rooms with bath and ski dorm accommodations; dining rooms and bar. Information: Darion Inn Ski Touring Center, East Burke, VT 05832. 802-626-5641.

MIDDLEBURY: Middlebury College Snow Bowl (13 m E on SR 125), extensive cross-country ski program; instruction available; N end of Vermont Ski Touring Trail starts here; downhill ski facilities with day lodge, snack bar. Information: Middlebury College Snow Bowl, Middlebury, VT 05753. 802-388-4356.

MOUNT SNOW: Mount Snow Ski Touring Center (off SR 100, 2 m from Mount Snow), 50 m of marked and groomed trails over meadows and through woodlands with occasional spectacular views; instruction and guided tours; rentals and waxing available; full-service resort area with extensive downhill ski facilities, variety of accommodations, restaurants, and après-ski; shops, services, and country store. Information: Mount Snow Ski Touring Center, Mount Snow, VT 05356. 802-464-3333. **The Hermitage Inn** (off SR 100 between Mount Snow and Wilmington; 3 m up on Cold-brook Rd.), 12 to 15 m of marked and maintained trails through fields, woods, and sugarbush for beginners to experts; trail fee ($2), map available; group and private instruction; guided tours; rentals; small country inn with accommodations and gourmet restaurant. Information: Jim McGovern, The Hermitage Inn, Box 457, Coldbrook Rd., Wilmington, VT 05363. 802-464-3759. Rentals and lessons: 802-464-5637. **Green Mountain House** (5 m N on SR 100 in West Wardsboro), 5 m of partly marked and maintained trails on unplowed roads, bridle paths, old logging roads, and hiking trails; no trail fee or map; instruction and rentals; family-oriented inn with accommodations for groups of up to 90; hearty home-style meals, trail and snack lunches also available. Information: Green Mountain House, Rt. 100, West Wardsboro, VT 05360. 802-896-8491.

NORTH HERO: Charlie's Northland Cross-Country Trails (US 2 on Lake Champlain; 30 m N of Burlington), 31 acres and 6 m of marked and groomed trails over rolling hills and meadows and through cedar grove; trail fee ($1); rentals available; housekeeping cottages and lodge accommodations; coffee, cocoa, hot spiced cider, and homemade doughnuts in the lounge. Information: Northland Inc., US 2, North Hero, VT 05474. 802-372-8822.

RANDOLPH: Green Mountain Touring Center (2 m W on SR 66; exit 4 off I-89), 25 m of marked and maintained trails on 1200 acres; beginner to expert terrain on open meadows and wooded mountainsides; trail fee ($2), free map; rentals and instruction; guided tours for inn guests only; lodging and home-cooked meals. Information: Bob Gray, Green Mountain Touring Center, Green Mountain Stock Farm, Randolph, VT 05060. 802-728-5575.

RUTLAND: Mountain Top Ski Touring Center (8 m NE via US 4 or US 7; 1.8 m N of Chittenden), 55 m of marked trails, 12 m of which are groomed, meander through the mountains, over open meadows, and around the Chittenden Reservoir at 2000-ft elevations; 600-acre property adjacent to **Green Mountain National Forest;** trail fee ($3), detailed contour trail map available; old Horse Barn has rental and retail shop, antique stoves in warming area and hot apple cider; EPSTI-certified instruction program includes group and private ski lessons, racing and winter camping classes; also, periodic clinics, seminars, and films; moonlight tours, guided overnight tours to country inns on Vermont Ski Touring Trail; accommodations and hearty food at Mountain Top Inn. Information: Mountain Top Inn, Chittenden, VT 05737. 802-483-2311.

STOWE: Edson Hill Ski Touring Center (3 m N on SR 108, then 2 m up on Edson Hill Rd.; halfway between Stowe village and Mt. Mansfield), about 40 m of interconnecting marked and maintained trails on 2000 acres, many trails groomed; beginner to expert terrain on gently undulating wooded hillside, some open fields, mostly facing south, affording sheltered trails and lovely views; all skiers must register at shop; daily small trail fee includes parking and mini-map; large detailed map ($1.50); group and private instruction, guided tours on request; rental and retail shop; trail food at ski shop, fireside lunches in Manor Lounge; choice of accommodations includes rooms with private bath, with fireplace, bunk rooms, and suites; dining room and fully licensed lounge; special lodging and touring package, family rates for rental equipment. Information: Edson Hill Ski Touring Center, RR 1, Stowe, VT 05672. 802-253-8954 or 7371. **Topnotch Ski Touring Center** (4 m N on SR 108), 50 m of marked and maintained trails on varied terrain of open fields and woodlands; trail fee ($1.25), trail map available ($1.25); private and group instruction, guided tours; rental and retail shop; candy, hot drinks, and energy snacks at trailhead warming shelter; luxury accommodations at Inn, continental cuisine, vintage wines, and entertainment in the bar. Information: Topnotch Ski Touring Center, Mount Mansfield Rd., Stowe, VT 05672. 802-253-8585. **Trapp Family Lodge** (4 m N off SR 108), one of the first ski touring centers in the country; 60 m of marked and maintained trails on wooded and open terrain with many beautiful views; trail fee ($2), trail map ($1.50); trails connect to other trail systems in area leading to Bolton Valley, Madonna Mountain Ski Area, and Edson Hill Manor (approximately 100-m trail system in the area); ski school, directed by Ned Gillette, former Olympic cross-country ski team member, offers group and private instruction for all skill levels from first-time skiers to advanced skiers interested in learning wilderness touring and winter survival; special price for 5 days of lessons, rentals, and trail fees; instruction in racing technique; backcountry guided tours with lunch in trailside mountain log cabin, 5 km from start; MAP accommodations at lodge. Information: Trapp Family Lodge, Stowe, VT 05672. 802-253-8511. **Cross Country Outfitters** (1 m N on SR 108), 15 m of marked and partly groomed trails on beginner to expert terrain of hardwood forest and open meadows; certified instruction, guided tours; trails link with Stowe area system of trails; no trail fee; rentals, family prices; light snacks available at ski shop. Information: Cross Country Outfitters, Mountain Rd., Box 1308, Stowe, VT 05672. 802-253-4582. **Ski Hostel Lodge** (6 m S of Stowe on SR 100; 4 m N of Waterbury; exit 10 off I-89), surrounded by acres of beautiful terrain with many m of unmarked but easy-to-follow trails for beginners to experts; accommodations for 80 guests in dorms or rooms; hearty meals served country style; game room with piano and fireplace; minutes from Stowe. Information: Martha Guthridge, Ski Hostel Lodge, Waterbury Center, VT 05677. 802-244-8859. Stowe area, with major downhill ski facilities has numerous accommodations, restaurants, shops and services. For information and reservations: Stowe Area Association, Stowe, VT 05672. 802-253-7321. Toll free: 800-451-3260.

STRATTON MOUNTAIN: Stratton Mountain Nordic Center (18 m E of Manchester, off SR 30 in Stratton Mountain), many m of marked trails; certified instructors offer group and private lessons; half-day and full-day guided tours, Wed.-night moonlight tour with wine and cheese backpack; rentals; extensive downhill ski facilities; full-service resort area with wide variety of accommodations, restaurants, and lots of apres-ski. Information: Stratton Mountain Nordic Center, Stratton Mountain, VT 05155. 802-297-2200. **Cracker Barrel Ski Shop** (E; at jct of SR 100 & SR 30, in Rawsonville), about 15 m of marked and maintained novice to expert trails with access to many more; 6-m trail to Gale Meadow Lake; no trail fee, map available; group and private instruction; guided tours; rentals (weekly package rates); abundant lodging, restaurants, and services in area. Information: Jeff Sullivan, Cracker Barrel Ski Shop, Box 263, Bondville, VT 05340. 802-297-1200.

WAITSFIELD: Tucker Hill Ski Touring Center (S off SR 100, then

1½ m W on SR 17), 15 to 20 m of marked, maintained, and groomed trails for all levels of skiers; many newly cut trails and old logging roads through wooded hills and flat areas for mostly intermediate skiers, plus some very tough trails; trail fee ($1.50), trail map available; group and private instruction; guided midmorning tours with rental, guide, and lunch included; Lunar Tours by reservation; Cross-Country shop (open daily 9 am-5 pm) has warming area with wood stove, retail and rental equipment; snowshoe rentals; comfortable lodging and home-cooked meals with fresh-baked bread at rustic Tucker Hill Lodge. Information: Tucker Hill Ski Touring Center, c/o Tucker Hill Lodge, Waitsfield, VT 05673. 802-496-3203. Lodge: 802-496-3983. **Ole's Cross-Country Center** (Sugarbush Warren Airport), rentals, sales, instruction, guided tours. Information: 802-496-3430. **Valley Ski Touring Guide Service** (East Warren Rd., Waitsfield), instruction and guide service specializing in family touring; nursery available; by appointment only. Information: 802-496-2242. **Sugarbush Ski Touring Center** (Sugarbush Inn in Warren), 50 m of marked trails on varied terrain for all skill levels; certified instruction; rental, repair, and retail shop; guided tours; weekly ski touring movies and equipment demonstrations. Information: Sugarbush Ski Touring Center, Sugarbush Inn, Warren, VT 05674. 802-583-2301. A 5.7-m part of the **Long Trail** is suitable for advanced intermediate and expert skiers; access by Sugarbush Valley Ski Area Gondola to Lincoln Peak, then follow red triangle markers N 2.9 m to Mt. Ellen at top of Glen Ellen Ski Area chairlift; trail continues N over undulating terrain another 2.8 m to General Stark Mtn. at top of Mad River Glen chairlift; notify area ski patrols before attempting trip; no less than 3 members to a party recommended; deep snow conditions required to cover rough terrain. Waitsfield/Warren areas with 3 major downhill ski areas (Sugarbush Valley, Glen Ellen, and Mad River Glen) offers numerous accommodations, restaurants, après-ski, and services.

WOODSTOCK: Woodstock Ski Touring Center (Woodstock exit off I-89, then W on US 4 to Woodstock, then S on SR 106, ½ m), over 50 m of marked and maintained trails, 25 m of which are groomed and periodically set with tracks; beginner to expert terrain on woodlands and pastures with excellent vistas of picturesque Woodstock village; trail fee ($2), trail maps available; EPSTI-certified group and private instruction; novice and intermediate picnic and nature tours guided by ski instructors trained in forestry and nature study; measure racecourse; snowshoeing permitted on designated trails, rentals available; touring center (open daily from 9 am) has retail and rental equipment, waxing room, locker rooms, showers, fireside bar and restaurant; warming hut with paddle tennis nearby; comfortable lodging at Woodstock Inn (½ m) with 122 rooms, ski/lodging plans; additional accommodations, restaurants in Woodstock. Information: John Wiggin, Director, Woodstock Ski Touring Center, Woodstock, VT 05091. 802-457-2114. **Skyline Trail** is a 12-m privately built and maintained trail from Barnard (N on SR 12) to Pomfret; trail well-marked with blue and orange diamond-shaped markers; 2 lean-to shelters for winter camping. Information at Woodstock Ski Touring Center.

VIRGINIA

For additional information, contact the individual area or Virginia State Travel Service, 6 North Sixth St., Richmond, VA 23219.

HARRISONBURG: George Washington National Forest (in several sections, partly in WV; hq in Federal Bldg., Harrisonburg), over 1 million acres of rugged mountainous terrain including Blue Ridge, Shenandoah, Allegheny, and Massanutten Ranges; there are no identified ski trails in the forest since the snow cover is generally inconsistent, but in good snow years, skiers are welcome to use the many miles of unplowed Forest Service roads as well as marked hiking trails (391 m) throughout the forest. The **Blue Ridge Parkway** (between Waynesboro and Roanoke) when closed by snow is excellent for touring and has breathtaking views of the Shenandoah Valley as well as views to the east. **Appalachian Trail** also follows along the ridge crossing the parkway several times. Information: Forest Supervisor, George Washington National Forest, 210 Federal Bldg., Harrisonburg, VA 22801.

HOT SPRINGS: The Homestead (on US 220, 75 m N of Roanoke) offers cross-country skiing when conditions permit; downhill ski facilities, day lodge, cafeteria, restaurant; Olympic-size ice-skating rink (rentals), sleigh rides, indoor pool, all-weather tennis; a year-round luxury resort hotel with fine food, superb service, evening dancing, concerts; 5600-ft commercial airstrip. Information: The Homestead, Hot Springs, VA, 24445. 703-839-5500.

MARION: Mount Rogers National Recreation Area, Crest Zone (near NC/TN border) includes 5729-ft Mt. Rogers, highest point in VA; has hilly, generally open alpine meadows with rock outcrops; some of the blazed hiking and horse trails plus Forest Service roads are suitable for cross-country skiing with enough snow cover; access to area is at Elk Garden Gap via SR 600 near Konnarock; **Appalachian Trail** also passes through the area, crossing Mt. Rogers and White Top Mtn. summits; no snowmobiles. Information: Ranger, National Recreation Area Headquarters, U.S. Forest Service, Marion, VA 24354. 703-783-5196.

SHENANDOAH NATIONAL PARK (300-sq-m park atop the Blue Ridge Mountains): **Skyline Drive** winds 105 m along the crest of the ridge with spectacular views of the Shenandoah Valley and the Piedmont from numerous overlooks; elevations to 4000 ft; abundant wildlife; 95 m of **Appalachian Trail** parallels Skyline Drive along ridge offering easy access; park is open year round, Drive is open except during periods of severe winter weather, most park facilities are closed during winter months; main access points at Front Royal (N) via I-66 and US 522, US 211 from Luray, I-64 from Charlottesville or Waynesboro. Information: Superintendent, Shenandoah National Park, Luray, VA 22835. 703-999-2241.

WASHINGTON

For additional information, contact the individual area or Washington Dept. of Commerce and Economic Development, Travel Development Division, General Administration Bldg., Olympia, WA 98504.

CHELAN: North Cascades National Park (NE; bisected by SR 20), cross-country touring opportunities are limited due to high avalanche risk; **Lake Chelan National Recreation Area** has an 11-m route that generally follows the Stehekin River and Stehekin Valley Rd. (access from Chelan via float plane, Chelan Airways daily charter, or via boat, Lake Chelan Boat Co.); side trails lead to Coon Lake and other points of interest; winter camping and snowmobiling permitted; accommodations and restaurant at North Cascades Lodge at Stehekin Landing. Information: Superintendent, North Cascades National Park, 800 State St., Sedro Woolley, WA 98284. 206-855-1331.

LONGVIEW: St. Helens Ranger District of **Gifford Pinchot National Forest** (I-5 N to Spirit Lake exit, then 50 m E on SR 504 to Spirit Lake/St. Helens area), 7–8 m of marked and maintained trails designated for skiers only; many m of roads for multi-use; 6 interconnecting trails marked with cross-country ski symbol at start, then blue diamond along the way; mostly easy terrain with gentle slopes, only several spots with moderate grades; 2 trails marked for both skiers and snowmobiles on forest roads with varied terrain offer excellent views of Mt. Adams and Mt. St. Helens; **Spirit Lake Snow Trails** map available with arrows showing suggested direction of travel and brief trail descriptions; restaurant in Spirit Lake Lodge (privately owned) open weekends. Accommodations, restaurants, and services in Castle Rock (50 m) and Longview (60 m). Information: District Ranger, St. Helens Ranger District, U.S. Forest Service, Cougar, WA 98616. 206-238-5244.

PORT ANGELES: Olympic National Park (17 m S), about 24 m of marked and mapped trails in the **Hurricane Ridge Area** with open subalpine meadows at 5000-ft elevations and spectacular views of surrounding peaks, glaciers, and the Strait of Juan de Fuca; 7 ski touring routes range from easy meadows near Hurricane Ridge Lodge to difficult routes with steep icy hillsides; route 1 and route 2 offer short tours over moderate terrain with drifts and bumps to challenge novice technique, good views within a short distance; 1.5-m route 3 climbs a broad windswept summit to a 360-degree panorama atop Hurricane Hill—advanced skiers will find this a rewarding tour; routes 5 & 6 follow unplowed road 11.5 m to 6000 ft above timberline Obstruction Point—steep sidehill and exposure to storms make this a difficult route recommended, under good conditions, for advanced skiers; Old Elwha Rd. route 4 descends through open meadows and wooded areas to Whiskey Bend and to Elwha Ranger Station—difficult tour subject to variable conditions;

cross-country skiers sign out and sign in; guided naturalist tours; overnight tourers check with a ranger for parking, weather, route and registration information; downhill ski facilities; Lodge (10 am-4:30 pm, weekends and holidays weather permitting) offers lunch, picnic area, alpine ski rentals, snowshoe rentals, waxing area, ski patrol, and first-aid services; no snowmobiles. Information: Superintendent, Olympic National Park, 600 East Park Ave., Port Angeles, WA 98362. 206-452-9236. Current weather forecast and snow conditions: 206-452-9235.

SEATTLE: The Cross Country Center (at Mt. Hyak Ski Area on Snoqualmie Pass, 55 m E via I-90; exit Hyak), about 30 m of marked and maintained trails with access to many more m of trails in Snoqualmie Pass Area; varied terrain from flat and rolling to steep alpine slopes in rugged Cascade Mountains with open scenic vistas including views of 8 lakes; Pacific Crest Trail passes within 2 m of area; trails machine-groomed with tracksled behind roller, at least one trail groomed at all times; trails patrolled by Nordic Patrol unit of the National Ski Patrol; Ski School offers one-day lessons, 3-week series of 3 days of lessons for beginners or intermediates, all-day flat running clinic for advanced skiers and racers, downhill clinic for instruction ᵣf telemark, parallel, and open turns; special program of instructioɩ and events for the blind, area hosted Nordic events of 1979 National Blind Games; competition and citizens' races; guided tours; no snowmobiles; rental and retail shop; downhill ski facilities with day lodge, cafeteria; lodging at Sundance Condominiums (206-434-6233). Public bus from Seattle area to Snoqualmie Pass. Information: The Cross Country Center, P.O. Box 118, Snoqualmie Pass, WA 98068. 206-434-6503. Snow report: 206-442-SNOW.

SPOKANE: Mt. Spokane Ski Area (30 m NE via US 395, US 2 and SR 206), 16 m of marked trails for beginner to expert skiers on old logging roads, trails along Brickle Creek and to Spirit Lake; no instruction, rentals available in Spokane; snowmobiles permitted; downhill ski facilities with day lodges, cafeteria, restaurant, cocktail lounge, après-ski; nursery. Deluxe lodging at area Snowblaze Condominiums (Rt. 1, Box 416-B, Mead, WA 99021. 509-238-4630). Information: Mt. Spokane Skiing Corp., N. 7322 Division St., Spokane, WA 99208. 509-238-6281. Snow report: 509-238-6223 or 6269.

TACOMA: Mount Rainier National Park (70 m SE; hq on SR 706 at Longmire), 14,410-ft snowcapped ancient volcanic peak surrounded by glacial system with dense forests below; 5 m of marked trails on moderate to difficult terrain at **Paradise** (E of Longmire) area recommended for touring; winter camping permitted at designated sites, Sunshine Point campground near Nisqually entrance open year round; Visitor Center and snack bar open daily at Longmire, weekends, holidays at Paradise; guided snowshoe tours; snowmobiles permitted in designated areas; park entrance fee ($2 per car). Accommodations, restaurant, services in Ashford. Information: Superintendent, Mount Rainier National Park, Star Route, Tahoma Woods, Ashford, WA 98304. 206-569-2341.

VANCOUVER: Wind River Ranger District of **Gifford Pinchot National Forest** (SR 14 E to Carson exit, then 27 m N on County Rd. N73 to Winter Sports Area), 12 m of marked and maintained interconnecting trails; Trail 1 is a 5.25-m scenic loop through dense timber and open clearcuts with some steep grades for intermediate or better skiers, a 1.5-m shortcut loop possible with gentle grades for beginners; Trail 2, a 1.5-m scenic tour into McClellan Meadows, features a log stringer snow bridge over Wind River, for intermediates; Trail 3 is rated easy for first 1.5 m, last 3 m for advanced skiers with a knowledge of winter survival; Trail 4 offers a safe and scenic 2-m tour for novice or expert; all trails tagged with luminous orange cards; snowmobiles on separate designated trails; no shelter or food service; plowed parking areas, cars must have State Sno-Park Permit (Office of Winter Recreation, Washington State Parks and Recreation, P.O. Box 1128, Olympia, WA 98504; annual fee $5). Accommodations, restaurants, and services in Stevenson (31 m). For trail map and information: District Ranger, U.S. Forest Service, Carson, WA 98610. 509-427-5645.

YAKIMA: White Pass Ski Area (52 m W on US 12), unlimited touring possibilities on subalpine and alpine terrain of surrounding Wenatchee National Forest; beautiful rolling, heavily wooded areas with little avalanche danger; marked trail system in the process of development as well as plans for instruction program and rentals; cross-country skiers permitted to use lower part of alpine ski area; lifts can be used to reach high country, particularly in the spring when the snow pack has settled; downhill ski facilities with day lodge, cafeteria, bar, locker room; lodging at area Village Inn; restaurant, grocery store, service station; heated pool. Information: White Pass Co., P.O. Box 354, Yakima, WA 98907. 509-453-8731. Additional accommodations and restaurants in Packwood (19 m W) and Rimrock Lake (9 m E).

WEST VIRGINIA

For additional information, contact the individual area or West Virginia Travel Development, Dept. of Economic and Community Development, State Capitol Bldg., Charleston, WV 25305.

DAVIS: Canaan Valley State Park (7 m S on SR 32), 5810-acre park with marked trails suitable for cross-country skiing; area accommodations include 250-room lodge and 15 fully equipped cabins; 34 trailer campsites; restaurant, cocktail lounge, convention facilities, lighted ice-skating rink; downhill ski area with day lodge, snack bar, restaurant and pub, nursery. Information: Canaan Valley Resorts, Rt. 1, Box 39, Davis, WV 26260. 304-866-4121. **Blackwater Falls State Park** (2 m W off SR 32), 1688-acre park dominated by waterfalls and deep river canyon has marked trails connecting to Canaan Mtn. Area of Monongahela National Forest; accommodations in beautiful natural stone and wood Blackwater Falls Lodge with 55 rooms; 25 fully equipped cabins, 65 trailer campsites; restaurant, snack bar; grocery store nearby. Information: Manager, Blackwater Falls Lodge, Davis, WV 26260. 304-259-5216.

MARLINTON: Watoga State Park (S off US 219), located in the Appalachian highlands, is largest of the state parks with 10,057 acres and many m of scenic trails and horseback paths suitable for cross-country skiing; adjoins Calvin Price State Forest. Lodging, restaurants, and services in Marlinton. Information: Superintendent, Watoga State Park, Star Rt. 1, Box 252, Marlinton, WV 24954.

MONONGAHELA NATIONAL FOREST: Cranberry Back Country (SW tip of forest; access points along SR 39, E of Richwood), 53,000 acres with about 80 m of interconnecting trails and unplowed roads suitable for cross-country skiing; beginner to advanced terrain ranges in elevation from 2600 to 4600 ft with wide forested ridges, narrow, steep-sided river valleys, and numerous rock outcrops; easy-to-follow backcountry trail map (free) has numbers, names, and mileages for all roads and trails; roads are signed at junctions; winter camping permitted, 9 three-sided shelters available along Cranberry River Rd.; roads and trails recommended for skiers include Highland Scenic Hwy., Forest Rds. nos. 76, 102, 108, and Cow Pasture Trail (access from Cranberry Mountain Visitor Center, 20 m E of Richwood on SR 39), Dogway Fork Rd. (2 m W of Visitor Center off SR 39), and Forest Rd. no. 77 (opposite North Bend Picnic Area on SR 39). Accommodations, restaurants, and services in Richwood and Marlinton. Map and information: District Ranger, U.S. Forest Service, P.O. Box 110, Richwood, WV 26261. 304-846-6558. **Canaan Mountain Area** (NE part of forest; off SR 32, just W of Davis), Forest Rd. no. 13 and foot trails in the area are recommended for cross-country skiing; trail map available at Blackwater Falls Lodge (see Davis). Information: District Ranger, U.S. Forest Service, Parsons, WV 26287. Two areas above are recommended by the Forest Service as best for cross-country skiing, although skiers are welcome on all trails and unplowed roads throughout the forest. Additional information: Forest Supervisor, Monongahela National Forest, Elkins, WV 26241.

PIPESTEM: Pipestem State Park (on SR 20, 17 m NE of Princeton exit off WV Turnpike), 4027-acre park with about 20 m of marked and maintained trails suitable for cross-country skiing; easy to difficult terrain, often rocky in areas, with beautiful overlooks of Mountain Creek Gorge; trail map available; rental equipment and ski clinics in the planning stage; snowmobiles permitted in certain areas. Accommodations at area lodge with 113 rooms, plus 25 housekeeping cottages; restaurant in lodge; snacks, sandwiches, and supplies in Black Bear Lounge. Additional restaurants, lodging, and services in Hinton, Athens, and Princeton. Information: Superintendent, Pipestem State Park, Pipestem, WV 25979. 304-466-1800.

SLATYFORK: Snowshoe (N on US 219; 42 m S of Elkins; 60 m N of Lewisburg), 31 km of beginner to advanced marked and maintained trails wind through tall spruce forests; average annual snowfall of over 200 inches; trail fee ($3), trail map available; class and private instruction; rentals; downhill ski area in NE-facing bowl with major center of activity and lodging located at top of mountain; cross-country skiers may ride the basin lifts back to the top; year-round second-home resort has day lodge with cafeteria, burger shack, dining room, bar, nursery; ski shop with alpine and Nordic gear; slopeside lodge and condominium accommodations for over 900; gourmet restaurants, lounges, and après-ski; package plans and group rates available. Information: Snowshoe Ski Area, Cross-country Ski Coordinator, Slatyfork, WV 26291. 304-799-6600; snow report: 304-799-6630.

WISCONSIN

For additional information, contact the individual area or Wisconsin Dept. of Business Development, Division of Tourism, P.O. Box 7606, Madison, WI 53707.

ANTIGO: Gartzke Flowage Trail (9 m E on Fifth Ave.), 2 marked loops totaling 3 km on rolling open and wooded terrain; open daylight hours. **Jack Lake Trail** (13 m N on US 45, then 2 m E on County Rd. J), 5.6 km of marked trails on hilly wooded terrain; shelter and restrooms at Veterans Memorial Park (1 m), open daylight hours. **Jack Lake Trail** (13 m N on US 45, then 2 m E on WI 54409. 715-623-4156. **Riverview Country Club** (4 m W on SR 64), 2 marked loops totaling 7.6 km on gentle open terrain; shelter, restrooms, and plowed parking area; open daylight hours. Food, lodging, and services in Antigo. Information: Riverview Country Club, Rt. 4, Antigo, 54409. 715-623-3623.

BARABOO: Devil's Lake State Park (5 m SE via SR 123 and County Rd. DL), 3 marked and partially groomed trails totaling 16.8 km; gentle rolling wooded terrain; restrooms at park hq, plowed parking area and trail maps at trailhead; open 6 am–11 pm; park sticker required; year-round camping. Information: Superintendent, Devil's Lake State Park, Rt. 4, Baraboo, WI 53913. 608-356-8301. **Mirror Lake State Park** (exit US 12 off I-90-94 to Fern Dell Rd., then 1.5 m S), 5.6 km marked trails on gentle wooded terrain;

restrooms; plowed parking area; park sticker required. Information: Superintendent, Mirror Lake State Park, Rt. 3, Box 92, Baraboo, WI 53913. 608-254-2333. **Devil's Head Ski Area** (exit SR 78 off I-94, then 10 m S on SR 78), 4-km marked trail; downhill ski facilities, cafeteria, restaurant; accommodations at area. Information: Devil's Head Ski Area, Box 38, Merrimac, WI 53561. 608-493-2251. **Christmas Mountain** (N to Wisconsin Dells, then 4.5 m W on County Rd. H), 11.2 km of marked trails on rolling terrain; rentals; downhill ski facilities, day lodge, restaurant, snack bar. Information: Christmas Mountain Ski Area, Box 1, Wisconsin Dells, WI 53965. 608-254-2531. **Woodside Ranch Resort** (NW; on SR 82, 7 m E of Mauston), 9.6 km of marked and groomed trails on rolling wooded terrain; trail map available; rentals; downhill ski facilities, sleigh rides, snowmobiling; accommodations, dining, and lounge at ranch. Information: Woodside Ranch Resort, Mauston, WI 53948. 608-847-4275.

BAYFIELD: Valkyrie Ski Trail (S on SR 13 to Washburn, then 8 m NW on County Rd. C to Mt. Valhalla Winter Sports Area), 3 marked and maintained, interconnecting loops of 1.9 m, 2.3 m, and 6.1 m; novice to intermediate, rolling wooded terrain in Chequamegon National Forest; trail map available; 3 rest areas en route; designated snowmobile trail; plowed parking area and shelter at trailhead, jct of County Rd. C and Forest Rd. 439. Food, lodging, and services in Washburn, Ashland, and Bayfield. Information: District Ranger, Washburn Ranger District, USFS, 103 East Bayfield, Washburn, WI 54891. 715-373-2667. **Port Mountain Ski Area** (3 m S on SR 13), 15 m of marked and groomed trails on rolling wooded terrain; rentals and instruction; downhill ski facilities, day lodge, cafeteria. Food, lodging, and services in Bayfield. Information: Port Mountain Ski Area, Box 239, Bayfield, WI 54813. 715-779-3227.

BLACK RIVER FALLS: Arrowhead Lodge Trail (1 m E off I-94 at SR 54), 11.2 km of marked and groomed trails on gentle wooded terrain; rentals available; accommodations and food at lodge. Information: Arrowhead Lodge, Black River Falls, WI 54615. 715-284-9471. **Black River State Forest** (SE to Millston, 4 m E on County Rd. O, then .75 m N on Smrekar Rd.), 6 marked loops totaling 12.8 km on hilly wooded terrain; restrooms; open 6 am–11 pm. Information: Supervisor, Black River State Forest, Rt. 4, Box 5, Black

River Falls, WI 54615. 715-284-5301. **Levis Mount Trail** (N to Merrillan, then E to jct of SR 95 & County Rd. J), 19.2 km of marked trails on gently rolling wooded terrain; toilets and plowed parking area. **Foster Trail-Rock Dam** (N via US 12 & County Rd. M to Rock Dam), 6.4 km of marked trails on rolling wooded terrain; toilets and plowed parking area. Information on preceding 2 trails: Clark Country Trails, Courthouse, Neillsville, WI 54456. 715-743-2490.

CHIPPEWA FALLS: Brunet Island State Park (24 m N via SR 178), 4.8 km of marked trails on gentle wooded terrain; plowed parking area; water at park office (7:45 am–4:30 pm). Information: Superintendent, Brunet Island State Park, Rt. 2, Cornell, WI 54732. 715-239-6888. **Lake Wissota State Park** (5 m NE on County Rd. O), 4 marked trails totaling 12.8 km on open and wooded slightly hilly terrain; restrooms, shelter, and plowed parking area; open 6 am–11 pm; park sticker required. Information: Superintendent, Lake Wissota State Park, Rt. 5, Box 188, Chippewa Falls, WI 54729. 715-382-4574. **Deepwood** (NW to Colfax, then 9 m NW on County Rd. N), 16 km of marked trails on rolling wooded terrain, plus open skiing on golf course; trail fee; rentals and instruction; downhill ski facilities; day lodge, restrooms; food and lodging at area; plowed parking area. Information: Deepwood Ski Area, Wheeler, WI 54772. 715-658-1394.

DODGEVILLE: Governor Dodge State Park (3 m N on SR 23), 2 marked trails totaling 10.4 km on rolling hilly wooded terrain; 50 yds of advanced trail must be walked; toilets and plowed parking area; park sticker required. Information: Superintendent, Governor Dodge State Park, Rt. 1, Dodgeville, WI 53533. 608-935-2315.

DOOR COUNTY: Potowatami State Park (4 m W of Sturgeon Bay on County Rd. C), 2 marked trails totaling 14.4 km on gentle wooded terrain on Sturgeon Bay; downhill ski facilities; restrooms, shelter; plowed parking area; open 6 am–11 pm; park sticker required; food, lodging, and services in Sturgeon Bay. Information: Superintendent, Rt. 8, Sturgeon Bay, WI 54235. 414-743-5123. **Peninsula State Park** (W of Ephraim), 3 marked loops totaling 19.2 km; toilets; plowed parking area; park sticker required. Information: Superintendent, Peninsula State Park, Fish Creek, WI 54212. 414-868-3258. **Omnibus Ski Area** (4 m N of Egg Harbor, or

S of Fish Creek), 3 marked and groomed trails totaling 16 km on open and wooded gentle terrain; access to many m of state trails; downhill ski facilities, day lodge, cafeteria, restaurant, cocktail lounge; ice skating. Food, lodging, and services in Fish Creek. Information: Omnibus Ski Area, Fish Creek, WI 54212. 414-868-3233. **Newport State Park** (5 m E of Ellison Bay via SR 42, then Newport Rd.), 12 marked trails totaling 36.8 km on open and wooded terrain on Lake Michigan; water, restrooms, and shelter; snowshoeing; winter camping; plowed parking area; park sticker required. Information: Superintendent, Newport State Park, Ellison Bay, WI 54210. 414-854-2500.

EAGLE RIVER: Gateway Lodge (N on US 45 to Land O'Lakes, then E on County Rd. B), 48 km of marked trails on rolling wooded terrain, most trails groomed; access to other area trails; rentals and instruction; downhill ski facilities; lodging, restaurant, cocktail lounge. Information: Gateway Lodge, Land O'Lakes, WI 54540. 715-547-3321. **Afterglow Trail** (N via SR 17 to Phelps, then 2.5 m N on County Rd. E to Forest Rd. 2565), 8 marked and groomed trails totaling 16 km on easy wooded terrain; access to national forest trails; trail fee, map available; restrooms, shelter, and plowed parking area; open 9 am–9 pm; cottage rentals. Information: Afterglow Lake Resort, Phelps, WI 54554. 715-545-2560. **Chanticleer Inn** (3 m E of Eagle River on SR 70), 6.4 km of marked and groomed trails on gentle open and wooded terrain; access to other area trails; rentals; open daylight hours; downhill ski facilities; ice skating, tobogganing, snowmobiling; year-round resort with variety of accommodations (package plans available); restaurant, cocktail lounge. Information: Chanticleer Inn, Rt. 3, Eagle River, WI 54521. 715-479-4486. **Anvil Ski Trail** (8.5 m E on SR 70), 11 m of marked interconnecting trails; gentle novice to hilly expert terrain in Nicolet National Forest; color-coded trail map; shelter en route; comfort station and plowed parking area at trailhead; winter camping; motorized vehicles not permitted without written permission. **Giant Pine Trail** (S on US 45 to Three Lakes, then 11 m E on SR 32 to Forest Rd. 2183 to Forest Rd. 2414, then N 1.6 m to parking area), 8 interconnecting marked loops totaling 8 m; wooded flat terrain in Nicolet National Forest, suitable for novice skiers; ski trail is designed and constructed for one-way traffic; trail map available; plowed parking area at trailhead; winter camping; no snowmobiles. Food, lodging, and services in Three Lakes and Eagle

River. Information for preceding 2 trails: Forest Supervisor, Nicolet National Forest, 68 S. Stevens St., Rhinelander, WI 54501. 715-362-3415. **Trees For Tomorrow** (in Eagle River), 1.6 km of marked trail open daily, 18.2 km of marked trails open weekends; rentals; instruction and seminars; lodging and food (reservations necessary for weekends). Information: Trees For Tomorrow, Ski Registrar, Box 609, Eagle River, WI 54521. 715-479-6456. **Pride O' The North Trail** (W on SR 70 to St. Germain, then 1.5 m NE on Birchwood Dr.), 2.4-km marked and groomed novice trail on wooded terrain; park along road; rental cottages (equipment furnished to guests). Information: 715-542-3793. **Musky Inn Trails** (W on SR 70 to St. Germain, then 1.75 m N off SR 155), 2 marked and groomed trails totaling 9.6 km on rolling to hilly wooded terrain; trail map; rentals; open daylight hours; lodging and food at area. Information: Musky Inn Trails, Rt. 1, St. Germain, WI 54558. 715-542-3768. **Eagle River Nordic Ski Center** (in Eagle River), more than 50 km of marked and groomed trails in Nicolet National Forest; rental and retail equipment; instruction, racing clinics, guided tours; overnight accommodations at lodge, gourmet food (package plans). Information: Eagle River Nordic Ski Center, Eagle River, WI 54521. 715-479-7285.

EAU CLAIRE: Carson, Fairfax & Riverview City Parks (in town) have marked trails on rolling wooded terrain suitable for cross-country skiing; maps available; toilets, shelters, and plowed parking areas; open 9 am–11 pm. Information: City of Eau Claire, Tourism Division, Eau Claire, WI 54701. 715-839-5025.

HAYWARD: Rock Lake Ski Touring Trail (NE via US 63 to Cable, then 7.5 m E on County Rd. M to Lakewoods Resort), 39.9 km of marked and partially groomed trails interconnecting for novice to intermediate skiers in Chequamegon National Forest (3 km of trail on private land connecting to forest land); map available; rentals; trailhead shelter, toilets, and plowed parking area; open daylight hours. **Namekagon Ski Trail** (NE via US 63 to Cable, then E on County Rd. M to County Rd. D to Forest Rd. 209), 3 interconnecting marked and groomed loops of 1.68 km, 2.4 km, and 2.2. km on gentle novice wooded terrain in Chequamegon National Forest; trail map available; open daylight hours; plowed parking area. Information for above 2 trails: District Ranger, Hayward Ranger District, USFS, Hayward, WI 54843, 715-634-4821. **Mt. Telemark**

(N via US 63 to Cable, then 3 m E on County Rd. M), one of the best touring centers in the country, known for its extensive, manicured trail system; 93 km of marked and groomed trails for novice to advanced skiers on wooded terrain; measured racing trails; trail fee, map available; rental and retail shop; group and private instruction for novice through advanced skiers, for telemark turns and racing technique; citizens' and Nastar races; downhill ski facilities; year-round resort with a variety of accommodations at Telemark Lodge (group rates and package plans), restaurants, cocktail lounges, entertainment; nursery; heated pool, saunas; shops. Information: Telemark Lodge, Cable, WI 54821. 715-798-3811.

Birkebeiner Trail is a 55-km trail that begins at Telemark Lodge and runs SW through Bayfield and Sawyer County forest lands to Hayward; Telemark hosts the American-Birkebeiner Race which draws several thousand enthusiastic competitors annually for what is reputed to be the nation's largest citizens' race. Information: Telemark Lodge (address above) or Hayward Chamber of Commerce, Hayward, WI 54843. Lodging, food, and services in Hayward.

Gull Lake Trail (SW on US 63 to US 53, then 6 m N of Trego on US 53, then 1.5 m E on County Rd. F, and 2 m N on Haynes Rd.), 8 km of marked trails on hilly wooded terrain suitable for advanced skiers; trail map available. **Nordic Woods** (SW; 14 m E of Spooner off SR 70 on Dugan Lake Rd.), 9.6 km of marked trails on rolling wooded terrain; map available; park along road. Information on preceding 2 trails: Washburn County Trails, County Hwy. Bldg., Spooner, WI 54801. 715-635-8725.

HUDSON: Willow River State Park (5 m NE on County Rd. A), 3 marked and groomed trails totaling 12.5 km on intermediate wooded terrain; winter registered camping; water, toilets, and plowed parking area; park sticker required. Information: Superintendent, Willow River State Park, Hudson, WI 54016. 715-386-5931. **Snowcrest** (10 m N on SR 35), 5 marked and groomed trails totaling 12.8 km on hilly open and wooded terrain; rentals and instruction; lighted trails for night skiing (open Sun.–Tues. 9 am–10 pm, Wed.–Sat. 9 am–11 pm); trail fee; downhill ski facilities, day lodge, cafeteria, restaurant; lodging, food, and services nearby. Information: Snowcrest, Rt. 1, Somerset, WI 54025. 715-247-3852. **Game Unlimited** (5 m NE on County Rd. E), 3 marked and groomed trails totaling 25.6 km on rolling open and wooded intermediate terrain; trail fee, open from 8 am; shelter, toilets, water at trailhead; lodging and cooking facilities for groups (by appointment); plowed parking area. Information: Game Unlimited, Rt. 2, Hudson, WI 54016. 715-246-5475.

HURLEY: Mecca 1 Trail (S on US 51; 1 m N of Mercer on US 51, then 4 m SW on County Rd. FF to Wagon Wheel Rd., 1 m to trail), 8.8 km of marked trails on intermediate rolling wooded terrain; facilities and maps available at Wagon Wheel Lodge. **Old Flambeau Trail** (SW on SR 77 at Montreal), 28.8 km of marked trails on wooded rolling terrain for intermediate skiers; water available; open daylight hours. Information on above trails: Iron County Trails, Iron County Forestry Dept., Hurley, WI 54532. 715-561-2697. **Whitecap Mountain** (7 m W via SR 77, then 3 m W on County Rd. E), 5 marked and groomed loops totaling 25 km on hilly wooded terrain; trail fee; rentals, instruction, guided tours, moonlight tours; downhill ski facilities, cafeteria, restaurant, cocktail lounge; lodging at area; winter camping. Information: Whitecap Mountain Ski Area, Montreal, WI 54550. 715-561-2227.

LA CROSSE: Mt. La Crosse (2 m S on SR 35), 2 marked trails totaling 3.2 km on rolling to hilly wooded terrain; rental and retail shop, instruction; downhill ski facilities; restaurant, cocktail lounge; accommodations, services nearby. Information: Mt. La Crosse Ski Area, Box 9, La Crosse, WI 54601. 608-788-0044. **Wildcat Mountain State Park** (E on SR 33, 1.5 m S of Ontario), 12 km of marked trails on wooded hilly terrain; toilets and plowed parking area; open 6 am–11 pm; camping (fee). Information: Superintendent, Wildcat Mountain State Park, Box 98, Ontario, WI 54651. 608-387-4775. **Perrot State Park** (NW via US 53 and SR 93; 3 m NW of Trempealeau off SR 93), 12 km of marked trails on hilly open and wooded terrain; trail map available; open daylight hours; shelter, toilets, and plowed parking area. Information: Superintendent, Perrot State Park, Trempealeau, WI 54661. 608-534-6409. **Tommy's River Forest Area** (N off US 53, 3 m S of Galesville), 22 km of marked and groomed trails on novice to intermediate, open and wooded terrain; trail fee, trail map available; rentals; instruction on weekends; shelter and restrooms (Mon.–Sat., 9 am–5 pm; Sun. 10 am–5 pm). Information: Supervisor, Tommy's River Forest Area, Rt. 2, Galesville, WI 54630. 608-582-2371.

LAKE GENEVA: Mt. Fuji (2 m NE at jct of SR 36 & Kreuger Rd.),

4.8 km of marked trails on rolling open and wooded terrain for intermediate skiers; trail fee; downhill ski facilities, day lodge, food service. Information: Mt. Fuji Ski Area, Lake Geneva, WI 53147. 414-248-6553.

MADISON: Goose Lake Wildlife Area (12 m E on Missouri Rd.), 4.8 km of marked trails on rolling terrain; unplowed parking area. **Brooklyn Wildlife Area** (12 m S on Hughes Rd.), 9.6 km of marked trails on rolling open and wooded terrain; unplowed parking area. **Mazomanie Wildlife Area** (16 m W on County Rd. Y), 9.6 km of marked trails on gentle, novice open terrain; unplowed parking area. Information on above 3 areas: Dept. of Natural Resources, Rt. 4, Madison, WI 53711. 608-266-0208. **Waterloo Wildlife Area** (E via I-94, then N off SR 89 on Springer Rd. or Lenius Rd.), 14.4 km of marked trails on rolling open and wooded terrain; parking area usually plowed. Information: Supervisor, Waterloo Wildlife Area, Dept. of Natural Resources, Courthouse, Jefferson, WI 53549. 414-674-2500, ext. 45. **High Pine** (W via US 14 to Black Earth, then 3.5 m S on County Rd. F), 9.6 km of marked trails on rolling open and wooded terrain; warming shelter and toilets; trail fee; tobogganing, ice skating; plowed parking area. Information: High Pine, Rt. 1, Black Earth, WI 53515. 608-767-2437. **Hoofbeat Ridge** (W via US 14 to Mazomanie, then 2 m S on Reeve Rd.), 9 interconnecting marked and groomed trails totaling 18 km; gentle to hilly terrain; trail fee; trail map available; rentals and instruction; warming shelter, restrooms; plowed parking area. Information: Hoofbeat Ridge, Rt. 2, Mazomanie, WI 53560. 608-767-3667. **Blackhawk Ridge** (NW via US 12 to Sauk City, then 2 m S on SR 78), 64 km of marked and partially groomed trails for beginner to advanced skiers; lighted trails for night skiing; heated shelter en route; trail fee; rentals and instruction; trailhead shelter, restrooms, store; limited lodging at area. Information: Blackhawk Ridge, Box 92, Sauk City, WI 53583. 608-643-3775.

MANITOWOC: Point Beach State Forest (NE on Lake Michigan, 4 m N of Two Rivers on State Forest Rd.), 11.2 km of marked and groomed trails on rolling wooded terrain; map available; trailhead shelter, toilets, plowed parking area (daily 6 am-11 pm); winter camping; park sticker required. Information: Supervisor, Point Beach State Forest, Rt. 3, Box 183, Two Rivers, WI 54241. 414-794-7480. **Calumet County Ski Area** (W via US 151 & SR 55 to

Stockbridge, continue 3 m N to County Rd. EE, then 1 m W), 3.2 km of marked and groomed novice to advanced trails on wooded terrain; downhill ski facilities; food service, restrooms. Information: Calumet County Ski Area, Rt. 2, Hilbert, WI 54129. 414-439-1008.

MARINETTE: Goodman Park (NW via SR 64 & US 141 to Wausaukee, then 20 m W on County Rd. C, then 10 m N on Parkway Rd.), 2 marked trails totaling 16 km on rolling wooded terrain; shelter, water, toilets; plowed parking area. Information: UWEX, Marinette County Courthouse, Marinette, WI 54143. 715-735-3371. **Mt. LeBett** (W via SR 64 and US 141 to Coleman, then 5 m W on County Rd. B), marked trails on gentle to hilly open terrain; rentals available; downhill ski facilities, day lodge, food service. Information: Mt. LeBett Ski Area, Rt. 1, Coleman, WI 54112. 414-897-2290.

MEDFORD: Sitz Mark Ski Touring Trail (4 m N of SR 64 on Forest Rd. 119, between Medford & Gilman), 2 interconnecting marked and groomed loops of 1.2 km and 4 km on rolling wooded terrain in Chequamegon National Forest; rentals, chalet and snack bar at Perkinstown Winter Sports Area (½ m from trail); trail open daylight hours, map available; plowed parking area; lodging, food and services in Medford. Information: District Ranger, Medford Ranger District, USFS, Medford, WI 54451. 715-748-4875.

MILWAUKEE: Brown Deer Park (7835 N. Green Bay Rd.), 2.7 km of marked and groomed trails for beginners on gentle open terrain. **Dretzka Park** (120th St. & Bradley Rd.), 4 km of marked and groomed trails on open hilly terrain. **Whitnall Park** (5879 S. 92nd St., Hales Corners), 2.7 km of marked and groomed trails on rolling wooded terrain. Above parks have shelter, restrooms, water, and plowed parking areas. Information: Milwaukee County Parks, Courthouse, 901 N. 9th, Milwaukee, WI 53233. 414-278-4354. **Emma Carlin Trail** (SW via SR 59 to Palmyra, then 2 m E on County Rd. Z), 3 marked loops totaling 9 km on hilly wooded terrain recommended for advanced skiers only. **John Muir Trail** (SW via SR 59 to Palmyra, then 3 m S on County Rd. H), 3 marked loops totaling 11.8 km on hilly wooded terrain; toilets at LaGrange Campground. **Nordic Trail** (SW via SR 59 to Palmyra, then 3 m S on County Rd. H), 5 marked loops totaling 14.4 km on hilly wooded terrain. **Scuppernong Trail** (SW via SR 59 to Eagle, then 5 m N on County Rd. ZZ), 3 marked loops totaling 8.3 km on hilly wooded terrain;

toilets. Preceding 4 trails have plowed parking areas. Information: Supervisor, Southern Kettle Moraine State Forest, Rt. 1, Box 87, Eagle, WI 53119. 414-594-2135. **Olympia Ski Area** (W on I-94 to exit 282; N on SR 67 at Oconomowoc), 13 km of trails on open terrain; downhill ski facilities; trail fee; year-round resort with variety of accommodations; restaurant, cocktail lounge, entertainment; heated pool, sauna, recreation room; nursery. Information: Olympia Ski Area, 1350 Royal Mile Rd., Oconomowoc, WI 53066. 414-567-0311.

PARK FALLS: Newman Springs Ski Touring Trails (12 m E on SR 182), 3 one-way interconnecting marked trails totaling 11.8 km on rolling wooded terrain in Chequamegon National Forest; trail map available; open daylight hours; plowed parking area. Information: District Ranger, Park Falls Ranger District, USFS, City Hall Bldg., Park Falls, WI 54552. 715-762-3294. **Gates Lake Trail** (N via SR 13 to Glidden, then 6.5 m SW on County Rd. N & D to Shanagolden, then Forest Rd. 167 to trail), 3 marked interconnecting trails totaling 4.7 km on rolling wooded terrain in Chequamegon National Forest; trail map available; plowed parking area. **West**

Torch River Trails (NW to Clam Lake via SR 13 & SR 77, 2.5 m S on County Rd. GG), 4 marked interconnecting color-coded trails totaling 19.1 km on gentle to rolling wooded terrain in Chequamegon National Forest; trail map available; plowed parking area. Information on preceding 2 trails: District Ranger, Glidden Ranger District, USFS, Glidden, WI 54527. 715-246-2511.

RHINELANDER: Consolidated's Ski Trails (10.5 m E on US 8, then .3 m S on Leith Rd.), 2 marked and groomed trails totaling 7.8 km on gentle wooded terrain suitable for novice and intermediate skiers; brochure and trail map available; plowed parking area. Information: Consolidated Paper Co., Wisconsin Rapids, WI 54494. 715-422-3956. **Holiday Trails** (5 m E off US 8), 3 marked and groomed trails totaling 17.6 km on wooded terrain for novice to advanced skiers; daily 9 am to dark; rentals; food and lodging at area. Information: Holiday Acres Resort, Box 460, Rhinelander, WI 54501. 715-369-1500. **Harrison Hills** (S via SR 17 to County Rd. B, then 1 m W), 7.2 km of marked trails on rolling wooded terrain; toilets and water; plowed parking area. **Otter Lake** (SW via US 8 to Tomahawk, then 9 m E on County Rd. D), 4.8 km of marked trails on intermediate wooded terrain; toilets and water; plowed parking area. Information: Lincoln County Trails, Forestry, Land & Parks Dept., Courthouse, Merrill, WI 54452. 715-536-7522. **Gerbick Lake Trail** (SW via US 8 to Tomahawk, then 5 m E on County Rd. D and 1.5 m S on County Rd. H), 3 marked and groomed trails totaling 37.5 km on novice to intermediate wooded terrain; trails connect with Otter Lake trails; rentals; food and lodging at area. Information: Birkensee Resort, Rt. 5, Tomahawk, WI 54487. 715-453-5103. **Skiniskis Touring Centre** (SW via US 8; 7 m N of Tomahawk on Wolf Rd.), 3 marked and groomed trails totaling 16 km on gentle to hilly, wooded terrain; trail maps available; rental and retail shop; instruction and guided tours; winter campsites; open Mon., Tues., Thurs., Fri. 10:30 am–4:30 pm and Sat., Sun. 9 am–6 pm. Information: Skiniskis Touring Centre, Terrace View Campsites, Rt. 3, Hwy. 8E, Tomahawk, WI 54487. 715-453-4796. **Palmquist Farm Trails** (SW; 20 m W of Tomahawk on US 8, then ½ m N on River Rd.), 4 marked and groomed trails totaling 30.4 km on novice to advanced wooded terrain; trail fee; rentals; sleigh rides; food, lodging, and sauna at area. Information: Palmquist Farm Trails, Rt. 1, Brantwood, WI 54513. 715-564-2558. **Dillman's Lodge Trail** (NW via SR 47 to Lac du Flambeau, then 3 m NE on Sand Lake Lodge Lane), 6.4 km of marked trails on rolling wooded terrain; dining, lounge and plowed parking area at lodge. Information: Dillman's Sand Lake Lodge, Lac du Flambeau, WI 54538. 715-588-3143. **Wildcat Lodge** (N via SR 47, US 51 and County Rd. M, 4 m N of Boulder Junction), 7 marked and groomed trails totaling 40 km on novice to advanced wooded terrain; trail fee; rentals; dining at lodge, rental cottages. Information: Wildcat Lodge, Box 138, Boulder Junction, WI 54512. 715-385-2421. **Escanaba Lake Trail** (N via SR 47, US 51; 7 m S of Boulder Junction on County Rd. M at Nebish Rd.), 14.5 km of marked trails on hilly wooded terrain recommended for experienced skiers; toilets, water, and plowed parking area. **Madeline Trail** (N on SR 47 to Woodruff, then 2 m SE on County Rd. J to Rudolf Rd.), 15.2 km of marked trails on gentle to hilly terrain for all skill levels; plowed parking area. **McNaughton Lake Ski Trail** (N on SR 47 to Kildare Rd.; 11 m S of Woodruff), 11.2 km marked novice trail on wooded terrain; plowed parking area. **Schlect Trail** (N via SR 47; 1.25 m S of Minocqua via US 51 to Leary Rd.), 3.5-km marked trail for expert skiers only; plowed parking area. Information for preceding 4 trails: Northern Highlands/American

Legion State Forest, Rt. 1, Box 45, Boulder Junction, WI 54512. 715-385-2727.

RICE LAKE: Hardscrabble (5 m E on County Rd. C), 16 km of marked trails on gentle to rolling wooded terrain; rentals and instruction; downhill ski facilities; chalet, cafeteria; open 9 am–dusk; accommodations, restaurants, and services nearby. Information: Hardscrabble, Rice Lake, WI 54868. 715-234-3412.

ST. CROIX FALLS: Interstate State Park (S of town on US 8), 11.2 km of marked trails on rolling wooded terrain; toilets, water, and plowed parking area; winter camping; park sticker required. Information: Superintendent, Interstate State Park, Box 429, St. Croix Falls, WI 54024. 715-483-3747. **Trollhaugen** (S to Dresser, then ¾ m E on County Rd. F), 4.8 km of marked trails on rolling to hilly wooded terrain; trail fee; rentals and instruction; downhill ski facilities; chalet and cafeteria. Information: Trollhaugen, Box 607, Dresser, WI 54009. 715-755-2955. **Nature's Way** (18 m E on US 8, then 4 m N on County Rd. V), 32 km of marked trails on rolling wooded terrain; trails groomed with track set; shelters en route; trail fee; rentals; hostel with food and sauna. Information: Nature's Way, Rt. 2, Turtle Lake, WI 54889. 715-986-2484.

SHEBOYGAN: Terry Andrae State Park (2 m S on Lake Michigan), 1.6 km marked trails on rolling open and wooded terrain; toilets, water, winter camping; park sticker required. Information: Superintendent, Terry Andrae State Park, Sheboygan, WI 53081. 414-452-3457. **Northern Kettle Moraine State Forest** (W via SR 23 and County Rd. G), 60 km of marked trails include 5 circular trails and one 40-km glacial trail with shelters en route; water, toilets, and plowed parking area at park hq; park open 6 am–11 pm; winter camping. Information: Supervisor, Northern Kettle Moraine State Forest, Box 426, Campbellsport, WI 53010. 414-626-2116. **Jellystone Park Camp Resort** (W on SR 23, then 3 m S on County Rd. G to County Rd. T), 12.2 km of marked and groomed trails on rolling open and wooded terrain; trail fee; rentals; restaurant; winter camping. Information: Jellystone Park Camp Resort, Rt. 1, Glenbeulah, WI 53023. 414-526-3407.

SUPERIOR: Pattison State Park (12 m S on SR 35), 8.8 km of marked one-way trails on rolling wooded terrain; shelter available for groups by reservation; water and plowed parking area. Information: Superintendent, Pattison State Park, Rt. 2, Box 435, Superior, WI 54880. 715-399-2115.

WAUPACA: Hartman Creek State Park (8 m SW off SR 54), 11 km of marked trails on rolling to hilly wooded terrain; trail maps en route; toilets, water, shelter, and plowed parking area; open 6 am–11 pm; park sticker required. Information: Superintendent, Hartman Creek State Park, Rt. 1, Waupaca, WI 54981. 715-258-2372. **Norseman Hill** (N; 5 m NW of Iola on County Rd. MM), 8 km of marked and groomed trails on wooded terrain; trail fee; warming shelter and restrooms. Information: Norseman Hill, 410 W. Iola St., Iola, WI 54945. 414-445-2476.

WAUSAU: Sylvan Hill Park (NE part of town on E. Sylvan St.), 5.7 km of marked and groomed trails; downhill ski facilities; chalet, food service. **Nine Mile Swamp Trail** (County Rd. N off US 51 bypass, then 4 m to Rosebud Rd.), 3 marked trails totaling 12 km on gentle to rolling wooded terrain; toilets; plowed parking area. Information on preceding 2 trails: Marathon County Trails, Courthouse, Wausau, WI 54401. 715-842-2141. **Rib Mountain** (3 m SW off US 51 bypass), 4 km of marked and groomed trails; trail fee; rentals; downhill ski facilities; chalet, cafeteria, cocktail lounge. Information: Rib Mountain Ski Area, Box 387, Wausau, WI 54401. 715-845-2846. **Underdown Wilderness Area** (N; 8 m N of Merrill via US 51, then 1 m E on County Rd. H to Copper Lake Rd.), 22 km of marked trails on rolling wooded terrain; plowed parking area; lodging, food, rentals in Merrill. Information: Lincoln County Trails, Forestry, Land & Parks Dept., Courthouse, Merrill, WI 54452. 715-536-7522.

WAUTOMA: Lake of the Woods Campground (10 m S at jct of County Rd. J & 14th Ave.), 24 km of marked trails on gentle wooded terrain for novice skiers; shelter, water, restrooms; winter camping; plowed parking area (fee). Information: Lake of the Woods Campground, Box 207, Rt. 1, Wautoma, WI 54982. 414-787-3601. **Green Lake Trails** (SE via SR 73 & SR 23; 3 m W of Green Lake on SR 23), 4 marked and groomed trails totaling 36.8 km on open and wooded gentle terrain with several steep spots; trail fee; rentals; daily 8 am–4:30 pm. Information: Green Lake Trails, Green Lake, WI 54941. 414-294-3231.

WEST BEND: Ridge Run Trail (in town, ½ m S of SR 33 on University Dr.), 2.1 km of marked trails on hilly terrain; shelter, toilets, and plowed parking area; open 7 am–9 pm. **Sandy Knoll Trail** (4 m SE off SR 33 on Wallace Lake Rd.), 4 km of marked trails on rolling terrain; shelter, toilets, and plowed parking area. Information on above trails: Washington County Park, 515 E. Washington St., West Bend, WI 53095. 414-334-3491. **Sunburst** (3 m N on US 45), 2 km of marked trails on rolling to hilly, open and wooded terrain; trail fee; rentals; downhill ski facilities, chalet, food service. Information: Sunburst, 8335 Prospect Dr., Kewaskum, WI 53040. 414-626-4605. **Pike Lake State Park** (SW off SR 60 on Pike Lake Rd.), 3.6 km of marked trails on hilly wooded terrain; trail map available; shelter, toilets, and plowed parking area; park sticker required. Information: Pike Lake State Park, Rt. 2, Hartford, WI 53027. 414-644-5248.

WISCONSIN RAPIDS: Ridges Inn (1 m S on SR 13, then ¾ m E on Griffith Ave.), 3 marked and groomed trails totaling 7.8 km on gentle to hilly wooded terrain; lighting for night skiing; trail fee; open 7 am–11 pm; winter camping. Information: Ridges Inn, 2311 Griffith Ave., Wisconsin Rapids, WI 54494. 715-424-1111. **Standing Rocks** (NE via SR 54 to Plover, then 5.75 m E on County Rd. B, 1.5 m S on town road, then 1.25 m E on town road), 2 marked and groomed trails totaling 7.2 km on rolling wooded terrain; downhill ski facilities; shelter and water on weekends; toilets and plowed parking area. Information: Standing Rocks, Portage County Parks, County-City Bldg., Stevens Point, WI 54481. 715-824-3949 or 346-3510. **Sky Line Ski Area** (S via SR 13; ¼ m N of Friendship), 400 acres with trails winding through woods, along streams, and into a Christmas tree plantation; rentals; downhill ski facilities, chalet, cafeteria, dining room, bar; motel accommodations, restaurants, services nearby. Information: Sky Line Ski Area, Friendship, WI 53934. 608-339-3421. **Sandhill Wildlife Area** (SW via SR 173; 1 m W of Babcock on County Rd. X or 5 m S of SR on County Rd. X), 4 interconnecting loops totaling 33.8 km on gentle terrain; trails marked and groomed; toilets and plowed parking area; open 7 am–7 pm. Information: Supervisor, Sandhill Wildlife Area, Babcock, WI 54413. 715-884-2726. **Puff Creek** (NW via SR 73 to Pittsville, then 7.5 m N on County Rd. A), 3 marked and groomed loops totaling 8 km on rolling wooded terrain; plowed parking area. Information: Wood County Park Dept., Courthouse, 400 Market St., Wisconsin Rapids, WI 54494. 715-423-3000, ext. 190.

WYOMING

For additional information, contact the individual area or Wyoming Travel Commission, 1-25 at Etchepare Circle, Cheyenne, WY 82002.

CODY: Sleeping Giant Ski Area (48 m W via US 14, 16, 20), access to cross-country skiing in the Wapiti Valley near the East Entrance to Yellowstone National Park; rentals and guide service; downhill ski area, day lodge, snack bar. Information: Sleeping Giant Ski Resort, P.O. Box 960, Cody, WY 82414. 307-587-4044 or 3409. **Pahaska Tepee** (W via US 14, 16, 20; 2 m E of Yellowstone National Park), guided tours into Yellowstone; year-round resort with lodge and cabin accommodations, dining room, tavern; lodge is Buffalo Bill's old hunting lodge. Information: Pahaska Tepee, Box 491, Cody, WY 82414. 307-587-5536 or 5537.

JACKSON: Grand Teton National Park (4 m N on US 26, 98, 187) has a spectacular range of peaks, beautiful glaciated canyons and lakes; about 40 m of valley trails are recommended for skiers; most mountain trails are not suitable for touring due to avalanche danger; Moose Visitor Center (daily exc. Dec. 25) offers ski tours, snowshoe hikes, tour suggestions, orientouring trails leaflet and compass; for skiers who seek short tours, a brochure is available with descriptions of 10 ski trails marked by orange diamonds or paint blazes; snowmobiles permitted on unplowed roads, and on Jackson and Jenny Lakes when frozen; food, lodging, services, rentals, and guides available in area (see below). Information: Superintendent, Grand Teton National Park, P.O. Drawer 170, Moose, WY 83012. 307-733-2880. Current road conditions, weather and facility information: 307-733-2220. **Flagg Ranch** (N on US 89 midway between Grand Teton and Yellowstone National Parks), access to unlimited ski touring; rentals; guided tours into Yellowstone National Park; lodging, dining room, bar, general store, campground. Information: Flagg Ranch, Moran, WY 83013. 307-543-2861; toll free (except WY): 800-443-2311. **Triangle X Ranch** (26 m N of Jackson; 13 m N of Moose off US 89, 189, 26), guided tours into Grand Teton National Park; cabin accommodations, lodge with dining room and lounge; American plan. Information: Triangle X

Ranch, Moose, WY 83012. 307-733-2183. **Powderhound Ski Tours** (12 m NW of Jackson on SR 390 at Teton Village) offer a variety of guided tours into Grand Teton National Park and Bridger-Teton National Forest; ½ day introductory tour includes instruction in basic touring technique, waxing instruction; full-day tour includes touring technique, waxing instruction, and 6–8 m scenic tour plus gourmet lunch; other tours include wildlife and winter ecology day tour, advanced day tour, igloo dinner tour for hearty beef stew; overnight igloo tour, designed for novice skiers, includes dinner, breakfast, and all necessary gear; private instruction; variety of vacation package plans. Information: Powderhound Ski Tours, Box 286, Wilson, WY 83014. 307-733-2208. **Teton Village** is a complete year-round resort at the base of **Jackson Hole Ski Area** (12 m NW of Jackson on SR 390); retail, rental, and repair shops; guide services; child care center; variety of lodge, motel, and condominium accommodations, economy to gourmet restaurants, bars; shops. Package plans available. Information: Teton Village Resort Association, Inc., P.O. Box 220, Teton Village, WY 83025. 307-733-4005. **Snow King Mountain** (6 blocks from downtown Jackson), a downhill ski area with cross-country rentals, instruction, and guided tours; popular 4-m trail begins at Ramada Snow King Inn (at ski area) and leads E into the Cache Creek Drainage of the **Bridger-Teton National Forest;** day lodge with cafeteria; food and lodging at ski area and in Jackson. Information: Snow King Mountain, Box R, Jackson, WY 83001. 307-733-2851. **Grand Targhee Resort** (42 m NW of Jackson; 12 m E of Diggs, ID off ID SR 33), many m of wooded trails and access to unlimited open terrain with deep powder snow on the western side of the Grand Teton range; rentals and instruction; year-round resort with downhill ski facilities, lodge, and condominium accommodations, restaurant, cocktail lounge, heated outdoor pool; nursery; package plans available; shuttle bus service (with 48 hours' advance notice; information and rates: 307-353-2308) from Idaho Falls, ID or Jackson airports. Information and reservations: Grand Targhee Resort, Alta, WY, via Diggs, ID 83422. 307-353-2308.

LARAMIE: Happy Jack Ski Area (off I-80, 10 m E), access to cross-country ski trails in Medicine Bow National Forest; rentals, instruction, guided tours; downhill ski area with day lodge and restaurant; accommodations, restaurants, and services in Laramie and Cheyenne (38 m E). Information: Happy Jack Ski Area, Box

3825, Laramie, WY 82070. 307-745-9583. **Medicine Bow Ski Area**
(32 m W via SR 130), marked cross-country trails in Medicine Bow
National Forest; downhill ski facilities, day lodge, cafeteria, beer
lounge; food, lodging, and services in Centennial and Laramie.
Information: Medicine Bow Ski Area, Box 121, Centennial, WY
82055. 307-745-5750. Area resorts and dude ranches that offer
cross-country skiing, food, and lodging include: Mountain Meadow
Cabins (3 m from Medicine Bow Ski Area), Box 157, Meriden
Route, Cheyenne, WY 82001. 307-634-1706. Vee Bar Ranch (21 m
W of Laramie on SR 130), Rex Route, Box 198, Laramie, WY
82070. 307-742-5741. Sand Lake Lodge (18 m SW of Arlington,
off I-80), Gene Alloway, 1634 Jim Bridger, Casper, WY 82601.
307-234-6064.

PINEDALE: White Pine Lodge (10 m NE of Pinedale on all-
weather U.S. Forest Service Rd.), cross-country skiing in Bridger
Wilderness Area; downhill ski facilities; lodging for 80 in rooms
and dormitories; snack bar and restaurant; package plans for
groups. Information: White Pine Lodge, Box 833, Pinedale, WY
82941. 307-367-2913.

SHERIDAN: Bear Lodge Resort (W via I-90 & US 14; ¼ m W of
Burgess Junction on US 14A), cross-country skiing in the Bighorn
National Forest; experienced guide service; year-round resort with
rustic cabins, lodge, dining room, bar, and lounge. Information:
Bear Lodge Resort, Bear Lodge, WY 82836. 307-655-2444.

YELLOWSTONE NATIONAL PARK, closed in the winter by
heavy snows, is beautiful, with a frosty cover of frozen steam
around the geysers and with blue, pink, yellow, and green hot-
water pools in the winter landscape; deer, moose, elk, and buffalo
may be seen in the park; the park is accessible only by skis, snowshoes, snowmobiles, and snowcoaches (heated passenger vehicles);
all unplowed roads and trails are open to cross-country skiers; most
trails are marked by orange metal markers on trees; trail information, maps, and detailed brochures of ski and snowshoe trails in the
Old Faithful area are available at Old Faithful and Mammoth Hot
Springs Visitor Centers; permit required for warming fires and
overnight camping; accommodations at Old Faithful Snow Lodge,
hearty meals served in dining room; adjacent Bear Den Ski Shop
offers ski and snowshoe rentals and repairs, instruction, group and

private guide service, narrated Nordic tours of the basin area, snowshoe discovery walks; package tours include snowcoach transportation from South Entrance (transportation from Jackson or Teton Village included) or from West Entrance to Old Faithful Snow Lodge, food and lodging; Mammoth Hot Springs Visitor Center and campground open year round (access from North Entrance at Gardiner, MT). Information and reservations: Yellowstone Park Company, Yellowstone National Park, WY 82190. 307-344-7311.

VOLUMES IN THE
AMERICANS-DISCOVER-AMERICA SERIES

Available from your bookseller or from William Morrow & Company, Inc., 6 Henderson Drive, West Caldwell, NJ 07006

Cross-country Skiing: A Guide to America's Best Trails, by Lucy M. Fehr. $6.95

Skiing USA: A Guide to the Nation's Ski Areas, by Lucy M. Fehr. $4.95

Canoeing and Rafting: The Complete Where-to-Go Guide to America's Best Tame and Wild Waters, by Sara Pyle. $5.95

Walking: A Guide to Beautiful Walks and Trails in America, by Jean Calder. $3.95

American Travelers' Treasury: A Guide to the Nation's Heirlooms, by Suzanne Lord. $5.95

Traveling with Children in the USA: A Family Guide to Pleasure, Adventure, Discovery, by Leila Hadley. $4.95

A Literary Tour Guide to the United States: Northeast, by Emilie C. Harting. $4.95 Travelflex, $8.95 hardcover

A Literary Tour Guide to the United States: West and Midwest, by Rita Stein. $5.95 Travelflex, $9.95 hardcover

A Literary Tour Guide to the United States: South and Southwest, by Rita Stein. $5.95 Travelflex, $9.95 hardcover

Also available:

The Flag Book of the United States, by Whitney Smith. $5.95 paper, $12.95 hardcover

Volumes in the Americans-Discover-America series are available from your bookseller or from William Morrow & Company, Inc.

When ordering, add 75¢ postage and handling for the first book, plus 10¢ for each additional book. Make checks payable to William Morrow & Company. Inc. (Prices subject to change without notice.)

To: William Morrow & Company, Inc.
     6 Henderson Drive
     West Caldwell, NJ 07006

Please send me:

Quantity   Price

____ Cross-country Skiing: A Guide to America's Best
      Trails ($6.95)   _____

____ Skiing USA: A Guide to the Nation's Ski
      Areas ($4.95)   _____

____ Canoeing and Rafting: The Complete
      Where-to-Go Guide to America's Best
      Tame and Wild Waters ($5.95)   _____

____ Walking: A Guide to Beautiful Walks and
      Trails in America ($3.95)   _____

____ American Travelers' Treasury: A Guide to
      the Nation's Heirlooms ($5.95)   _____

____ Traveling with Children in the USA: A
      Family Guide to Pleasure, Adventure,
      Discovery ($4.95)   _____

____ A Literary Tour Guide to the United States:
      Northeast ($4.95 Travelflex, $8.95
      hardcover)   _____

____ A Literary Tour Guide to the United States:
      West and Midwest ($5.95 Travelflex, $9.95
      hardcover)   _____

____ A Literary Tour Guide to the United States:
      South and Southwest ($5.95 Travelflex,
      $9.95 hardcover)   _____

____ The Flag Book of the United States ($5.95
      paper, $12.95 hardcover)   _____

                                   Postage _____

              Sales tax if applicable _____

                                      Total _____

NAME

STREET

CITY   STATE   ZIP